UNIVERSITY OF NORTH CAROLINA AT CHAPEL HILL
DEPARTMENT OF ROMANCE LANGUAGES

NORTH CAROLINA STUDIES
IN THE ROMANCE LANGUAGES AND LITERATURES

Founder: URBAN TIGNER HOLMES
Editor: MARÍA A. SALGADO

Distributed by:

UNIVERSITY OF NORTH CAROLINA PRESS
CHAPEL HILL
North Carolina 27515-2288
U.S.A.

NORTH CAROLINA STUDIES IN THE
ROMANCE LANGUAGES AND LITERATURES
Number 239

EL ÁNGEL DEL HOGAR

EL ÁNGEL DEL HOGAR
GALDÓS AND THE IDEOLOGY
OF DOMESTICITY IN SPAIN

BY

BRIDGET A. ALDARACA

CHAPEL HILL

NORTH CAROLINA STUDIES IN THE ROMANCE
LANGUAGES AND LITERATURES
U.N.C. DEPARTMENT OF ROMANCE LANGUAGES

1991

Library of Congress Cataloging-in-Publication Data

Aldaraca, Bridget, 1938-
　El ángel del hogar: Galdós and the ideology of domesticity in Spain / by Bridget A. Aldaraca.
　p. – cm. – (North Carolina studies in the Romance languages and literatures; no. 239)
　Includes bibliographical references.
　ISBN 0-8078-9243-2
　1. Pérez Galdós, Benito, 1843-1920 – Criticism and interpretation. 2. Women in literature. 3. Sex role in literature. 4. Family life in literature. I. Title. II. Series.
PQ6555.Z5A637　　1992　　　　　　　　　　　　　　　　　　　91-30892
863'.5–dc20　　　　　　　　　　　　　　　　　　　　　　　　　　　CIP

© 1991. Department of Romance Languages. The University of North Carolina at Chapel Hill.

ISBN 8087-9243-2

DEPÓSITO LEGAL: V. 2.749 - 1991　　　I.S.B.N. 84-599-3244-3

ARTES GRÁFICAS SOLER, S. A. - LA OLIVERETA, 28 - 46018 VALENCIA - 1991

In memoriam Mary B. Codd

... I discovered that if I were going to review books I should need to do battle with a certain phantom. And the phantom was a woman, and when I came to know her better I called her after the heroine of a famous poem, The Angel in the House. It was she who used to come between me and my paper when I was writing reviews. It was she who bothered me and wasted my time and so tormented me that at last I killed her. You who come of a younger and happier generation may not have heard of her – you may not know what I mean by the Angel in the House. I will describe her as shortly as I can. She was intensely sympathetic. She excelled in the difficult arts of family life. She sacrificed herself daily. If there was chicken, she took the leg; if there was a draught she sat in it – in short she was so constituted that she never had a mind or a wish of her own, but preferred to sympathize always with the minds and wishes of others. Above all – I need not say it – she was pure.

        Virginia Woolf, *Professions for Women* (1931)

TABLE OF CONTENTS

	Page
ACKNOWLEDGMENTS	13
PROLOGUE	15
INTRODUCTION	25
1. THE PERFECT WIFE: FROM COUNTER-REFORMATION TO ENLIGHTENMENT	33
2. EL ÁNGEL DEL HOGAR: THE SPIRITUALIZATION OF WOMEN IN NINETEENTH-CENTURY SPAIN	55
3. EL LUJO: WOMEN AND CONSPICUOUS CONSUMPTION	88
4. LA FAMILIA DE LEÓN ROCH: DOMESTICITY AND DIVORCE IN SPAIN	118
5. TORMENTO: BOURGEOIS MORALITY AND THE PRIVATIZATION OF VIRTUE	139
6. LA DE BRINGAS: THE MYTH OF PRIVATE AND PUBLIC SPHERES	160
7. LO PROHIBIDO: THE LITERARY CREATION OF AN ANGEL	185
EPILOGUE: TRISTANA: THE DEATH OF AN IDEAL	231
SELECTED BIBLIOGRAPHY	253

ACKNOWLEDGMENTS

My research on medical thought and hysteria in nineteenth-century Spain was partially supported by a grant from the Program for Cultural Cooperation Between Spain's Ministry of Culture and United States Universities. Additional assistance was also provided by the same institution in 1990 in the form of a publication subsidy awarded to the North Carolina Romance Languages and Literatures Series. I am grateful to the Program for Cultural Cooperation for their financial assistance and for their interest in my work. I would like also to thank José Luis Peset for facilitating my access to the Real Academia de la Medicina in Madrid, and Pablo Sanz, the curator, for his unfailingly cheerful assistance.

Chapter 2 appeared in a slightly different form as "*'El ángel del hogar':* The Cult of Domesticity in Nineteenth-Century Spain" in *Theory and Practice of Feminist Literary Criticism,* eds. G. Mora and K. S. Van Hooft (Ypsilanti, Michigan: Bilingual Press, 1982), pp. 62-87. An abbreviated version of Chapter 6 appeared earlier as "The Revolution of 1868 and the Rebellion of Rosalía Bringas" in *Anales Galdosianos,* XVIII (1983), pp. 49-60. An edited version of Chapter 5 was published in Spanish as *"Tormento:* La moral burguesa y la privatización de la virtud" in *Texto y Sociedad: Problemas de Historia Literaria,* eds. B. Aldaraca, E. Baker, and J. Beverley (Amsterdam: Rodopi, 1990), pp. 215-229. The section in Chapter 7 entitled "Hysteria: The Language of Silence" was originally presented as a paper for the Asociación Internacional de Galdosistas at the November, 1987 meeting of the Midwest Modern Language Association.

I would like to thank Farris Anderson for his meticulous reading of the original manuscript, and Harriet Turner for her helpful suggestions near the end. Antonio Ramos-Gascón gave me much encouragement at an important early stage of this work.

The necessary isolation of any sustained intellectual endeavor has been made easier by the intellectual companionship, emotional support and invaluable friendship of various people. I would like to take this opportunity to thank them: José Álvarez Junco, John Beverley, Alda Blanco, María Brey de Rodríguez Moñino, Susan Kirkpatrick, Ileana Rodríguez, Geraldine Scanlon and Joan Connelly Ullman. A special thanks to my dear friend Michael Predmore, who guided me through the final labyrinth of publication. I also owe a debt of gratitude to my friends Drs. Pilar de Miguel and Luis Fernández Fau for encouraging my interest in the fields of psychoanalysis and psychiatry, for their many hours of conversation on mental illness, and for helping me to avoid a layperson's errors on medical questions.

My sons, Andrew and Jaime Aldaraca have played an important, if often involuntary, part in my intellectual and emotional considerations of feminism. I have learned tolerance from them, and hope. From Edward Baker, I have learned the most important lesson of all: the only limits to our creative endeavours are those which we ourselves choose to impose.

PROLOGUE

My preliminary research for this book followed the trail of numerous articles with titles like "La misión de la mujer," "La educación de la mujer," and "Influencia de la mujer," which appeared in the fashion and family magazines in Spain during the latter half of the nineteenth century. These magazines, with names such as *La Guirnalda* (The Garland); *La Margarita* (The Daisy); *El Pensil del Bello Sexo* (The Flower-Garden of the Fair Sex), echoed the sentimental tone of similar magazines published in England and France. The names of other magazines indicated their family orientation: *El Museo de las Familias, La Defensa de la Familia,* or simply, *La Familia*. Also of tremendous importance to the growing middle-class feminine readership was the introduction of fashion magazines such as *El Correo de la Moda* (Fashion's News) and *La Moda Elegante Ilustrada* (Illustrated Magazine of Elegant Fashion). What emerged gradually from this plethora of recipes for women's role in society was something equivalent to a manual on how to create in real life the sweet, pure angel-women who lived in the pages of Victorian fiction, in the novels of Charles Dickens, for example, or in Coventry Patmore's emblematic poem of Victorian domesticity, which he called "The Angel in the House."[1]

When I came across a magazine entitled *El Ángel del Hogar* (The Angel in the House) edited by María Pilar Sinués de Marco, an

---

[1] See Nina Auerbach, *Woman and the Demon: The Life of a Victorian Myth* (Cambridge and London: Harvard University Press, 1982), pp. 66-69. According to Auerbach, the title of the poem became "a convenient shorthand for the selfless paragon all women were exhorted to be, enveloped in family life and seeking no identity beyond the roles of daughter, wife and mother. 'Angel' and 'house' became virtual synonyms" (p. 69).

author whose articles I had already found in other similar magazines, I felt justified in acclaiming the existence of a Spanish "Angel in the House" that could be considered, at the very least, a close cousin of her English counterpart. However, when I discussed with women friends in Spain my discovery of their *ángel del hogar*, they talked to me about another woman, the "perfect wife" ("la perfecta casada"). I was of course familiar with Fray Luis de León, the Spanish Counter-Reformation author of *La perfecta casada*, but I was surprised to find his book still circulating among contemporary Spanish women, resting on their mother's bookshelves, given to them on occasion as a wedding present by a concerned mother-in-law to be. The juxtaposing of the ethereal Victorian domestic angel and Fray Luis de León's perfect wife, whose roots are woven in with the 'strong woman' of the Bible, impelled me to pose the following question: how can an image change so radically yet apparently stay the same?

The study of an ideology must encompass a territory much more vast than that which needs to be excavated in order to retrieve a single image or icon. The word ideology itself suggests both idea and ideal. Raymond Williams, in his book *Keywords: A Vocabulary of Culture and Science* [1976], locates the original use of the term in the French Enlightenment: *idéologie*, a word proposed by Destutt de Tracy in 1796, to refer to the philosophy of the mind, or the science of ideas as distinguished from the *ancien régime*'s concept of metaphysics.[2] Williams cites the first pejorative use of the word to mean fanatical and/or revolutionary in Napoleon's attack on the idea of democracy and other enlightenment principles as 'ideology', that is, as the conscious attempt to uphold or impose a social theory.[3] According to Williams, it is Marx and Engels who, by emphasizing the gap between theory understood as an abstract system of ideas and the material conditions of life, initiate a new interpretation of the word ideology as, in Williams' words, "false consciousness, illusion, unreality, or upside-down reality."[4]

The Marxist use of the term ideology as 'false consciousness' speaks to the use of ideologies to explain or justify the *status quo* of material life. Rationalizations which explain 'reality' are consciously

---

[2] Raymond Williams, *Keywords: A Vocabulary of Culture and Society* (New York: Oxford University Press, 1976), p. 126.
[3] Williams, p. 126.
[4] Williams, p. 128.

derived from abstract reasoning but rely inevitably upon false logic, since the motives or class interests underlying the arguments are disguised or hidden from the ideologist; hence, he/she reasons or thinks in a state of 'false consciousness.' Williams affirms that, in general, the widest historical use of the term ideology is that of "the set of ideas which arise from a given set of material interests,"[5] and he reminds us, citing Marx and his *Contribution to the Critique of Political Philosophy* [1859] that both the sense of ideology as a conscious production of ideas in the service of material interests and that of ideology as illusion or false consciousness are present in Marxist writings.[6] In *A Dictionary of Marxist Thought*, the authors comment on the use of ideology in the writings of Lenin, Lukács and Gramsci. They maintain that after Lenin: "Ideology is no longer a necessary distortion which conceals contradictions but becomes a neutral concept referring to the political consciousness of classes, including the proletarian class."[7]

Leaving aside the difficulty of discussing, in a post-Freudian context, the degree of awareness of motives or intentions that is ascertainable by individual consciousness, it should be emphasized that today the term ideology is most frequently used to denote a putatively logical system of ideas which may or may not reflect a specific set of material circumstances – an ideology may be antiquated or purposely utopian. Nevertheless, all ideologies, whether current or outmoded, have social roots and therefore functioning ideologies do not remain on the level of utopian abstraction as desire but are also realized in concrete forms of social practice, in such social institutions as the state, the family, the legal system, the production and distribution of popular culture, and so forth.

The term bourgeois ideology, then, encompasses both the theoretical writings of bourgeois thinkers – Rousseau, Paine, Adam Smith, et al. – who helped to forge bourgeois class consciousness, but also the social representations of ideological practice: the laws of the bourgeois state, its political and social institutions. In the case of feminist ideology, to cite another example, the belief in either an innate or a socially constructed gender identity which transcends or displaces, either continuously or momentarily, other elements of

---

[5] Williams, p. 129.
[6] Williams, p. 128.
[7] *A Dictionary of Marxist Thought*, eds. T. Bottomore, L. Harris, V. G. Kiernan, R. Miliband (Cambridge: Harvard University Press, 1983), p. 222.

cultural identity such as race or class, and the belief that gender identity can be transformed into the politically organizable sentiment of female solidarity are necessary, indeed, inevitable components of feminist theory, since feminism is a political movement which relies on the organizing tactic of female solidarity to achieve its goals.

The concept of ideology is particularly useful when bringing under critical discussion ideas which, because of their profound roots in the tradition of modern Western thought, are so familiar to us that they often function in popular discourse as truisms: I refer to concepts such as democracy, freedom, the family and so forth. For example, it can be useful to discuss the *ideology* of democracy in the case of third-world countries still fighting colonization where a fetichized electoral process organized and judged "democratic" by foreign interests is used to justify control by an imperialist power. What this example seeks to emphasize is that all ideologies function in the service of political and economic goals, either to reinforce and maintain power of one class or group or, in the opposite case, to combat the status quo of the dominant class or group.

I have made a distinction between the archeological recuperation of an artistic or literary image, and the investigation of the dynamics of an ideology defined not only as an abstract theoretical system but also as the concrete set of social practices which this theoretical system seeks to explain and justify. The relation of the *ángel del hogar*, a specific literary image in nineteenth-century literature, to the ideology of domesticity is this image's capacity to synthesize in a single phrase (or painting or poem or literary character), the complexity of the changes and developments in urban bourgeois culture – as distinct from feudal, seignorial or contemporary peasant societies – of a variety of new attitudes and practices concerning family life, the raising and education of children, and the role of women in the domestic sphere.

As the first three chapters will show, the ideology of domesticity is a specifically bourgeois ideology and therefore relies on other components of bourgeois thinking such as a belief in the radical separation of social existence into two contiguous but distinct and unrelated spheres of public and private, the stated belief in the social *and* political equality of men and women – the idea of 'women's influence' compensating for direct political participation, and a newly emphasized importance of the child as the center of family life. It is in the interests of bourgeois ideologues, in order to sustain their position as the dominant class, to perpetuate those ideas which theoretically maintain the non-existence of class and therefore the untenability of class conflict. Thus such globalizing phrases as "all men are created equal," and the "rights of man" maintain not only what should be but also purport to tell us what already is. This gap between what ideology insists *should be*, and what the evidence of material existence teaches us *is*, pinpoints the contradiction in the ideological system which the illusion of rhetoric – or laws or social institutions – seeks to mask.

The ideology of domesticity is forced to maintain and to disguise two glaring contradictions. First, a bourgeois democracy is a classless society and therefore it is possible to speak of all women without remarking upon any distinction of class; and second, the materiality of sexual desire is non-existent in normal women. In any consideration of bourgeois ideology in Spain, Marx's famous statement in the *German Ideology* [1846] that "The ruling ideas of each age have ever been the ideas of its ruling class..."[8] must draw our attention to Spain's lag in the development of a dominant bourgeois class. This historical lag – in relation to the capitalist industrial economies of England, France and Germany – partially explains a rhetorical support for the ideology of domesticity in the absence of wide-spread material circumstances which would sustain the habits and customs of European bourgeois family life in Spain. In Victorian England, poor and working-class women were certainly unable to live as angels in their *own* house. Nevertheless, the material wealth of the middle and upper-middle classes was sufficient to strengthen the illusion that *all* women could live out this male fantasy.

Class structure and class identity do not and cannot erase the concept of gender. The identification of the *ángel del hogar* as bourgeois ideology is not contradicted by my statement that the *ángel del hogar* is also a male fantasy. In Spain, the iconization of woman as an eternally young and virginal mother has much more to do with a nostalgic longing for home, that is, with a return to the relationship between male child and mother, than it does with the relation-

---

[8] *Marx and Engels on Literature and Art*, eds. L. Baxandall and S. Morawski, (St. Louis: Telos Press, 1973), p. 72.

ship between adult men and women in marriage or outside of marriage. The fact that many women upheld the values of domesticity and tried to conform to this idealized version of womanhood is perhaps the most cogent defense of the concept of ideology as false consciousness, for the end result of placing women on a pedestal was to justify and maintain almost *all* women's exclusion from public life and their restriction to the domestic sphere of activity. It also needs to be noted that while the exaltation of home and hearth is in part a reaction to the pernicious effects of industrialism on society, the idea that women's social value and validation depends solely on their role as wives and mothers gains strength at a moment in history when women in England and the United States are attempting to break down barriers to the presence of their sex in the university and in professions such as medicine, journalism, health care and teaching.

The pejorative sense of ideology as too political, closeminded or fanatical – a sense which speaks as much to the disrepute of the political as it does to the low esteem in which ideology is held – is especially evident in the choice of the phrase 'personal philosophy' rather than personal ideology when referring to an individual's particular set of opinions, values or theories. In the nineteenth century, the aesthetics of Naturalism idealized the scientific attitude and tried to realize in narrative the supposed value-free and objective perspective of the scientist. The goal of scientific objectivity purported to eradicate ideology, at least in the scientist's laboratory. A goal of ideological neutrality is likewise implicit in the realist novelist's attempt to use the novel to mirror reality, to narrate what is rather than what should be, or might have been.

Nevertheless, once the concept of ideology is accepted as a workable premise, what is eradicated is the possibility of an ideology-free cultural product, since culture is the ideological representation of social relations, which are, in turn, governed by the relations of production. The social relations between capital and labor, in which labor produces the commodity and capital consumes the profit is often relatively obvious; for example, in the case of the employees of a fast food chain. What is perhaps less obvious is the relation of the author to the reader or consumer of his product. The apparently direct relation between the author's words and our response to them is, in reality, mediated by capital – the publishing house's control, the effects of advertising, etc. – so that the novelist cannot write or sell his product, nor can we read it, from some place outside the web of capitalist social relations. This is so especially in the case of authors like Galdós or Dickens, or Balzac, who lived by the sale of their novels and articles. And just as there is no ideology-free novel, nor can there be literary criticism which is without an ideological perspective.

Under the rubric of realism, the novelist must reconstruct a fictional reality which is not only material, psychological and social but which also takes ideology into account. The 'realistic' representation of social relations in narrative form implies the unveiling of the lived contradictions of class and gender – that camouflaged empty space between the abstract ideal and the real or material, which ideology seeks to hide. The novels of Benito Pérez Galdós lend themselves to a discussion of the ideology of domesticity not only because women and domestic life provide much of the material for his narrative, but also because Galdós' own critical posture towards nineteenth-century Spanish society, his political and historical awareness and his self-consciousness as a realist novelist results in a continual revision of the broad canvas which he calls the Contemporary Novels.

The five novels which I have selected do not mark the ultimate parameters of Galdós' treatment of women and domesticity but establish, within a chronological continuum, a kind of beginning and ending of a certain stage in Galdosian narrative. *La familia de León Roch* [1878] marks a turning away from the historical novel, and the so-called novels of thesis, and defines his new contemporary novel as belonging to the genre of domestic realism, concerned with the mores and drama on a small-scale of urban family life and related themes of education, child-rearing, work and conspicuous consumption.

From the start, Galdós establishes a critical perspective towards what he sees as the spiritual lack within the middle- and upper-class family institution in Spain. He rewrites nineteenth-century standards of married happiness to include an awareness of female sexuality and begins to develop his own formula for domestic bliss, a formula which will come to fruition in *Lo prohibido* [1885]. In *Tormento* [1884], the seductive fantasy of the *ángel del hogar* – the male perspective – is played off against an impoverished woman's economic dependence and her need for both emotional and financial security – the woman's perspective. In *La de Bringas* [1884], the social respectability of an emotionally tepid and economically precarious marriage becomes the context in which the limits to ambition for the middle-class wife is explored.

My decision to limit my discussion of the ideology of domesticity in Galdós' works to five novels is based on the opposite reasons for not pausing to analyze in depth some of the fascinating texts which come under consideration in the first three chapters: such texts as *La perfecta casada*, Josefa Amar y Borbón's *Discurso sobre la educación física y moral de las mugeres*, and Pedro Felipe Monlau's *Higiene del matrimonio*. The thematic organization of the material of the first three chapters has as its goal an overview of the roots and the evolution of attitudes towards women and family life in Spain from the Catholic Counter-Reformation through the Spanish Restoration. As such, these chapters constitute my own narrative of an ideology, and the object – for she cannot be a subject – of this history of an idea, is the Spanish Angel in the House.

The analysis of a literary text must take into account not only the question of ideology, but also the specific problem of literary genre, in this case, that of the realist novel. In order to avoid simply measuring Galdós' novels against my own narration or reconstruction of the ideology of domesticity in Spain, I decided that each novel must be analyzed as an artistic whole, and placed as much as possible within the larger framework of Galdós' literary production. This approach afforded a close look at how the ideology of domesticity affects a wide spectrum of related themes within each novel: conspicuous consumption, the myth of private and public spheres, female and male sexuality, male and female hysteria, and especially, the precarious circumstances of the Spanish middle-class in which the *ángel del hogar* supposedly resided.

The question of class is never absent in Galdós' novels, but his masterful analysis of class conflict and the class limits of the ideology of domesticity will not take place until the writing of *Fortunata y Jacinta*. In this novel, the important question of maternity will be given a class context, when Jacinta's sterility is paired with Fortunata's fecundity. An adequate analysis of this literary masterpiece constitutes another or a different book, and I have chosen to end the main section with *Lo prohibido*, which represents both a moment of closure and an opening on to a new stage in Galdós' own ideological and literary development, a stage in which the fairy-tale ending of the story of Camila and Constantino in *Lo prohibido* is virtually impossible. The epilogue on *Tristana* constitutes a final commentary on patriarchal power, the pernicious effects of the ideology of domesticity upon women, and finally, Galdós' inability to see anything salvagable for either men or women in the claustrophobic prison of William Blake's 'marriage hearse.'

BRIDGET ALDARACA

May, 1990

INTRODUCTION

> Women are generally much better than they are judged to be; they are angels created by God in order to share our suffering, to wipe away our tears and to produce for us the only happiness that exists on this earth: love and the family.
>
> (La mujer es mucho más buena de lo que generalmente se la juzga; es un ángel creado por Dios para sufrir con nosotros, enjugar nuestro llanto y producirnos las únicas felicidades que hay en la tierra: el amor y la familia.)
>
> Antonio Fernando García, *El Correo de la Moda*

Students of the enormous corpus of prescriptive literature which defines the essence of women and their role in Spanish society are immediately faced with an obvious contradiction, one which is partially revealed by asking this question in relation to the quote which heads our introduction: when was it written? Although the answer given might err by a matter of decades, certain characteristics of language, style and content place it within a period no earlier than the late eighteenth century and probably not extending beyond the First World War. The inverse of this statement is that this quotation could not possibly have been extracted from a work like *La perfecta casada*, published in 1583 and considered to be the paradigmatic expression of the traditional ideal Spanish woman.[1]

---

[1] See María del Pilar Oñate, *El feminismo en la literatura española* (Madrid: Espasa-Calpe, S. A., 1938), p. 141:

> The ideal of woman dedicated exclusively to the home, expressed by Solomon and repeated from ancient times by the Church Fathers and other Christian writers, found its definitive interpretation in Fray Luis de León. After *The Perfect Wife*, all that was left to do was to spread out

The fact that this passage, marked as it is by both sentimentality and a hyperbolic albeit defensive praise of women and the family, is identifiably an artifact of nineteenth-century Spanish culture (it was written in 1877) calls into question the general acceptance of a monolithic static image of the traditional ideal woman, passed down from generation to generation, at times placed in opposition to new images of 'the modern woman' but basically faithful to itself and unchanging. Yet is the modern upper-class woman of the Spanish Enlightenment, with her varnish of French, music, drawing and dance, more or less modern than the middle-class woman who supports herself as a governess or who establishes herself as a *literata*, a literary woman,[2] in the nineteenth century? At this point, the firm dichotomy between traditional and modern becomes blurred.

In the opinion of a small, elite, urban minority, the women in 1790 who read French novels in the original and held evening gatherings to which both men and women were invited, had indeed progressed. But in the opinion of a majority whom we customarily refer to as traditionalists, these same women formed part of a general ambience of moral decay. The terms traditional and modern are therefore being used to express value judgments on a specific historical reality. But the fact that these terms must be utilized in relation to specific historical circumstances in order to have meaning does not negate the fact that an image of a perfect wife, *la mujer de su casa* (the housewife), defined and interiorized as an unchanging ideal, does indeed exist.

---

in innumerable pages of turgid prose that which the erudite Augustine monk had condensed into the brief chapters of his immortal work.

(El ideal de la mujer consagrada exclusivamente al hogar, expresado por Salomón y glosado desde antiguo por los Santos Padres y otros escritores cristianos, había encontrado intérprete definitivo en Fr. Luis de León. Después de *La perfecta casada* no cabía más que deluir en numerosas páginas de amazacotada prosa lo que el erudito agustino había condensado en los breves capítulos de su obra inmortal.)

[2] See Susan Kirkpatrick, *Las Románticas: Women Writers and Subjectivity in Spain 1835-1850* for an excellent study of three major 'literatas'. See also, Alda Blanco, "Domesticity, Education and the Woman Writer: Spain 1850-1880," in *Cultural and Historical Grounding for Hispanic and Luso-Brazilian Feminist Literary Criticism*, Ed. H. Vidal (Minneapolis: Institute for the Study of Ideologies and Literature, 1989), pp. 371-94, and María del Carmen Simón Palmer, "Escritoras españolas del siglo xix o el miedo a la marginación," *Anales de Literatura Española de la Universidad de Alicante* 2 (1983): 477-90.

In spite of radical changes in the social function of women in their role as housewife from the sixteenth through the nineteenth centuries, this image, *mutatis mutandi,* has remained sufficiently stable to be recognizable and to be utilized as a powerful ideological tool. Our next step must therefore be an attempt to abstract the essence of the ideological construct which surrounds the image of the perfect wife in order to discuss which parts have remained stable and which parts have changed, and why.

We defined the literature under discussion as prescriptive, that is, written by self-proclaimed authorities: clergy, educators, doctors of medicine, philosophers, theologians, etc. for the purpose of teaching women what they should be and what they should do. As prescriptive literature, all these works have two elements in common. One is the frequently minute delineation of the activities women should engage in, often defined in the negative, that is, proscribed activities for women. The other is the rationalization which justifies the mandated activities, usually based on an ontological definition of woman as genre, a kind of separate species or racial sub-set, a definition commonly expressed in the negative, what woman is not. *What* women can or cannot be allowed to do varies considerably within certain set limits, and the rationalizations vary extravagantly. But there is a third element, that which defines the spatial parameters placed upon female activity, which varies so little as to be, in effect, an unchanging factor, that is, *where* women must do their work and *where* they must be. The essence of the ideal woman is not that she is modest, industrious, thrifty and, in the nineteenth century, *ilustrada* (educated), but that she embodies all of these virtues in and only in the house. The ideal woman is ultimately defined not ontologically, not functionally but territorially, by the space which she occupies. The frontier of her existence as a virtuous woman begins and ends at her doorstep: "...and so the Good Woman who, from her doorstep inward will be quick and lively, from her doorstep out must be considered lame and dull-witted." ("...assí la buena mujer quanto, para sus puertas adentro ha de ser presta y ligera, tanto para fuera dellas se ha de tener por coxa y torpe.")[3]

---

[3] Fr. Luis de León, *La perfecta casada*, reimpresión de la tercera edición, con variantes de la primera, y un prólogo, ed. Elizabeth Wallace (Chicago: University of Chicago Press, 1903), p. 98. There is an out of print English translation by Alice

This constant, the physical circumscription of female activity to a specific social space, the domestic interior, must be discussed in relation to a second constant: women are different from men. This difference is expressed in both negative and positive terms; women are either superior or inferior to men. This apparent contradiction only obfuscates the underlying tenet that women's difference is defined in relation to a commonly accepted male standard. In the literature which describes and prescribes the ideal wife, these two constants are linked in a variety of combinations. As the following graph illustrates, either tenet can function as both cause or effect, creating infinite possibilities of tautological reasoning.

CAUSE: RATIONALIZATION   EFFECT: IMMUTABLE MATERIAL FACT

1. Women are (always)   They must be (do)
   in the house.   (therefore)   different from men.

2. Women are (do) different   They must remain
   from men.   (therefore)   in the house

These two premises form the essence of the traditionalist stance on women and can be synthesized into one law: The innate difference between men and women explains/necessitates a society structured upon the sexual exclusivity of social space. The following brief analysis of three representative quotes from different historical junctures confirms the presence of this core concept of the necessity of sexual apartheid, while illuminating important changes in the perception of social space.

Our first quote is taken from *La perfecta casada*, a work published twenty years after the final session of the Council of Trent in 1563.

> Just as men are meant for public life, so women are meant to be secluded: and just as men are meant to speak out and to show themselves, so women should shut themselves inside and hide from the public eye. Even in Church, where the service of God and the duties of religion require them to go, Saint Paul desires them to be covered up in such a way that men may not look

---

Philena Hubbard (Sister Felicia), of the Order of St. Anne, published in 1943 in a limited edition by the College Press of the Texas State College for Women (Denton, Texas). I have consulted this text for my own translations of quotes taken from *La perfecta casada*.

upon them, and would he therefore permit that they go wandering at will through the city squares and streets, showing themselves off? What have women to do outside their house, since they are not equipped with any of the requisite talent which public affairs demand? As experience has shown, since they do not have the intelligence to deal with weighty matters, they will necessarily be given over to petty and unimportant ones. Inevitably, since they are not equipped to treat profound and intellectual matters, they will be caught up in what is shameful and frivolous. And inevitably, since it is not their business nor their nature to be courageous, they will act with timidity. And so, those who make their homes better by closing themselves inside them and going about their household duties, destroy their homes when they leave them to go gadding about. And those who please their husbands and provide them with a good example by bustling around their home and hearth, when they appear on the street, poison the hearts and weaken the souls of all who look upon them; these women, who because they are themselves weak, were born to live inside the darkness and secrecy of their own four walls.

(Como son los hombres para lo público, assí las mugeres para el encerramiento: y como es de los hombres el hablar y salir a luz, assí dellas el encerrarse y encubrirse. Aun en la Iglesia, adonde la necessidad de la religión las lleva, y el servicio de Dios, quiere S. Pablo que estén cubiertas que apenas los hombres las vean, y consentirá que por su antojo buelen por las plazas y calles, haziendo alarde de sí? Que ha de hazer fuera de su casa, la que no tiene partes ningunas, de las que piden las cosas que fuera della se tratan. Forzoso es que, como la experiencia lo enseña, pues no tienen saber para los negocios de substancia, traten saliendo, de poquedades y menudencias: y forzoso es, que pues no es de su oficio, ni natural, hazer lo que pide valor, hagan el oficio contrario. Y assí es que las que en sus casas cerradas y occupadas las mejoran, andando fuera dellas las destruyen. Y las que con andar por sus rincones ganarán las voluntades y edificarán las consciencias de sus maridos, visitando las calles, corrompen los corazones agenos: y enmollecen las almas de los que las veen, las que por ser ellas muelles, se hizieron para la sombra, y para el secreto de sus paredes.)[4]

---

[4] Luis de León, pp. 98-9.

The exclusion of women from the public world of men is justified in two ways: first, women do not possess the capabilities to perform those activities which take place outside the home; and second, their weakness *(por ser muelles)*[5] is a defect which contaminates the men with whom they might come in contact in public life. Social space, that is, space in which communitary activities – important and weighty matters – take place, is perceived exclusively as public *(lo público)*,[6] a terrain which is the common property of men. The space within the house has no social relation to the outside male community. It is an enclosed space, existing within the public world, but hidden off from it and inaccessible. Women can preserve the sacrosanct quality of this secret space only by remaining in it. A woman (wife) outside the house becomes a public woman, and by extension the intimate enclave of the house becomes public. The house, then, is perceived as an ultimate feudal preserve, and woman its guardian, the key to the walled city which contains the man's possessions, among them, his wife: "...God created woman, and gave her as companion to her husband, in order that she might guard his home and be, as it were, the key to it." ("...el fin para que ordenó Dios la muger, y se la dió por compañía al marido, fue para que le guardasse la casa... y fuesse como su llave...")[7]

Our second quote, taken from a feminist text written by Doña Josefa Amar y Borbón and published in 1790, while reflecting the

---

[5] The Corominas etymological dictionary defines *muelle: "flexible, blando, suave."* (flexible, soft, smooth). Fr. Luis' use of the word *muelle* always carries a direct reference to female physiology as well as an implicit reference to female moral weakness, for example: "God gave women little strength and weak limbs, because he didn't create them to go travelling about but to sit quietly in their corners." ("Porque les dió a las mugeres las fuerzas flacas, y los miembros muelles, sino porque les crió no para ser postas, sino para estar en su rincón assentadas."), pp. 97-8. His fear that the physical presence of disgustingly soft women in the street will have a morally contaminating effect on men, will "weaken *(emollecen)* their souls," gives to the word *muelle* a misogynistic and censorious overtone which will find its way into nineteenth-century vocabulary as *"la vida muelle,"* the easy life, of the Spanish prostitute.

[6] The Covarrubias dictionary defines *público: "lo que todos saben y es notorio, pública voz y fama."* (what is well-known and notorious, public voice and reputation.) *Lo público*, that which is appropriated for common use, is contrasted not to private but to secret, *secreto: "todo lo que está encubierto y callado."* (all that is covered up and silenced.) This contrast between public life and secrecy underscores the fact that social life took place in the public eye, and outside the home. Female virtue is so weak, it can only thrive in the darkness and obscurity of the house. The sunshine of the plaza reveals woman's physical and moral defects.

[7] Luis de León, p. 97.

influence of the Spanish Enlightenment in its support for education for upper-class women, still maintains the traditional position that women do not belong in the public world:

> The order or disorder of private families transcends the family and influences public well-being and tranquility. The particular occupation of women is located within these private families: that is, the management and governing of the household, the care and raising of the children, and above all, the intimacy and perfection of her husband's society.
>
> (El orden y desorden de las familias privadas trasciende y se comunica a la felicidad y quietud pública. En estas familias privadas tienen las mugeres su particular empleo. Este es la dirección y gobierno de la casa, el cuidado y crianza de los hijos, y sobre todo la íntima y perfecta sociedad con el marido.)[8]

What distinguishes this quote from our previous one is the concept of a private social world, that of the family, which although restricted to the fixed perimeter of the house, exists in relationship to the public world. In theory, women are no longer excluded from public life, since the order and prosperity which is created autonomously within the family transcends the walls of the house and effects the well-being of all. Essential to this viewpoint is the author's definition of the State: "The more or less numerous grouping of individuals and families." ("La congregación más o menos numerosa de individuos y de familias.")[9]

The physical space of the house is no longer primarily a strongbox for the husband's possessions; it has been given a social content, and the social life in which the woman participates is no longer the harem-like exclusion of Fray Luis' enclosure. The private intimacy between husband and wife, and the family unit of parents and children form an individual microcosm of public society. It is a complete structure, and therefore perfect.[10]

---

[8] *Discurso sobre la educación física y moral de las mugeres* (Madrid, 1790), prólogo, XII.

[9] Amar y Borbón, prólogo, I.

[10] The concept of privacy, both bodily privacy and the idea of a private social life away from the public eye comes into existence throughout the seventeenth and eighteenth centuries. Even then, the evolution of a private domestic life is a direct function of the material abundance which permits the development of a taste for privacy. See Phillipe Ariès, *Centuries of Childhood: A Social History of Family*

Our third quote taken from an article published in *La Guirnalda* in 1873 is prototypical of the florid prose which predominates in the women's magazines which begin to proliferate towards the end of the 1840's:

> Woman does not need political rights; she requires respect, consideration and protection. By her very nature, she is not called upon to perform the coarse labors of the stronger sex; her mission is one of peace and tranquility; her kingdom resides within the bosom of the family; it is there that she has her throne.
>
> (No necesita la mujer derechos políticos sino respetos, consideraciones y cuidados. No está llamada por su naturaleza a las rudas faenas del sexo fuerte; su misión es de paz y tranquilidad; su reinado reside en el seno de la familia; allí tiene su trono.)[11]

Once again the innate physical weakness of women precludes their participation in the work done by men outside the home. But the concept of public life has changed radically to include the idea of limited participation in the governing of the state. The author equates an undefined power within the institution of the family with political rights. The real exercise of political rights in the public sphere is, however, one of the "coarse labors" which only men can perform.

The family, as an institution, has taken the place of the physical fortress, the house. Now it is the family which protects woman from the arduous tasks of public life and at the same time provides a private kingdom over which she can rule. The claustrophobic image of a throne within the bosom of the family spells out only too well the limitations of her realm.

Life (New York: Alfred A. Knopf, 1962), pp. 394-5, 405-7; see also Fernand Braudel, *Capitalism and Material Life 1400-1800*, trans. M. Kochan (New York: Harper and Row, 1974), pp. 224, 240; and Lawrence Stone, *The Family, Sex and Marriage in England: 1500-1800* (New York: Harper and Row, 1977), pp. 253-7.

[11] F. M. Tubino, "La mujer y su reforma moral," *La Guirnalda*, año VII, núm. 147, 1 (febrero 1873), pp. 9-10.

CHAPTER ONE

THE PERFECT WIFE: FROM COUNTER-REFORMATION TO ENLIGHTENMENT

Our introduction has brought into relief the fact that different historical manifestations of traditional ideology concerning the role of women in Spanish society change not only in literary style but also in content. To understand how Fray Luis' ideal wife of the Spanish Catholic Counter-Reformation evolves into the nineteenth-century *ángel del hogar*, we must return to the late sixteenth century and analyze the relation between Fray Luis' ideological position and the specific class interests it seeks to vindicate.

Although virtually nothing is known about Doña María Valera Osorio,[1] the woman to whom Fray Luis dedicates *La perfecta casada*, it is evident throughout the text that the author directs his advice to a woman of the upper class. In addition, the constant strictures against visiting, gossiping, shopping in stores, parties and the mere presence of women in the plaza or street[2] implies a critique of the customs of urban rather than rural women.

The author proposes a general solution to the problem of women based on an adoption of the modes of country life by all women both urban and rural. He sets up a moral hierarchy for all economic activity in which that kind which precludes the use of money – the "natural" agrarian economy of the self-sufficient landed estate – is morally superior to the world of commerce, or, coming down the scale, to the artisan, soldier or the salaried day-laborer, although

---

[1] Luis de León, prólogo, XI.
[2] Luis de León, pp. 99, 51-52.

these kinds of employment are virtuous to the extent that they require industriousness.[3] This moral hierarchy is, in effect, a revindication of that class which perpetuates itself through the system of the entailed country estate, and the duties which Fray Luis imposes upon the perfect wife reflect his interest in the preservation of this class through the preservation of its property.

The primary duty of the perfect wife is that of custodian and judicious administrator of the inherited patrimony of her marriage partner. Her function in the domestic economy is based on a strict division of labor: men produce wealth and women conserve it:

> Just as man's obligation is to acquire, so does woman have the obligation to preserve and to save: and this conservation is like a payment or salary which by right she owes to her husband for the sweat of his labor.
>
> (Y como el hombre está obligado al trabajo del adquirir, assí la muger tiene obligación al conservar y guardar: y que aquesta guarda es como paga y salario, que de derecho se debe a aquél servicio y sudor.)[4]

Fray Luis' description of this division of labor – men produce and women administer consumption or spending – masks the reality in which the class of property owners is maintained by the *"sudor"* [sweat] of a laboring class composed of both sexes. But this passage also serves to ennoble the function of the estate owner and to establish his hierarchical position in relation to his marriage partner within the ruling class.

According to the laws of pre-capitalist agrarian economy, wealth is non-renewable. To spend is to deplete the estate. Fray Luis' insistence on the wickedness of the spendthrift woman[5] is in part a result of his denial of the moral right to enrich oneself through the investment of capital:

---

[3] Luis de León, pp. 32-36.

[4] Luis de León, p. 29. Fray Luis de León relies on Aristotle's description of the biological differences between men and women: women are cold and humid, men are dry and hot, to justify the division of labor into the passive task of preserving and the active task of acquiring: "woman, who is by nature frail and cold, inclines to a lack of movement and to scarcity, and is suited to frugality" ("...la mujer, que por ser de natural flaco y frío es inclinada al sossiego y a la escasez, y es buena para guardar") [p. 22].

[5] Luis de León, p. 26, pp. 60-90.

>...with her [the perfect wife] he is content with the land that he inherited from his ancestors and with cultivating its fruits, rather than going into debt, or becoming entwined with the dangers and uncertainties of other kinds of profits and affairs... to live by one's property is an innocent and sinless life, and any other kind of livelihood remains blameless only by a miracle.
>
> (...que con ella se contenta con la hazienda que heredó de sus padres, y con la labranza y fruto della, y que ni se adeuda, ni menos se enlaza con el peligro y desassossiego de otras grangerías y tratos,... bivir uno de su patrimonio, es vida innocente y sin pecado, y los demás tratos por maravilla carecen del.)[6]

The wife's careful administration of the household economy is seen as a financial asset; by not spending, the inheritance will automatically increase and the husband will not be forced to enter into other kinds of money-earning activities:

> ...having her to keep his household well-stocked and rich, he is not forced to sail the seas, nor to go to war, nor to place his monies out to earn interest, nor to get mixed up in vile and unjust affairs. By working his inherited lands and gathering the fruit of his labors, and having her to safekeep and administer what he has reaped, he possesses sufficient wealth.
>
> (...teniéndola a ella, para tener su casa abastada y rica, no tiene la necessidad de correr la mar, ni yr a la guerra, ni de dar sus dineros a logro, ni de enredarse en tratos viles e injustos, sino que con labrar él sus heredades cogiendo su fructo, y con tenerla a ella por guarda y por beneficiadora de lo cogido, tiene riqueza bastante.)[7]

In addition to the perfect wife's duty to preserve the estate through the exercise of thrift *(economía)*, she must also increase her husband's wealth through her own industry. The question of how this is to be accomplished provokes a two-page panegyric on the virtue of the spinning wheel.[8] The image of the virtuous wife at her spinning wheel is charged with the moral values of the period,

---

[6] Luis de León, p. 23.
[7] Luis de León, p. 22.
[8] Covarrubias defines *hilar* [to weave]: "the exercise and occupation of domestic and industrious women." ("exercicio y ocupación de mugeres caseras y hazendosas.") This definition underlines the fact that spinning is, *by definition*, woman's work. It is also the specific occupation by which the virtuous wife is defined.

foremost among them the belief that idleness *(el ocio)* is the source of wickedness.⁹ The fact that this belief is itself an ideological by-product of the system which Fray Luis defends is cogently expressed by José Antonio Maravall in a section of his work *Estado moderno y mentalidad social*, sub-titled "El mito de 'trabajar más' como supervivencia de una sociedad estacionaria" (The Myth of 'always working' as a Product of Static Societies).

> The social recognition of the moral superiority of the very industrious and his depiction as a paradigm for an entire population, has a rural origin and is linked to those cultures of a predominantly agrarian character. The cliché, "idleness is the devil's handmaiden" is coined and perpetuated in a rural ambience. While the urban centers from an early date always attempted to implement a regimented and limited work schedule,... in the rural environment, work was seen as unending labor. Not being able to be without an occupation, without doing some kind of task, is a virtue typical of an archaic and static rural society.
>
> (El reconocimiento social de la superioridad moral del muy trabajador y su presentación como paradigma a toda una población, tiene un origen rural y está ligado a las culturas de predominante carácter agrario. El tópico "la ociosidad, madre del vicio" se forma y desarrolla en un medio campesino. Mientras que el mundo urbano procura siempre desde temprana fecha, un trabajo reglamentado y limitado... en el mundo rural el trabajo aparece como ocupación de todas las horas: el no saber estar sin hacer algo, sin ocuparse en algo, es una virtud típica de una sociedad estática y campesina arcaizante.)¹⁰

Covarrubias thus reinforces our interpretation that Fray Luis would have the perfect wife spin, not only for the value of her product, but also because this activity is emblematic of the good woman. Sebastián de Covarrubias, *Tesoro de la lengua castellana o española*. Según la impresión de 1611, ed. Martín de Riquer (Barcelona, 1943).

[9] Covarrubias defines *ocio*: [idleness or inactivity]: "it is not as common a word as idleness, idle, he who does not busy himself with any occupation." ("no es tan usado vocablo como ociosidad, ocioso, el que no se ocupa en cosa alguna.") We are a long way from the modern concept of work as wage-labor measured by the clock, and its negation, so-called free-time, measured as time left over from work-time. The modern translation of *ocio* as leisure would therefore be inaccurate. See Sebastián de Grazia, *Of Time, Work and Leisure* (New York: The Twentieth Century Fund, 1962), esp. pp. 63-68.

[10] José Antonio Maravall, *Estado moderno y mentalidad social*, vol. 2 (Madrid: Revista de Occidente, 1972), p. 392.

The participation of the mistress of the household in the production of cloth, and especially, in the confection of wearing apparel and bed-clothes is seen by Fray Luis as both a money-saving and a money-earning activity, since private domestic production meant that these articles did not have to be purchased at current inflationary prices.[11] Maravall cites the concern of the court as early as 1544 concerning the impact of salaries on the price of ready-made goods: "the workmanship costs more than the silks and the fabric of the clothes..." ("questan más las hechuras que las sedas y el paño de la ropa...")[12]

But Fray Luis, cognizant of the disdain which upper-class women shared with upper-class men for manual labor,[13] exhorts them to industry by arguing their obligation to serve as exemplar for the lower classes:

> ...let them pick up their distaff, and arm their fingers with needle and thimble, and surrounded by their ladies-in-waiting, and in their midst, together sew pieces of beautiful fancy work, so that with this pastime, they wile away part of the evening and do not succumb to slothful sleep but rather make use of their time, and that these tasks may occupy the youthful thoughts of their handmaidens, who, inspired by the example of the lady of the house, will compete among themselves to see who can work the hardest...
>
> (...tomen la rueca y armen los dedos con la aguja y dedal, y cercadas de sus damas, y en medio dellas hagan labores ricas con ellas, y engañen algo de la noche con este exercício, y hurten se al vicioso sueño para entender en el, y occupen los pensamientos mozos de sus doncellas en estas haziendas, y hagan que animadas con el ejemplo de la señora, contiendan todas entre sí procurando aventajarse en el ser hazendosas.)[14]

---

[11] Luis de León, p. 40.

[12] Maravall, p. 359.

[13] Luis de León, p. 32. "But they will protest, perhaps, the delicate ladies of today, that this description is vulgar, and that the married woman who spins and weaves is the wife of some laborer, and belongs to a different social rank than they do, and they want to hear nothing more about it." ("Pero dirán, por ventura las señoras delicadas, de agora, que esta pintura es grossera, y que aquesta casada es muger de algún labrador, que hila y texe, y muger de estado diferente del suyo, y que assí no habla con ellas.")

[14] Luis de León, p. 37.

As this quote makes clear, the social role of exerting moral influence is the exclusive prerogative of upper-class women. Exemplary virtue, as well as property, is the patrimony of the aristocracy and the wealthy gentry.

The transmission of the family estate through the patriarchal line places an additional and essential duty upon the wife, that of absolute sexual fidelity:

> ...the woman's fidelity... is the foundation upon which this whole edifice is built, in a word, it is the being and the essence of the married woman: because if she is not faithful she is not a woman; she is a treacherous whore and vile, putrid filth; of every kind of offal, she is the most rank and despised.
>
> (...el ser honesta una muger... es como el subjeto sobre el qual todo este edificio se funda, y para dezirlo en una palabra, es como el ser y la substancia de la casada: porque si no tiene esto no es ya muger sino alevosa ramera, y vilissimo cieno, y vassura la más hedionda de todas, u la más despreciada.)[15]

Any weakening of patriarchal authority undermines the divinely ordained social structure. The ultimate rebellion against male authority is female sexual infidelity; such an event can only be imagined in apocalyptic terms:

> It must be understood that for a woman to deceive her husband is the same as if the stars were to cease to shine and the heavens to fall: such a thing breaks the laws of nature and returns everything to its former state of primordial chaos.
>
> (Entendiendo que el quebrar la muger a su marido la fe, es perder las estrellas su luz, y caerse los cielos, y quebrantar sus leyes la naturaleza, y volverse todo en aquella confusión antigua y primera.)[16]

The husband maintains control over his wife by secluding her within his house and by preventing any foreign influence from penetrating from the outside.[17] After a warning against go-betweens, (*celestinas* or *trotaconventos*), who disguise themselves as poor women

---

[15] Luis de León, p. 19.
[16] Luis de León, p. 20.
[17] See Oñate, p. 117.

in need of charity, Fray Luis continues with an additional remonstrance against novels and gossip. The paranoia and the xenophobia of the political ambience of the Counter-Reformation is succinctly expressed in the analogy which the author uses to illustrate his point:

> In well-organized Republics, those kinds that were formerly organized by law, nothing was more forbidden than communication with foreigners or with those of different customs.
>
> (En las repúblicas bien ordenadas, los que antiguamente las ordenaron con leyes, ninguna cosa vedaron más, que la comunicación con los estraños, y de diferentes costumbres.)[18]

In conclusion, Fray Luis' ideal of the perfect wife is one which places her within a pre-capitalist agrarian economy. She is not an industrious bourgeois urban housewife, but the administrator of a large estate with powerful if limited authority over her household servants and slaves. Although she may be completely restricted to this estate, the house is large, and within its limits it is still possible, if she so desires, to participate in productive labor which will directly benefit the economic unit of which she is a member. Her duties are not to provide a spiritual haven for her husband but to help him protect and preserve the estate. Nor is motherhood a sacred charge as it will be in the nineteenth century.[19] Her obligation as mother is primarily to bear her husband's children rather than those of another man. Although she is exhorted to breastfeed them, she should do so mainly to prevent their contamination (bastardization) through the milk of lower-class and slave wom-

---

[18] Luis de León, p. 56.

[19] Fray Luis' preoccupation with female extravagance completely outweighs his interest in the mother-child relationship. Indeed, children, except for the nursing infant, are absent entirely from his description of the domestic scene. For a discussion on Fray Luis' inattention to children's education see, Alain Guy, "L'Ethique Familiale, Politique et Sociale," in *La Pensée de Fray Luis de León* (Limoges: Imprimerie A. Bontemps, 1943). Guy provides additional proof of the durability of Fray Luis' image of the perfect wife by praising her as: "a model of good manners and good sense, very suitable for guiding the conscience and the heart of a young woman of the 16th century and... is it necessary to say, the very spirit of her twentieth-century sisters?" ("...un modèle de finesse et de bon sens, très apte à dirigir la conscience et le coeur d'une jeune femme du XVIe siècle et... faut-il le dire? l'esprit même de ses soeurs du XXe siècle" (p. 655).

en.[20] The perfect wife of the Counter-Reformation is an efficient, industrious albeit unequal business partner to her upper-class husband. If she sits surrounded by anyone, it is not her children but her servants, whose spinning she directs, and if she is absolutely perfect, she is at the wheel herself.

The Tradition of Patriarchal Authority in the Home

The revindication of patriarchal authority within the framework of the upper-class family, the owners of the 'great houses', is enunciated at length in an early eighteenth-century moral treatise by Fray Antonio Arbiol, entitled *La familia regulada con doctrina de la Sagrada Escritura y Santos Padres de la Iglesia católica,* first published in 1715 and read in subsequent editions throughout the century.[21] Written as a post-tridentine apology for the institution of marriage, this text is firmly entrenched within a wider cultural change that Marcel Bataillon calls the "secularization of piety."[22] While this process followed a different trajectory in the Protestant countries, where the marriage of the clergy institutionalized the fusion of the interest of the Church and the landed gentry under the protection of the civil state,[23] Arbiol's treatise exemplifies Bataillon's statement that "The question itself of marriage... was connected to and, in a certain way, complementary to that of ecclesiastical and monastical celibacy."[24] Some of Arbiol's most energetic pages are dedicated to the

---

[20] Luis de León, pp. 102-6.

[21] Fray Antonio Arbiol, *La familia regulada con doctrina de la Sagrada Escritura, y Santos Padres de la Iglesia católica,* first published in 1715, ed. (Madrid, 1783). Arbiol, a Franciscan, was born in 1651 and died in Saragossa in 1726. He wrote numerous religious works, among them: *Los desengaños místicos, La religiosa instruida,* and *Estragos de la lujuria y sus remedios. La familia regulada...* is cited by Vicente Palacio Atard as one of the most widely-read monographs on Christian instruction in the eighteenth century. See *Los españoles de la Ilustración* (Madrid: Ediciones Guadarrama, 1964), n. 37, p. 70.

[22] Marcel Bataillon, *Erasmo y España: Estudios sobre la historia espiritual del siglo XVI,* vol. 1 (México: Fondo de Cultura Económica, 1950), p. 334.

[23] See Christopher Hill, *Society and Puritanism in Pre-Revolutionary England,* esp. Ch. 12, "The Spiritualization of the Household" (London: Secker and Warburg, 1964); see also John Bossy, "Counter-Reformation and the People of Catholic Europe," *Past and Present,* no. 47 (May, 1970), pp. 51-70, for a consideration of the effect of the Tridentine reforms on the modern institution of the family.

[24] Bataillon, p. 334. "La cuestión misma del matrimonio... era conexa, y en cierto modo complementaria, de la del celibato eclesiástico y monástico."

condemnation of the abuse of the father's authority over his children known as the right of *patria potestas*, which often resulted in enforced monastic vocations or the prevention of a son's marriage in order to maintain tutelage over his property.[25]

The sanctification of marriage – its dignification by the Church as a sacrament rather than a civil contract – demanded a softening of the traditional ecclesiastic position on the dichotomy between asceticism-sainthood and carnality-damnation, in order to include a space for legitimate sexual activity within a marriage blessed by the Catholic Church. With this purpose in mind, the entire first section of Arbiol's treatise is given over to a catalogue of non-celibate, (married) saints. Philippe Ariès' statement that "...the progress of the concept of the family and of the religious rehabilitation of the layman followed parallel paths..."[26] is substantiated by Arbiol's use of the Holy Family as a model for perfect conjugal harmony in the service of God. The image of the chaste Joseph, and Mary, the virgin Mother of God, while in apparent conflict with the need to destigmatize legitimate sexual activity, serves to incorporate marriage into an ideological spiritual realm maintained and regulated by the Church.[27]

The main purpose of the marriage institution, according to the Church, is to provide a structure which not only permits but is conducive to the salvation of the soul. The negative aspect of St. Paul's dictum, "it is better to marry than to burn", is deemphasized as marriage is vindicated as an opportunity to carry the cross, perhaps the only kind of "harsh labor" ("ruda faena") for which the weaker sex is particularly suited.[28]

The marginal position of St. Joseph in relation to the fervent cult of the Virgin Mary fomented by the Catholic Church through-

---

[25] Arbiol, pp. 480-1, 483.

[26] Ariès, p. 357.

[27] Arbiol, p. 60. The various Tridentine reforms of the Catholic marriage rite demonstrate that the Catholic Counter-Reformation hoped 1) to establish clerical hegemony over the means of contracting marriage and 2) to reaffirm and to legitimize the idea of the Parish and the authority of the Parish priest in the performance of religious rites. See *Canons and Decrees of the Council of Trent*, trans. Rev. J. Waterworth (London, 1848), pp. 194-204. See also Bossy, cited, n. 23.

[28] Arbiol, p. 73. "Consider that, since it has been thus ordained or permitted by Our Lord God, it must be to the benefit of their soul's salvation, to carry their burdens and their cross with great patience." ("Considere, que cuando así lo dispuso, o lo permitió para la salvación de su alma, llevando sus trabajos, y su cruz con mucha paciencia.")

out the middle ages constitutes a problem for Catholic propagandists. In order for the image of the Holy Family to reflect the dominant ideology which upholds absolute patriarchal authority, St. Joseph must be rehabilitated into Catholic mythology as a wise and active head of the family, rather than the passive and obedient recipient of God's plan for the birth of his Son. Arbiol resolves this problem, following the thinking of the Church, by separating moral superiority – delegated to the Virgin – from social authority,[29] which resides exclusively in the male, by reason of his likeness to the male Christ, head of the communion of saints:

> The mystic head of the male is Christ Our Lord, and the head of woman is the male, her husband,... The male is the image and the glory of God, and woman is the glory of her husband,...
>
> (La cabeza mística del varón es Cristo Señor nuestro, y la cabeza de la muger es el varón su marido,... El varón es imagen, y gloria de Diós, y la muger es gloria de su marido,...)[30]

According to Arbiol, the family unit, headed by the husband, extends downward to wife, children, servants and slaves. So precisely defined is the hierarchy, he even includes a brief final chapter on the duties of dwarfs and pygmies. The wife's duties are defined according to her place in the hierarchy and can be synthesized into one rule: "The subordination and affectionate obedience which the wife owes to her husband..." ("La sujeción, y afectuosa obediencia, que debe tener la muger a su marido...")[31] This submission to male authority is two-fold: intellectual or moral and physical. Arbiol admits of a possible relationship between the education of women and the undermining of patriarchal power when he says: "Let women not turn themselves into doctors [of philosophy], but rather let them remain subject to their man." ("...que no se hagan doctoras, sino que estén sujetas a su varón...")[32]

Particular emphasis is placed on the physical submission of wives to the sexual demands of their husbands. Even though the wife is continually exhorted to model her behavior on that of the

---

[29] Arbiol, p. 71.
[30] Arbiol, p. 68.
[31] Ibid.
[32] Arbiol, p. 66.

Virgin Mary, the Virgin's purity must not be a pretext for avoiding the payment of the wife's debt to her husband:

> Some inconsiderate women are deceived by the enemy [the devil] under the false pretext of a greater purity, and are unable to understand that by submitting their will in order to pay that which they owe [to their husbands] for the love of God, is an act deserving of eternal life.
>
> (A algunas mugeres inconsideradas las engaña el enemigo con pretexto falso de más pureza, y no acaban de entender, que el vencerse a pagar lo que deben por el amor de Dios, es acto meritorio de vida eterna.)[33]

Arbiol hints that marital satisfaction of sexual needs is a mutual obligation but all egalitarian sentiment is neutralized with the blunt reminder that: "The man should love his wife as he loves himself, and the wife should love and fear her man." ("El varón ame a su muger, como a sí mismo, y la muger ame, y tema a su varón.")[34]

The reign of terror which the husband is authorized to exercise over the subjects under his tutelage in order to maintain his position of authority is given particular emphasis in those chapters which touch upon the education of the children.[35] The basic assumption is that children are evil: "The evil tendencies of the child are continually increasing,..." ("La malicia de las criaturas de día en día

---

[33] Arbiol, p. 68. It is clear from Arbiol's frequent comments on the subject that wives used church attendance as a means of escaping the house and their husband's constant surveillance. The conflict between patriarchal secular authority (the Family) and patriarchal ecclesiastical authority (the Church) is expressed with much more intensity in Arbiol's works, while it is only alluded to in *La perfecta casada*. Arbiol's attempt at a solution is to develop a model in which Church authority will reinforce patriarchal domestic authority and vice-versa. The husband is urged to correct his wife's excess devotion with tenderness: "...it is not desirable that in order to make her more moderate, she would lose her sense of piety and abandon it [religious devotion] entirely" ("...no sea que por hacerla moderada, la vuelva indevota, y lo dexe todo") [p. 63].

[34] Arbiol, p. 66.

[35] The practice of whipping and other physical punishments to discipline children throughout the sixteenth, seventeenth, and eighteenth centuries has been thoroughly documented in both Ariès and Stone (see intro, n. 10 for references). Arbiol insists that: "the father who truly loves his child, will whip him frequently" ("el padre que en verdad ama a su hijo, le azota con frequencia") [p. 231]. Nor does his wife escape: Arbiol approves "some moderate punishment" ("algún moderado castigo") [p. 436], except during pregnancy, because of the danger of aborting the foetus.

va de aumento,..."); and only the rod will cure them of their vices: "...better teach them to cry than to laugh." ("...antes les enseñarás a llorar que a reir.")[36]

Scandalous behavior that reflects on the good name of the family, defined as the male lineage and therefore embodied in the male surname, must be prevented by a rigid and inviolable separation of the sexes on all levels of the hierarchy, including that of brother and sister.[37] The role of the mother in the education of her daughters is reduced to a pale reflection of the authoritarian posture of the father. Although she is charged with custodianship of her daughters in the normal order of sexual apartheid,[38] the burden of discipline falls upon the father in the case of overly recalcitrant daughters:

> The truth of the matter is that there are some daughters so restless and bad that anything a poor father might do is insufficient to repress them and it would be useful for the resolute father to spit in their face, thus says the Sacred Text, that they might be shamed in the blush of their unsightliness, and put a stop to their wicked ways.
>
> (Verdad es, que hay algunas hijas tan inquietas, y malas, que no basta el cuidado de un pobre padre para reprimirlas; y sería conveniente, que el padre resuelto escupiese en la cara, dice el Sagrado Texto, para que ellas se confundiesen con el rubor de su fealdad, y pusiesen raya a sus malos pasos.)[39]

La familia regulada... is of special interest to us as a text which captures and portrays the tensions born of irreconcilable conflicts of interest between master and servant, traditionally considered to be part of the upper-class family. This social unit is no longer bound together by reciprocal ties of feudal loyalty, but by the servant's need for employment and the hope of an inadequate wage, all too often in arrears.[40] The idealized image of domestic harmony between the mistress and her maids portrayed in Fray Luis' *La perfecta casada* has vanished. The servants, by reason of their relative economic autonomy, belong more to the public world than to the private realm of

---

[36] Arbiol, p. 488.
[37] Arbiol, pp. 492, 510, 578.
[38] Arbiol, p. 576.
[39] Arbiol, p. 489.
[40] Maravall, pp. 386-92.

the family. While the traditional moral obligation of the master to serve as an exemplar for his servants is remarked upon, they are not united by any affective ties; on the contrary, "man's enemies are his servants" ("los enemigos del hombre son sus domésticos").[41] What must be avoided at all costs is the possible alliance between the children of the house and the servants. The position of the children and the servants in relation to male parental authority is singularly parallel, since the total subjection of the children is not yet alleviated by modern concepts of education, nor is the mother allowed to mediate between them, if indeed she wished to do so.[42]

The final image of the extended patriarchal upper-class family, as described by Arbiol, is one in which the lone patriarch, beset on all sides by children, servants and perhaps an unsubmissive wife, argues, cajoles, attempts to bargain, and finally demands that his household subjects acquiesce to his natural-divine right to dispose of their destinies.

WOMEN IN THE SPANISH ENLIGHTENMENT

It is in light of our examination of power and authority within the extended patriarchal family of the *ancien régime*, that we return to a more detailed study of the social values enunciated by the Spanish Enlightenment figure, Doña Josefa Amar y Borbón. Her *Discurso sobre la educación física y moral de las mugeres* is mainly a defense of the right of upper-class women to have access to the cultural life of their husbands. She argues, as did Benito Feijóo y Montenegro twenty-five years earlier in his "Defensa de la muger" [1765], that the apparent frivolity of women is a result of their lack of education, rather than an innate characteristic of the female sex.[43]

---

[41] Arbiol, p. 491. One indication of an increasing sense of a private life is the presence throughout the text of a threatening amorphous *pueblo* [people], perceived as a social entity separate from and antagonistic to the family.

[42] Arbiol, p. 71.

[43] Amar y Borbón, p. 230. It is interesting that Feijóo also attributes the inferiority of feminine discourse not only to their lack of a formal education, but also to the deprivation of social stimuli which results from their forced seclusion within the home. See Benito Feijóo y Montenegro, "La Defensa de las mugeres," *Teatro crítico universal,* tomo primero, Discurso XVI (Madrid, 1765), pp. 408-9, 448-9.

What distinguishes Amar y Borbón from her contemporaries on the subject of education for women, is her sympathetic understanding of the tedium experienced by those wealthy women who chose not to enter into the shallow pastimes of their class: the salon life of the perpetual *tertulia*, the choosing of a *cortejo*, a kind of lap-dog lover and official fan-waver, and in general, the world of vanity and ostentation so brilliantly described by Carmen Martín Gaite in her book *Usos amorosos del dieciocho en España*.[44] Although the goals of reform outlined by Amar y Borbón do not transcend the interests of the women of her own class, she justifies the need for women's education on a concept of marriage based not on the mindless submission of wife to husband but on the harmony born of communication between intellectual and moral equals:

> The marriage institution presupposes a structure of two people who must live in eternal and mutual union and society: for that reason, the communication of ideas as well as of interests is necessary; for unless this is so, a marriage will never be united and tranquil.
>
> (La institución del matrimonio supone el designio de dos personas que han de vivir perpetuamente en mutua sociedad y unión: para esto, es necesaria la comunicación de ideas, como la de intereses; y de otro modo no serán nunca los matrimonios unidos y pacíficos.)[45]

Amar y Borbón's new definition of the 'companionate marriage'[46] reevaluates the rigid authority with which the husband controls the wife:

> The subjection of the wife to her husband is so declared by Saint Paul in his letter to Tito; but his reign must be comparable to a political one which fosters the common good, rather than the control which the parents exercise over their children, which is more like a royal and sovereign power.
>
> (La sujeción de la mujer al marido la declara S. Pablo en su Epístola a Tito; pero el imperio de este ha de ser semejante al

---

[44] Carmen Martín Gaite, *Usos amorosos del dieciocho en España* (Madrid: Siglo Veintiuno, 1972).

[45] Amar y Borbón, prólogo, IX.

[46] I have borrowed the term from Lawrence Stone, *The Family, Sex and Marriage in England 1500-1800*, Chapter 8.

de la política, en el cual se promueve la utilidad común, distinto del que tienen los padres sobre los hijos, que es parecido al dominio real y soberano.)[47]

This passage is more than a plea for a rule of enlightened despotism within the family. Amar y Borbón is asking that Enlightenment ideology penetrate the archaic family power structure. Although she judges it suitable that children continue to live under the *ancien régime,* women should be afforded the status of citizen, with the right, if not of vote, at least of voice in the ordering of family affairs.

One of the most common arguments against higher education for women is that their daily life of domestic labor within the household makes any but the most rudimentary education unnecessary. This argument is frequently accompanied by an expression of concern that time dedicated to study would be subtracted from the all-consuming task of serving the husband and children. Amar y Borbón defends herself against these prejudices, as will apologists for female education in the nineteenth century, by continually paying homage to the wife's responsibility for her domestic duties:

> Handiwork [sewing, etc.] and the governing of the household are the characteristic talents of women; that is to say, that even when they develop others, which is very well advised, the former remain the primary and most essential ones...
>
> (Las labores de manos y el gobierno doméstico son como las prendas características de las mujeres; es decir que aun cuando reunan otras, que será muy conveniente, aquellas deben ser las primeras y esenciales...)[48]

But she also argues that:

> ...study and reading make the seclusion of the home pleasant, and wipe away or distort that idea of servitude consistent with the never-ending care and governance of the household;...
>
> (...el estudio y la lectura hacen agradable el retiro de la casa, y borran o desfiguran aquella idea de servidumbre, que representa el continuo cuidado y gobierno doméstico;...)[49]

---

[47] Amar y Borbón, p. 285.
[48] Amar y Borbón, p. 150.
[49] Amar y Borbón, p. 197.

This argument becomes much more persuasive when combined with the veiled threat of what may happen if women are not provided with the means to alleviate the tedium of their solitude: "they will try to amuse themselves at any price." ("se procura buscar la distracción a cualquier precio.")[50]

It comes as no surprise that Amar y Borbón does not advocate that women leave the home in order to receive more education. They would have to attend the university with men, or separate schools would have to be built for them, and this would creat "disorder".[51] Her acceptance of the basic immutability of the social structure is stated early in the prologue: "Let us not form any kind of unrealistic plan: let us try only to rectify as much as possible that which is already established." ("No formemos pues un plan fantástico: tratemos sólo de rectificar en lo posible el que está ya establecido.")[52]

Her suggestions for reform are not seen as antagonistic by the official censor Miguel de Manual y Rodríguez, who reviewed her book for the Council of the Supreme Inquisition, which had been revived under Carlos IV as a result of the general reaction of the Spanish rulers to the French Revolution.[53] The censor praises her ideas effusively:

> I can only find much to be admired in this Discourse; far from containing anything against religion, Royalty or the law, everything in it is doctrine in complete conformity with Catholicism and with the State.
>
> (Yo no he encontrado sino mucho que admirar en este discurso; tan lexos de contener cosa alguna opuesta a la religión, a la regalía y a las leyes, que todo él es un conjunto de doctrina la más conforme con el Catolicismo y la política.)

His comments indicate a growing appreciation of the social importance of women, and he supports the Discourse in the hope that it can be:

---

[50] Amar y Borbón, p. 167.
[51] Amar y Borbón, prólogo, XXX.
[52] Amar y Borbón, prólogo, XXXII.
[53] See Richard Herr, *The Eighteenth Century Revolution in Spain* (Princeton University Press, 1969), pp. 241, 266.

> ...a stimulating force that will help to bring about the successful attainment in Spain of that excellent education which we so desire for our women, and the advantages which the State can expect to gain from this noble and considerable part of its individuals.
>
> (...el movil de maior impulso para que se logre en nuestra España la buena educación que tanto se desea en las mugeres, y los beneficios que el Estado puede esperar de esta noble y considerable parte de sus individuos.) [54]

Although the activity of middle and upper-class women is still confined almost exclusively to the domestic sphere, their role as educators of the family's children gives them a social function which links them to the public sphere. The fact that the feminist demands of Amar y Borbón for female higher education are praised by the official Inquisition censor as progressive reveals the slowly changing fabric of Spanish social values as Spain edges her way towards the nineteenth century, but also underlines the potential for assimilation of certain feminist demands – at least at the level of propaganda – into a still rigidly classist and anti-feminist society.

Another important element which distinguishes this text from our previous ones, is the author's belief in the Lockean idea of the malleability of the infant and child, and the consequent importance which this gives to the parent-child relationship. Education is no longer the negative process of controlling the vicious instincts of the child with the rod, but rather one by which the ideas and the moral example of the educator mold the formless substance of the child. [55] Any rod may serve, but only the parent can or should create his child, since the example which he or she provides is the primary pedagogical tool. [56] The obligation of the upper class to live a model Christian life as an exemplar for the lower classes has become a social obligation which functions mainly in relation to their own children. Although lip service is paid to the traditional duty of the masters to Christianize their servants, the same Lockean tenets which make the role of parents indispensable in the education of

---

[54] Quoted in Manuel Serrano Sanz, *Apuntes para una biblioteca de escritoras españolas*, in Biblioteca de Autores Españoles, vol. 268 (Madrid, 1975), p. 28.
[55] Amar y Borbón, p. 251.
[56] Amar y Borbón, p. 261-62.

their children, relieve them of responsibility for the moral character of the servants:

> ...the servants come into the house already grown up; that is to say, educated, or rather one should say, without any education at all; and since they do not consider themselves to be as dependent as the children, they do not possess the same docility.
>
> (...los criados se admiten ya grandes; esto es, educados, o mejor decir, sin educación alguna; y como no se consideran tan dependientes como los hijos, no tienen la misma docilidad...)[57]

As the servants are isolated out of the extended family unit, so is the relation between parents and children tightened and intensified around the awesome burden of education. The idea of a parent-child bond is both new and problematic, so difficult to maintain that it can only function: "...by the reciprocal love which binds together this tie" ("...por el recíproco amor que estrecha este vínculo.")[58]

Amar y Borbón's acceptance of the immutability of the class structure of Spanish society permits her to state the exact limits of educational reform:

> It would seem that the proposal for a system of education should include all the classes of the State, but this is impossible in practice, if one takes into account that in this world everything is relative. It is true that the essential obligations belong to every class of people without distinction; but the same education is not needed by all in order to fulfill them. Consequently, we will not speak about women of the vulgar class, for whom it is sufficient to know how to perform the mechanical tasks of the house. In the normal order of things, their destiny will be to join together with common men like themselves, for whom a certain kind of attraction is not necessary. In these marriages, mutual happiness is achieved if the husband dedicates himself to his work, and the woman helps him according to her abilities. Not everyone regards happiness from the same perspective; and for that same reason, the number of dissatisfied is not large. The Wise Distributor of goods and talents has given to some a more simple way of thinking, in order that they may easier fulfill their

---

[57] Amar y Borbón, p. 291.
[58] Amar y Borbón, p. 252.

needs and desires, while others, possessed of a greater sensitivity and energy, find their discontent in that very same delicacy and variety of their desires.

(Parece que proponiéndose un sistema de educación, debiera comprender todas las clases del estado, mas esto es imposible en la execución, si se advierte que en el mundo todo es respectivo. Es cierto que las obligaciones esenciales son de todo género de personas sin distinción; pero no se requiere igual instrucción para cumplirlas. Por tanto no se hablará de aquellas mugeres de la clase común, que les basta saber por sí mismas los oficios mecánicos de la casa. Su suerte por lo regular será unirse con los hombres también rudos, para los cuales no es preciso cierto atractivo. En estos matrimonios se consigue la mutua felicidad con que el marido sea aplicado al trabajo, y la mujer le ayude según sus fuerzas. No todos miran la felicidad bajo un mismo aspecto; y esto hace que sea menor el número de los desgraciados. El sabio distribuidor de los bienes y talentos ha dado a unos ideas más sencillas, para que puedan más facilmente contentar sus deseos y necesidades, al paso que otros, dotados de mayor sensibilidad y energía, encuentran su amargura en la misma delicadez y variedad de sus deseos.)[59]

Two separate and distinct images of women – and of men – emerge here, each a logical extrapolation of an upper-class definition of class difference. Sensitivity, creative energy and a certain refinement of taste – those talents necessary to produce "culture" – are the prerogatives of the ruling class. Physical strength, which translates into "mechanical tasks," is identified with the lower classes of *both* sexes. The dichotomy between emotional sensitivity and physical strength, here divided along class lines, will become transformed into a feminine/masculine principle in the nineteenth century as the production of ideology evolves upon the bourgeoisie.

Buried in this passage is another important concept, one which the author dismisses perfunctorily, but which will be developed by the playright L. Fernández de Moratín, especially in *La comedia nueva*, produced on the stage for the first time in 1792, two years after the publication of Amar y Borbón's *Discourse*. We refer to her statement that the men and women of the lower classes can expect to achieve *mutual* happiness within marriage if the husband is indus-

---

[59] Amar y Borbón, prólogo, XXXIII-XXXIV.

trious and the wife assists him "according to her abilities." The patronizing attitude which concedes to the lower classes the right to a menial kind of happiness does not negate the importance of the fact that this happiness is seen as the product of a partnership in a common enterprise. Unlike the image of Fray Luis' "perfect wife," which can only be projected by *maintaining* the class division (the perfect wife serves as a model for the female servants and is an efficient manager of their labor), the model of the companionate marriage is one which is relatively transferable to the working class since it focuses exclusively on the relation between the sexes.

The role of middle and lower-class women in the partnership of marriage is Moratín's point of departure in *La comedia nueva*, and the reason for the juxtaposition of Doña Mariquita and Doña Agustina who laments that "for the educated woman, fecundity is a torment" ("para las mujeres instruidas es un tormento la fecundidad"). [60] The heroine of the play and the model of feminine behavior is the enchanting Doña Mariquita who certainly knows what she wants, although she may not be entirely successful in achieving it:

> No sir, if I am ignorant, all the better for me. I know how to write and to keep an account, I know how to cook, I know how to iron, I know how to sew, I know how to mend and darn, I know how to embroider, I know how to keep house; I'll take care of my own, and my husband, and my children, and I'll raise them up myself. Well, sir, don't I know enough?
>
> (No señor, si soy ignorante, buen provecho me haga. Yo sé escribir y ajustar una cuenta, sé guisar, sé planchar, sé coser, sé zurcir, sé bordar, sé cuidar de una casa; yo cuidaré de la mía, y de mi marido, y de mis hijos, y yo me los criaré. Pues, señor, ¿no sé bastante?) [61]

Moratín also bases his play *El sí de las niñas* on the theme of female education and its prejudicial effect on the moral character of young girls taught to hide their feelings, to be insincere, even to lie as long as they please those who have authority over them. Moratín underlines the fact the the prescribed lessons in proper behavior effectively taught women the humiliating means of resistance to

---

[60] L. Fernández de Moratín, *La comedia nueva*, ed. Dowling and Andioc (Madrid: Clásicos Castalia, 1969), p. 102.
[61] Fernández de Moratín, p. 102.

authority employed by the disenfranchised: lying, hypocrisy, manipulation, deceit: "...what is called an excellent education is that which fills them with fear, deceitfulness and the silence of a slave." ("...se llama excelente educación la que inspira en ellas el temor, la astucia y el silencio de un esclavo.")[62]

Arbiol, writing in 1715, reiterates the traditional reservation against any education for women that might modify her status of subjugation to male authority. Thus writing, which signified the power to elude surveillance, was consistently frowned upon. He insists: "And I am of the firm opinion that the proper upbringing of our daughters does not require teaching them to write..." ("Y soy de firme dictamen que no conviene para la buena crianza de las hijas el enseñarles a escribir...").[63]

Seventy-five years later, Amar y Borbón states firmly:

> To learn to read and write is appropriate for all women, and even more so now that they have done away with the mistaken notion that it is not a good thing for women to know how to write,...
>
> (El aprender a leer y escribir es conducente a todas, y más desde que se ha desterrado el error de que no conviene que las mujeres sepan escribir,...)[64]

The fact that Moratín's heroine Doña Mariquita, a woman on the fringes of the lower class, feels no need for Latin and Greek in order to exercise her profession as housewife is not as important to our study of the ideal wife as is her claim that she can already read, write, and keep the household accounts, in addition to the traditional knowledge of cooking and sewing, and that she assumes these new skills to be necessary to fulfill her responsibilites in the home.

P. Rodríguez de Campomanes, the chief advocate for popular education during this period, supports the education of lower-class women for economic reasons: "families will live in abundance with the universal application of both sexes" ("las familias vivirán abun-

---

[62] Moratín, *El sí de las niñas*, ed. Dowling and Andioc (Madrid: Clásicos Castalia, 1968), p. 263.
[63] Arbiol, p. 490.
[64] Amar y Borbón, p. 168.

dantes con la universal aplicación de ambos sexos"), but he also cites moral reasons:

> If they do not share a similar education, the wives and daughters of the artisans will continue to be shiftless; and they will not be able to inspire in their sons and husbands the kind of diligent behavior which they themselves find unfamiliar and wearisome.
>
> (Si la educación no les es común, las mujeres e hijas de los artesanos perseverarían ociosas; y no podrían inspirar a sus hijos y maridos una conducta laboriosa, de que ellas mismas vivirían distantes y tediosas.)[65]

In spite of the fact that we see here the nucleus of the nineteenth-century ideology which embodies virtue in the female sex, regardless of class origins, Campomanes makes clear that the social function of providing a model of morality is still primarily the responsibility of the aristocracy:

> It is very true that the education of the young girls of the wealthy nobility, who will be mothers of families one day, by their model and example, provides the firm base for the industriousness of the common women.
>
> (Es cosa cierta, que la educación de las niñas nobles y ricas, que un día han de ser madres de familias, es lo que ha de echar cimientos sólidos a la laboriosidad de las mujeres plebeyas, a su imitación y ejemplo.)[66]

While it is beyond our capacity to document completely the process by which, in the nineteenth century, the social function of providing a model for moral behavior is extended beyond the aristocracy to include, at least in the rhetoric of the period, *all* "mothers of families," we have seen in the texts studied that the crucial link between motherhood, education and the role of exemplar is already being given limited expression during the Spanish Enlightenment.

---

[65] Pedro Rodríguez y Campomanes, *Discurso sobre la educación popular de los artesanos, y su fomento* (Madrid, 1775), p. 358.
[66] Campomanes, p. 337.

CHAPTER TWO

EL ÁNGEL DEL HOGAR: THE SPIRITUALIZATION OF WOMEN IN NINETEENTH-CENTURY SPAIN

The exceptional importance placed upon the moral education of children by their mothers in the home provides the main rationalization for the doctrine of separate spheres of male and female influence. The doctrine raises the social status of women, at least theoretically, but it also becomes a new justification for the indispensability of women in the home, and exercises much more suasion over women than does the coercive stance of the Catholic Church. The manifestation of the doctrine of separate spheres of influence in Spain during the period between 1845 and 1900 is characterized by an important contradiction. On the one hand, the relation of the family to the total social structure is constantly emphasized: "What is the *State*, but the exact image of the family? What is the *Nation*, in its earliest conception, but the union or association of fathers?" ("¿Qué es el *Estado*, sino la exacta imagen de la familia? ¿Qué es la *Patria*, en su más primitiva acepción, sino la reunión o asociación de los padres?")[1] On the other hand, the intimacy of domestic life is placed in opposition to the activities which take place in the public sphere.

The institution of the family and the public sector are perceived as separate social spheres, complementary and interdependent on a theoretical level, but in fact, more often depicted as antagonistic and mutually exclusive:

---

[1] Pedro Felipe Monlau, *Higiene del matrimonio*, 3rd ed. (Madrid, 1865), pp. 292-93.

Virtue, pure love and tranquility of spirit dwell in the family; the large crowded salons and places of public entertainment are filled with vice, destructive passions and temptations that provoke impure desires.

(En la familia residen la virtud, el amor puro y la calma del espíritu; en los salones de grande reunión y en los espectáculos públicos están el vicio, el oleaje de las pasiones y el incentivo de los deseos impuros.)[2]

Such phrases as "the lethal contact of the world" ("el contacto letal del mundo"), "that gloomy door called *business*" ("esa puerta llena de sombras que se llama *negocios*"), "politics... the social form of revolution" ("la política... forma social de la revolución")[3] are used to paint an image of a world given over to materialism and the primary law of self-interest. The public sphere of finance and politics is portrayed as corrupt, unstable, chaotic and most important of all, to a great degree, unfathomable and unknowable. The following quote from an early women's magazine, *El Pensil del Bello Sexo*, exemplifies how this belief in a materialistic and dangerous public world provokes in turn the creation of an idealized image of an isolated feminine domestic sphere which can be a timeless spiritual refuge and stable locus outside the turbulent flow of history.

As for those of you who talk about the emancipation of women, you do not realize that the very word itself could break the only link which binds us together in the chain of ages, that what lies beyond the profanation of woman is the abyss. Those of you who wish to assimilate woman into man, those of you who wish to fill her heart with your passions for a million dreams of gold and iron, you do not realize that if you go against the nature of the only being in whom we can still find some traces of primitive grace, we will become lost in the world, without anything which ties us to the past and nothing to guide us into the future.

(Si como vosotros los que habláis de la emancipación de la mujer, no sabéis que esa sola palabra puede cortar el único eslabón que nos sostiene en la cadena de los tiempos, que detrás de la

---

[2] Ángel F. Pulido, *Bosquejos médico-sociales para la mujer* (Madrid, 1876), p. 30.
[3] R. de Latorres, "Estudios filosóficos sobre la mujer," *El Pensil del Bello Sexo* (18 enero 1846). Pilar Sinués de Marco, "Contra el lujo," *El Correo de la Moda* (2 septiembre 1883), p. 258. Juan de Luz, "Una receta casera," *La Margarita* (30 julio 1871).

profanación de la mujer está el abismo. Vosotros los que queréis asimilar la mujer al hombre, los que queréis llenar su corazón de sus pasiones con mil ensueños de hierro y oro, no sabéis que si desnaturalizáis los únicos seres en que se hallan algunos rastros de la gracia primitiva, nos vamos encontrar perdidos en el mundo, sin nada que nos ate a lo pasado y nada que nos encamine al porvenir.)[4]

As this passage demonstrates, the language which is used to discuss public and private space is characterized by a certain vagueness, a tendency to hyperbole and a reliance upon the clichés of the period. The author here expresses the idea that the role of women is to provide spiritual support for men and that to do so they must themselves remain pure, "unprofaned" by any contact with the world. Women, and by extension, the place where they reside, are filled with primitive grace, an image reminiscent of the biblical Eden prior to Adam's fall from grace after tasting the apple from the Tree of Knowledge. Innocence is thus organically linked with ignorance. In the nineteenth century, an image of "primitive" grace also suggests the Rousseauian debate on "natural" versus "civilized" man and woman. And we are reminded that Rousseau's Emile and Sophie are not to be measured by the same yardstick. The idea that the female of the species is more natural than the male, that is to say, less corrupted by the pernicious influence of urban civilization, effectively designates the former as a kind of noble savage and provides the justification for isolating women from modern history under the guise of protecting and preserving the purity of their "natural" nobility.

The lack of specificity in describing the social space allocated to women results in part from the fact that what is being described is the "space" within the institution of the family. It is a metaphorical space which describes the role of women within a particular set of social relations rather than the actual physical occupation of a house, be it a mansion, a solitary room, or the rose-covered cottage of Dickens and Michelet. Thus we find, given the subjectivity inherent in the idealizing process, that the world of domesticity and the family can be described as both "sweet slavery" and, in the same text, as "a vast theatre" depending upon the author's need to empha-

---

[4] R. de Latorres, ibid.

size the inevitable submission of women to their social role, or the importance which this role exerts upon society.[5]

An important result of the contradiction between public and private spheres which are theoretically interdependent but consistently depicted as mutually exclusive manifests itself in the difference between the relation of each sex to the sphere he or she occupies. Although man is the natural occupant of the public sphere, he is *not* responsible for the corrupt environment in which he moves. He survives in this hostile terrain by virtue of his superior strength, intelligence and moral character. The home, defined not as a physical space but as a spiritual atmosphere, is, on the contrary, the creation of the woman who occupies this domain. She is, says one writer for the *La Moda Elegante Ilustrada,* "...the tie which binds together the most noble sentiments, the guardian of order and economy, the rainbow of peace, the source of everyone's happiness and well-being." ("...el vínculo de los más nobles afectos, la reguladora del orden y de la economía, el iris de paz, la inspiradora del contento y bien estar de todos.")[6] *Order,* the preservation of the status quo – a concept which includes economy or living within one's means but also in accordance with one's social position; *peace,* generally equated with harmony, that is, the absence of strife; and *happiness* or well-being; herein are expressed the social values to which the rising Spanish bourgeoisie aspires.[7]

The symbiotic relation between the house and the woman who occupies it had been previously emphasized by Fray Luis in a language worthy of the naturalist novelist, Emile Zola:

---

[5] A. P., "Influencia de la mujer en la sociedad," *El Museo de las Familias,* 21-22 (1863), p. 126. "As a matter of fact, while we aspire to independence, they want to give and to receive a state of sweet slavery." ("En efecto, mientras que nosotros aspiramos a la independencia, ellas desean dar y recibir una dulce esclavitud."), also Ruperto García Cañas, "Sobre la influencia de las mujeres en nuestras sociedades modernas," *El Museo de las Familias,* III (1845), p. 73. "Certainly, in the bosom of the family there exists a vast theatre where mother, wife, sister, and all those who are tied by blood exert a profound influence on the future of society." ("Seguramente en el seno de la familia hay un vasto teatro donde la madre, la esposa, la hermana y demás que se hallan ligados con el vínculo de la sangre ejercen poderoso influjo en el porvenir de la sociedad.")

[6] A. Pirala, "De la influencia e instrucción de la mujer," *La Moda Elegante Ilustrada* (30 abril 1873), p. 125.

[7] Social order is of such importance that peace and happiness are perceived as strictly a function of the maintaining of that order. See José Luis Aranguren, *Moral y Sociedad* (Madrid: Editorial Cuadernos para el Diálogo, S. A., 1976), p. 94.

...because the house and its state of cleanliness will necessarily smell like the woman who is charged with its care and cleaning: and to the extent that she is clean or unclean, just so one will find the house, as well as the table and bed, clean or dirty.

(...porque la casa forçosamente, y la limpieza della oliera a la muger, a cuyo cargo está su aliño y limpieza: y quanto ella fuera asseada, o desasseada, tanto assí la casa como la mesa y el lecho, tendrán de suzio o limpio.)[8]

Fray Luis insists here upon the concrete, physical relation between the woman and her surroundings. But although cleanliness certainly remains a virtue in the nineteenth century, of far greater importance is women's capacity to engender a holy light of peace and contentment which nurtures spiritually the family members: "Woman has one principal mission in life, to be the home's delight and joy." ("La mujer tiene una misión principalísima en la vida, la de ser el encanto y la alegría del hogar...")[9]

The precise details of the methods by which women are to accomplish their life mission often dissolve into a diffuse rhetoric in which, logically, that virtue which is the antonym of the self-interest which rules the public sphere is acclaimed as the supreme female virtue: the negation of self, self-denial, renunciation, self-abnegation:

Self-abnegation! How beautiful a word; how it brightens the woman's crown and makes beautiful her mission here on earth. Without woman's self-abnegation, domestic happiness would not exist, and men would oftentimes fail to reach those great destinies to which society calls him. How rich in benefits is the emotion of self-abnegation. Self-abnegation is the spirit's strength, the forgetting of one's own well-being for the good of another, and for that reason this virtue is necessary above all for the housewife:...

(¡La abnegación! Qué bella palabra; cómo realza la corona de la mujer y embellece su misión sobre la tierra. Sin la abnegación de la mujer no existiera la felicidad doméstica ni llegaría a veces el hombre a los grandes destinos a que le llama la sociedad. ¡Qué sentimiento tan rico en beneficio es la abnegación! La abnega-

---

[8] Luis de León, p. 110.
[9] "Algo para las mujeres," *El Correo de la Moda* (2 julio 1881), pp. 195-98.

ción es la fortaleza del espíritu, el olvido del bienestar propio para pensar en el ajeno, y por eso esta virtud es necesaria sobre todo al ama de casa:...)[10]

The generally accepted notion that women exist to please men, a notion given additional legitimization in nineteenth-century Spain by the popularity of Rousseau's treatise on education, *Emile,* is one of the keys to our understanding of the creation of the ephemeral *ángel del hogar.* In a period of history during which the social individual is acquiring a new definition and importance, woman is often perceived not as an individual but as a *genre* or type: "In respect to their character and even their soul, one finds less difference between women than between men: women remain closer to their nature than we do to ours." ("Respecto al carácter y aun al espíritu, encuéntranse menos diferencias de mujer a mujer que de hombre a hombre: apártanse menos de su naturaleza las mujeres, que nosotros de la nuestra.")[11]

The negation of any possibility of conflict of interests between husband and wife, the primary tenet upon which ideal (harmonic) family life is predicated, results in a consequent lack of need to address the topic of daily domestic life in problematic terms. It is therefore the conscious or unconscious negation of real experience which creates the conditions under which women may be idealized. It is only possible to understand the image of woman as muse, inspiration, pure spirit, and the concomitant lack of specificity in the rhetoric surrounding the *ángel del hogar* within the context of the idealization process, which takes as its starting point the negation of woman's existence as individual; that is, as an autonomous social and moral being. The idealized woman gains spiritual strength to the degree that she loses physical concreteness, ultimately becoming a Dulcinea-like omnipresent spiritual force, characterized as much by her corporal absence as she is by her capacity to inspire. Don Quixote's Dulcinea, given substance and personality, becomes Teresa Panza.

---

[10] Baronesa de Olivares, "La vida en familia," *El Correo de la Moda* (2 diciembre 1884).

[11] A. P. (cf. note 5), see also Monlau, pp. 164-65: "In women, individuality is much less pronounced than in men: the latter is much more selfish, less resigned. Women live more for the species than for themselves." ("En la mujer, la individualidad está mucho menos pronunciada que en el hombre: éste es más egoísta, menos sufrido. La mujer vive más para la especie que para sí misma.")

One justification for the restriction of non-working-class women to the home continues to be, in the nineteenth century, a belief in female weakness, now lauded as an enchanting feminine characteristic. The weakness of women, which Fray Luis defined as moral weakness and righteously condemned, is transformed into graceful feminine frailty. Women's despised softness is now perceived as womanly tenderness and vulnerability, inspiring in men the masculine instinct of protection. Fray Luis, with unconscious misogyny, insisted that women be restricted to the home in order that they not contaminate the men with whom they might come in contact.[12] Now however, it is women who must be protected from the contamination of a corrupt public world.

Beneath the cover of an egalitarian marriage contract, that is, one supposedly entered into freely by two parties of equal legal status, the *modus operandi* of bourgeois marriage is the feudal formula of service in return for protection, the wife tied to her husband by bonds of total fealty. But protection against what or whom? The Catholic traditionalists insist that women must accept male protection within marriage for the simple reason that they have no alternative. According to S. M. Fábreques, who is writing in a women's fashion magazine in 1871, the emancipation of women "...are words ill-suited to those who must always live, or almost always, dependent upon the other sex, because He who is all-powerful has thus ordained it." ("...son palabras que no sientan bien a las que han de vivir siempre, o casi siempre, bajo la dependencia de otro sexo, porque así lo dispuso *El* que todo lo puede.")[13] Considerable effort is required to sustain the inherent disjunction between an ideology which pretends to worship women as morally superior to men, and a social structure which reasserts the right of *patria potestas* through the imposition of the Napoleonic Code and, consequently, maintains a legal and economic sexual hierarchy within the family. In the case of Fábreques, as well as many other propagandists of the feminine ideal, there are curious and sudden lapses from the chivalric posture of male protector. Fábreques concludes his article on an overtly threatening note, as he makes clear to his reader that male protection is not something freely sought and granted or purchased in a free

---

[12] Luis de León, pp. 98-9. See also, intro, n. 4.
[13] S. M. Fábreques, "La mujer casada y San Pablo," *La Moda Elegante Ilustrada*, 30, 2 (1871), p. 15.

market, but rather a permanent aspect of the "natural" condition of women. Rebellion against the divinely mandated condition of female dependency must be paid for by social ostracism: "...it is better to depend upon a man, whether he be father, brother or husband, than to live abandoned in shame..." ("...vale más depender del hombre, llámese éste padre, hermano o marido, que vivir abandonada a la ignominia...")[14]

While it is safe to say that the economic and legal restrictions on middle-class women, reinforced by a long tradition of female decorum, provided a strong motive for internalizing the dogma of female dependency clothed as it was in the seductive garb of romantic chilvalry, one can still find buried in the myriad of articles which finally overwhelm the reader in their triteness and pomposity, an occasional voice which takes exception to the conventional posture. In an article entitled "No hay sexo débil" (There is no Weaker Sex), the author pinpoints how an insistence on female weakness may serve to mask the reality of male despotism within the family:

> Men want women to be weak so that they may exercise in the home a tyrannical rule which allows them to calm if not to extinguish their feverish desire, their burning thirst for a greater domination over the universe. Men want women to be weak to make her his plaything, in order to exploit her weakness...
>
> (El hombre quiere débil a la mujer para ejercer en su hogar un predominio tiránico que le permite calmar, ya que no extinguir, la febril ansiedad, la ardiente sed que siente de una dominación más vasta sobre el universo. El hombre quiere débil a la mujer para hacerla su juguete, para explotar su debilidad...)[15]

Much of the wrath of those who adhere to the doctrine of separate spheres is logically directed against the feminist position which is unwilling to accept the false status of separate but equal. The following commentary, written by a regular woman contributor to *La Moda Elegante Ilustrada*, is an excellent synthesis of the reaction by the middle-class male (and quite often the female as well) to the provocative phrase, women's emancipation:

---

[14] Ibid.
[15] María de la Concepción Gimeno, "No hay sexo débil," *La Moda Elegante Ilustrada* (22 junio 1874), p. 187.

For most men, the phrase "women's emancipation" signifies the resistance of the weaker sex against the stronger, the abandonment of her duties, an absence of all virtue, of all decorum, a lack of restraint, in a word, licentiousness.

(Para la generalidad de los hombres, la palabra "emancipación de la mujer" significa la resistencia del sexo débil contra el fuerte, el abandono de los deberes, la ausencia de toda virtud, de todo decoro, el desenfreno, el libertinaje en fin.) [16]

The argument of the traditionalists that Christianity had freed woman from her position as slave and concubine and raised her to a status of equality with men in her role as "wife and companion" is used to explain away feminist demands for equal political rights and access to the productive sector. Equal rights for women, which despite the lack of a feminist movement in Spain is the subject of heated debate,[17] signified primarily the right of middle-class women to a degree of economic independence. And it is at this point that the bourgeois origins of the ideology of domesticity are most clearly revealed. The material pre-conditions for the realization of the *ángel del hogar* are obviously a house in which the Angel can perform her duties, whether the house of father, brother or husband, and a man who will support the Angel at a level of middle-class decency throughout her life. For the lady of the house to work, especially given the absence of genteel occupations for women in Spain, is a manifestation of the husband's lack of economic power and, consequently, an overt sign of downward class mobility. Thus the Lady *(la dama)*[18] cannot work if class status is to be maintained; it is her position as Lady, not as Angel, which ties her to the economic fortunes of the head of the household.

---

[16] Robustiana Armiño de Cuesta, "La mujer emancipada," *La Moda Elegante Ilustrada*, 3, 2 (1871), p. 15.

[17] See Geraldine M. Scanlon, *La polémica feminista en la España contemporánea: 1868-1974* (Madrid: Siglo XXI de España, 1976). This seminal study is a thorough documentation of the traditionalist and liberal viewpoints on the subject of the "woman's problem." Of particular value is the author's careful reconstruction of the historical circumstances within which middle-class women attempted to live out the myth of the ideal woman.

[18] The idea of the Lady or *la dama* refers to class origin regardless of the married state. While the image of the Lady and the Angel in the House overlap at certain points (asexuality, good manners, modesty), the Angel is more specifically a model for middle-class women. Although she may not work outside the home, she is responsible for the care of the men and children and for maintaining the house in order.

The propagandists for the *ángel del hogar* consistently refer to woman or women without any apparent class distinction. The problems of working-class women – whether factory workers or engaged in domestic service – who are forced to "abandon their children" are seldom if ever mentioned in the women's and family magazines which are directed to an aspiring bourgeoisie whose principal concern is to draw a sharp line between itself and the lower classes. The fact that "woman" is referred to as a homogeneous universal is a sharp departure from the practice of writers prior to the nineteenth century. As our commentary on earlier texts has shown, a strong sense of class consciousness and an awareness of the fact that lower-class women do not share in the privileges of the upper classes or have the same social obligations is a distinguishing trademark. In the case of nineteenth-century ideologues, the linguistic eradication of class lines is, in part, a result of the failing prestige of the aristocracy as a model for the community. But the creation of an ideological world in which men and women become universals, with no history grounded in class origins, also reflects the tendency of the dominant bourgeoisie to impose its ideology on the rest of society. One could say that in the process of fabricating their image of the ideal wife and mother, the propagandists fall victim to their own illusion of an egalitarian society.

The moral banner of the Spanish bourgeoisie, still steeped in the traditions of patriarchy and regency, is altar and throne, family and private property. Our analysis of the ideological significance of the *ángel del hogar* is greatly clarified by underlining the fact that it is the family which is on the pedestal, high up and out of the mire, rather than a lone Venus or Pietà figure. The image of the Angel is never presented in isolation, but always with the necessary accoutrements that bring her into existence: the cradle, the thimble and sewing box, and if not a spinning wheel in the late nineteenth century, perhaps a sewing machine. But above all she is surrounded by the family members, for she exists *only* to serve them.[19]

---

[19] The hyperbolic praise of women tends to mask the fact that the ideal wife exists only as a function of the family. The family as an institution did not suddenly gain importance in order to provide an occupation for the bored *ama de casa* (housewife). The fact that the ideology of domesticity centers on the family and not on the housewife has become much clearer in the twentieth century. The family is still rigourously defended as the ultimate preserve of the individual, at the same time that prestige for the role of housewife and mother has declined

The revindication of women's rights must therefore necesssarily be perceived by the Catholic traditionalists as a direct threat to their position which links together Christianity and the sanctity of the bourgeois family. The following quote, taken from an article entitled "La emancipación de la mujer," exemplifies the tautological reasoning essential to any perception of the world which sees in the status quo its own justification:

> Jesus Christ came into this world because woman, in order to fulfill the generous mission which God had chosen for her, needed Jesus Christ to come here: as a slave, she kept safe in her heart, like the sanctuary guards the Divinity, her own redemption: and because in order that she might be deemed worth of it, titles were needed to exhibit to the succeeding generations, God granted her the title of Mother: that is woman's supreme honor. Well and good: in the heart of our Christian society, perhaps to complete the series of painful aberrations, we have seen in the light of progress this unholy threat of emancipation which offends by its very thought, and even though it is contrary to every Christian precept, this horrendous idea, like other insanities of the Nineteenth Century, has enthusiastic supporters in countries which considered themselves to be very cultured. What Satanic will is it, at the foot of the Cross, that tears at the banner of Christianity, nor what else but this can be expected from modern philosophy?...

> (Jesucristo vino al mundo porque la mujer, para cumplir la misión generosa que Dios le tenía fijada, necesitó que viniera Jesucristo: esclava, guardó en su seno, como el santuario guarda la divinidad, su propia redención: y como para merecerla títulos debía exhibir a la faz de las generaciones, Dios le dio el título de Madre: esa es la dignidad suprema de la mujer; Ahora bien: en el seno de nuestra sociedad cristiana, acaso por completar la serie de las aberraciones dolorosas, se vio a la luz del progreso esa amenaza de emancipación impía que hasta de pensamiento ofende: y aunque contrario a todos los preceptos cristianos, también esa funesta idea, como otros delirios del Siglo XIX, cuenta con entusiastas defensores en países que se tienen por

---

radically, in part as a result of women's growing importance in the work force and the rise of the "two-salaried household." For a classic neo-conservative defense of the family see Christopher Lasch, *Haven in a Heartless World: The Family Besieged* (New York: Basic Books, 1977).

muy cultos, ¿qué voluntad satánica rasga así, al pie de la cruz, la bandera del cristianismo, ni qué puede esperarse más que eso de la filosofía moderna?...)

And in an unusually straightforward style colored by uninhibited petulance, the author concludes by defining precisely the limits of women's equality to men: "...women should never be equal to men in social rights, she should be his companion." ("...la mujer no debe ser nunca igual al hombre en derecho social, sino su compañera.")[20] The strident tones used to defend the inviolability of home and motherhood may be said to serve as a linguistic barometer which measures the gap between the projected male ideal of the perfect wife and mother, and the inevitable failure of women to realize it. The quaintness of the author's use of theological catch-phrases ("what Satanic will?", etc.) does not, however, take away from the very modern attempt to professionalize housewifery and motherhood, making this activity the only possible career open to women. Men will earn degrees as doctors and lawyers; women, to realize their social role must fulfill the title imposed upon them by Christ. Until they enter into the sacred state of motherhood, there is no space for them in modern Christian civilization. Until they exist as mothers, they do not exist at all.

Traditional Female Education and the Concept of Modesty

The contradiction between a perception of the public and domestic spheres as two antagonistic worlds, and the belief that the family is the basic cell in an organic whole which is, in turn, the state, the nation or in the case of the Krausists, the harmonious community of nations, is resolved at the level of rethoric by allocating to women the social responsibility for exerting a civilizing influence upon the members of the family within the structure of the Christian home. Female influence thus becomes quite literally embodied in the husband and male children so that through them, and only through them, is this influence able to transcend the domestic sphere. In an article entitled "Instrucción y educación"

---

[20] A. P. A., "La emancipación de la mujer," *El Correo de la Moda* (2 noviembre 1875), p. 321.

published in the popular family magazine, *El Museo de las Familias*, which ran from 1843 to 1879, the author begins by asserting that "One could say that education is man's moral instruction..." ("La educación puede decirse que es la instrucción moral del hombre...") and concludes that "[There is] nothing more moral, nothing more instructive and useful for humanity than the school of Christianity." ("Nada más moral, nada más instructivo y provechoso para la humanidad que la escuela del cristianismo.")[21] Christianity should define women's attitudes and actions. The author leaves no doubt as to the content of women's influence in the home, as well as the status of female influence in relation to patriarchal authority:

> What springs to mind is Christianity's beneficial influence, because Christianity provided women with dignity, and granted to her the wonderful right to serve as a link to society. As concerns the gradual process of education, woman participates in the moral influence of the male. The child grows up and is formed in the heart of the family, under the father's authority, but also with the tender caresses of the mother;... In this distribution of education's duties, it is incumbent upon us to recognize that both influences march together in search of unity. The father's influence provides the image of authority, the mother's that of submission...
>
> (Sin solicitarlo, estamos recordando la saludable influencia del cristianismo, porque el cristianismo dio a la mujer su dignidad, y la concedió el maravilloso derecho de servir de vínculo a la sociedad. En cuanto a la marcha gradual de la educación, la mujer participa de la influencia moral del hombre. El niño crece y se forma en el seno de la familia, bajo la autoridad del padre, pero también bajo las tiernas caricias de la madre;... En esta distribución de deberes para la educación, es preciso reconocer que ambas influencias marchan de consuno en busca de la unidad. La influencia del padre por la imagen de la autoridad, la de la madre por la imagen de la sumisión...)[22]

Throughout the nineteenth century, the traditionalists' concept of adequate female education never really transcends elementary

---

[21] J. A. Bermejo, "Instrucción y educación," *El Museo de las Familias*, 12 (febrero, 1854), pp. 25, 28.
[22] Ibid., p. 36.

literacy, sewing and fanciwork, all crowned with a firm indoctrination in Catholic dogma, since:

> ...this angelical companion belongs to us, first of all, by God's will, and then through Christianity... Without [Christian] virtue, conjugal society would be a horrendous and thorny labyrinth, which would wound the heart and torment the soul.
>
> (...esta compañera angelical, después de Dios la debemos al cristianismo... Sin esta virtud la sociedad conyugal sería un laberinto funesto erizado de espinas, que lastimarían el corazón y tormentarían el alma.)[23]

One of the most widely repeated clichés of the period, that men make the laws and women the customs (in Spain, a statement which also speaks to the failure of attempts from the Counter-Reformation through the eighteenth century to codify social behavior through the Sumptuary Laws),[24] also reflects a growing awareness of the family institution as a socializing agent in which dominant values, such as women's submission to male authority, are or are not perpetuated. Education, conceived of as *moral* education, therefore revolves around the correct development of instincts and sentiments manifested by the children in socially approved comportment, rather than the development of the intellect and the capacity to reason.

The arguments which emphasize women's superior authority in the terrain of emotions evolve from an extrapolation of the belief in the basic intellectual inferiority of women to men. Since the rationalization of separate but equal spheres precludes the notion of inferiority, the realm of sentiment, of emotions, must be elevated and dignified in order to provide a balance of power between mind and heart and thus maintain the illusion of equality:

---

[23] Cañas, p. 73.

[24] The Sumptuary Laws are defined by Juan Sempere y Guarinos as laws, "to restrict excesses in food, and extravagances in clothes, furniture, new fashions, and other kinds of luxury goods." ("Para contener los excesos en la comida, y las demasías en los trages, muebles, modas, y demás de luxo.") See *Historia del luxo y de las leyes suntuarias de España*, I (Madrid, 1788), pp. 8-9. Attempts to regulate those aspects of daily life which by the 18th century were no longer considered to be the rightful domain of the State, resulted in the revolt of the people against Prime Minister Esquilache in 1766. For one account, see Charles E. Kany, *Life and Manners in Madrid: 1750-1800* (Berkeley: U. of California Press, 1932), pp. 220-24.

Heaven denied to women the physical and intellectual strength and energy which it granted to men; but on the other hand, it endowed her abundantly with a creative and lively imagination, with a sensitive and generous heart...

(Nególe el cielo a la mujer la fuerza y la energía física e intelectual que concediera al hombre; pero dotóla en cambio ricamente de una imaginación vivaz y creadora, de un corazón sensible y generoso...)[25]

writes one of the contributors to *El Correo de la Moda* in 1877.

Yet by defining women as brainless creatures ruled by an instinctive need to love and be loved, by sensibility rather than sense, a kind of Frankenstein's monster is created over whom the master may, in any given moment, lose control. One of the controlling agents used to keep women within defined limits of socially accepted behavior is the insistence on the existence of an innate sense of feminine modesty. That modesty is a "natural" or ontological characteristic of women is a reiteration of the belief in the essential difference between the male and the female nature. But we must turn back to Fray Luis de León, unencumbered as he is by nineteenth-century romantic chivalry, in order to see in the clarity of his logic how the image of the demure woman rises out of a profound belief in women's intellectual inferiority, or rather, in man's superiority over her.

Because, as we have said and will continue to say, just as Nature made women that they might remain secluded within the home: so did she also oblige them to keep silent... Because speech is born of understanding, and words are nothing more than images or signs of that which is born of the spirit: for which reason just as the good and honest woman was not made by Nature to study science, or for difficult affairs, but rather only for simple domestic labor, so thus did [Nature] limit her understanding, and consequently, her words and wit.... Woman's estate in comparison to her husband is a humble estate: and moderation and modesty [shame] are Nature's dowry to her.

(Porque, assí como la naturaleza, como diximos, y diremos, hizo a las mugeres para que encerradas guardassen la casa: assí

---

[25] Fermín Gonzalo Morán, "La mujer," *El Correo de la Moda* (10 noviembre 1877).

> obligó a que cerrassen la boca.... Porque el hablar nasce del entender, y las palabras no son sino como imágenes, o señales de lo que el ánimo concibe en sí mismo: por donde assí como a la muger buena y honesta, la naturaleza no la hizo para el estudio de las sciencias, ni para los negocios de difficultades, sino para un solo officio simple y doméstico, assí las limitó el entender, y por consiguiente les tassó las palabras y las razones.... El estado de la muger en comparación del marido es estado humilde: y es como dote natural de las mugeres la mesura, y vergüença...)[26]

For Fray Luis, the modest woman's silence follows logically upon the fact that no woman can have anything worthwhile to say. A woman who speaks is grotesque, in the order of a dancing bear or, more to the point perhaps, a talking bird. If Saint Paul ordained that woman be silent in God's house, man, in imitation of the deity, should follow suit in his own.

In spite of such cover-up phrases as "feminine influence," "women's sphere," and the "companion-wife" the belief in female submission to male authority remains intact throughout the nineteenth century. But the form that this submission takes does change as a result of the new model of family life: the ideal of bourgeois domesticity includes not only physical shelter for the family but also the private society of wife and children for the husband to enjoy. The ideal bourgeois wife is an educated woman, *"la mujer ilustrada,"* who adorns not only her body but also her mind in her new role as companion to her husband. Female education is defended by both traditionalists and progressives, although each group conceives of the content of this education in different terms. This defense of education for women is not surprising, given the fact that a modicum of education is equated with gentility. An educational varnish is supported on the grounds that "an educated woman makes home-life more smooth and pleasant." ("una mujer ilustrada hace más suave y fácil la vida del hogar.")[27] A wife's submission to her husband can now be defended as one more example of decorous or modest behavior: fighting, arguing, any form of defiance is uneducated, improper comportment.

---

[26] Luis de León, pp. 93-94.

[27] Concepción Gimeno de Flaquer, "La mujer estudiosa," *El Correo de la Moda*, 36, 45 (1886), p. 358.

In addition to the definition of modest and proper female behavior in the home as silent or sweetly vocal obedience to the male head of the household, the question of prescribed female comportment in the public sphere forms an essential element of the canons of decorum. In 1715, Father Arbiol warns his reader:

> Modesty is the most necessary virtue in a young maiden: and the depth of her virtue should be well-known... because if there should happen to be a scandal in the neighborhood, nobody would believe evil of such a prudent young lady.
>
> (La virtud más necesaria en una doncella, es la modestia: y conviene que por extremada, a todos sea notorio... para que si en el barrio sucede un escándalo, de la doncella tan recatada nadie crea cosa mala.)[28]

The idea that a woman's modest behavior is her only protection against public opinion and that her own self-restraint is all that restrains society's watchdog from attacking her, emphasizes again two previously noted elements of the public sphere: 1) it is a male terrain; women who leave home forfeit the right to male protection, and 2) men are not responsible for what occurs in their terrain. The ultimate social authority, public opinion, is an impregnable power; nameless and faceless, the public voice emanates from no definable source. It is free to create and destroy reputations and cannot be controlled.

Decorum or proper behavior defined as obedience to the prescribed social conventions of a given historical period is necessarily a question of fashion or *la moda*. Was there a particular style of decorum to which the proper young lady of the middle and upper classes aspired in the nineteenth century that distinguished her from her predecessors?

> Modesty... is more valued if it is inscribed in a sincere and tranquil gaze, in a mouth upon which plays the smile of innocence, and in cheeks that are stained pink with modesty's inimitable blush.
>
> (La modestia... es de mayor precio si se retrata en una mirada tranquila y honesta, en una boca por donde vaga la sonrisa de

---

[28] Antonio Arbiol, p. 493.

> la inocencia, y en unas mejillas que tiñe el carmín infalsificable del pudor.) [29]

writes Severo Catalina, who together with his French counterparts, Legouvé and Michelet, is one of the most widely read and quoted writers in Spain on the subject of women during this period.

Well and good, we may say, but what does a smile of innocence look like? The very vagueness of the description tightens the author's control over his image. The modest woman wears an ephemeral smile recognizable only by the creator of the idealized image. That the signs of proper comportment are as much dependent on individual interpretation as they are on a supposedly objective norm is revealed by two quotes from the same ecclesiastical authority, Father Arbiol:

> Women's wickedness can be recognized by the change in her face... and since you know the sign, do not disregard that which is of such great importance to you.
>
> Let their eyes reveal their modesty, let them look with diffidence, and blush...
>
> (La maldad de la mujer se conoce en la mutación de su rostro... y pues tienes la señal, no te descuides en lo que tanto te importa...
>
> Que guarden modestia en sus ojos, para mirar con encogimiento y rubor...) [30]

And the same law of arbitrary subjectivity which permits our eighteenth-century moralist to read the female blush as both innocence and guilt continues to function in the nineteenth century. In a widely read medical text which circulated in an abbreviated form from 1843 and from 1879 in an updated and complete edition, "modesty's inimitable blush" eulogized by Catalina is now cited as one of the possible symptoms of incipient nymphomania, the dreaded disease also referred to as *furor uterinus* in the nosology of the great eighteenth-century clinician, Philippe Pinel (1745-1822), and in Spain as *el furor uterino*. [31]

---

[29] Severo Catalina, *La mujer, apuntes para un libro*, 2nd ed. (Madrid, 1862), p. 119.

[30] Antonio Arbiol, p. 488.

[31] Fabre y D'Huc, *Tratado elemental de las enfermedades de la mujer y del niño*, ed. and trans. Rogelio Casa de Batista, 3rd. ed. (Madrid, 1872), p. 421.

This antithetical interpretation of a presumably standard sign which should lend itself to only one single reading agreed upon by social convention undermines the argument that a woman's decorous comportment will defend her against the wrath of public opinion. Women can control, within the financial and educational resources available to them according to their class, certain exterior signs: their apparel or the sedate gait and lowered voice directly associated with the demure and sheltered lady who need not leave her house to quarrel with the fish monger or butcher because she can send a servant in her stead. But she does not have the power to define herself as a good and modest woman; this power resides in the public sphere with those who, hidden behind the anonymous mask of "public opinion," will arbitrarily interpret her actions and appearance.

When Severo Catalina insists that "Woman is undefinable, because she is uneducated" ("La mujer es un ser indefinible, porque es un ser ineducado") and then goes on to say that "The main secret of education does not consist in forming wise women: it should consist in forming modest ones" ("El principal secreto de la educación no consiste en formar mujeres sabias: debe consistir en formar mujeres modestas"), [32] it is evident that he conceives of education as an additional means of control over women, and even perhaps a means of realizing at last that all too evasive ideal of the perfect wife. [33]

The idea that women do not exist in their own right, that they are undefined, genre or type rather than individual, clay upon which man places his imprint, becomes, as in the case of the physician and hygienist, Pedro Felipe Monlau, a means of reassuring the bourgeois patriarch that he still controls his world and his women:

> *Man makes the woman...* woman's nature is essentially good, docile and engaging: however little education she may have received, it is easy to complete it: *man makes the woman...*
>
> *(El hombre hace a la mujer...* la naturaleza de la mujer es esencialmente buena, dócil y simpática: por poca educación que haya recibido, es fácil completarla: *el hombre hace a la mujer...)* [34]

---

[32] Catalina, pp. 106, 115.
[33] For further discussion of *"la mujer ilustrada"* in the nineteenth century, see Scanlon, op. cit., pp. 15-57.
[34] Monlau, p. 129.

But the fact that men will control female education and therefore its results, does not reassure those reactionaries who have long relied on the premise that the principal means of control over women is their own ignorance. The mother's duty is to "conserve two things in her daughters: the mind's ignorance and the heart's goodness," ("conservar dos cosas en sus hijas: la ignorancia de la inteligencia y la bondad del corazón,")[35] writes the famous author of *La gaviota*, Cecilia Böhl von Faber [Fernán Caballero] to Teodoro Guerrero in a letter published posthumously in 1877.

This ambivalent attitude of the traditionalists toward female education is revealed concretely in the results of the pedagogical congresses held throughout the nineteenth century, documented by G. Scanlon in the work previously cited. Education, perhaps, but within limits: "What is absolutely certain is that one should not promote nor even less encourage in them [women] the desire to leave their proper sphere." ("Lo que no ofrece duda es que no debe fomentarse, ni menos excitar en ella, las aspiraciones a salir de su propia esfera.")[36]

Middle-class women who dared to aspire to a career or profession seemed to have been aware that their goals posed a threat to their male counterparts. One woman, writing in *El Correo de la Moda* in 1882 warns her readers: "An educated woman needs to be very humble so that they will not call her a pedant. Be studious and modest, dear readers! Make the woman doctor attractive." ("Una mujer ilustre necesita ser muy humilde para que no le denominen pedante. ¡Sed estudiosas y modestas, lectoras mías! Haced simpático el tipo de la mujer médico.")[37] And Catalina declares that "Modesty is not humilliation; but it borders on humility." ("La modestia no es la humillación; pero está tocando con la humildad.")[38] Modesty, then, is seen to be an awareness and gracious acceptance of the "humble estate" which defines women by reason of their sex. But as the pitifully servile and ingratiating manner of the majority of Spanish women who defended their right to education and work effectively demonstrates, humility, when forcibly imposed by external forces, does indeed become humilliation.

---

[35] Fernán Caballero, *El Correo de la Moda* (2 mayo 1877).
[36] Mariano Carderea, *Actas del Congreso Nacional Pedagógico* (Madrid, 1882), p. 317; quoted in Scanlon, p. 27.
[37] Concepción Gimeno de Flaquer, "La mujer médico," *El Correo de la Moda* (2 diciembre 1882), p. 358.
[38] Catalina, p. 117.

FEMALE SEXUALITY AND THE PRAISE OF MOTHERHOOD

One of the reasons why even lip service can be paid to the idea of education for women is that the traditionalists have at their disposal a whole new set of arguments defining male/female difference that forms part of a modern and ostensibly scientific discourse. These arguments serve to quiet the fear that men may be losing control of the weaker sex, even while the new discourse foments an image of women as possessing animal instincts that may drive them to repulsive, barely imaginable extremes.

Our previous discussion has shown that the romantic feminine ideal masks in reality a profound and unchanged disdain for women's intellectual and physical weakness, as well as a long, historically rooted male/female relationship of antagonism and distrust. This disdain is made explicit, forming the other side of the Janus head, in the medical literature, both in the textbooks and in important medical journals such as *El Siglo Médico*, as well as family magazines like *La Medicina Popular* and *La Salud*.

The following passage exemplifies the eagerness and satisfaction with which the arbiters of women's destiny accepted the contemporary biological rationalization of female dependency:

> Women will never take the men's place, as is feared, because the centuries and centuries during which our companion has been all love and humility, all self-abnegation and disinterest, are sufficient guarantee against such an event; in addition, no matter what may be the social conditions in which the fair sex lives, she will never be able to exempt herself from the laws of nature which hurl her into our arms.
>
> (Nunca la mujer se impondrá al hombre, según se teme, porque tantos y tantos siglos en que nuestra compañera fue toda amor y humildad, toda abnegación y desinterés, son suficiente garantía contra el caso expuesto; además, sean cuales fueran las condiciones sociales en que viva el sexo hermoso, jamás se podrá eximirse de las leyes de la naturaleza, que le arrojan en nuestros brazos.)[39]

---

[39] José Moreno Fuentes, "Reparos y obligaciones acerca del destino natural de la mujer," *El Correo de la Moda* (26 septiembre 1885), p. 286.

One of the most important distinctions between the rhetoric which idealizes women as the spiritual guardians of morality, and the language of the physicians is a more frequent and overtly expressed disgust and fear of women. The ideal of scientific objectivity imposes upon men of science the obligation of defining women according to materialist or scientific categories. Such a definition must be reached through empirical observation and would supposedly be free of superstition and prejudice.

In accordance with this model of scientific materialism, even though the doctors concur in the general opinion that women are all love and sensibility, the physical center of women is not the heart but the womb:

> The womb is the most important organ in a woman's life; it is one of the poles of feminine organization... Inevitably, all women's physical and moral affections reverberate in her womb, the uterus makes the woman what she is.
>
> (La matriz es el órgano más importante en la vida de la mujer; es uno de los polos de la organización femenina... En la matriz retumban indefectiblemente todas las afecciones físicas y morales de la mujer, el útero hace que la mujer sea lo que es.)[40]

According to the physician, what women may or may not want is irrelevant. Their reproductive potential defines and limits them to a unique social role, motherhood. So adamant is Monlau on this point that he insists: "Women should not be permitted to marry without having previously ascertained their physical capability to give birth." ("A las mujeres no se les debiera permitir el matrimonio sin que previamente constase su aptitud física para el parto."[41] Staunchly defending the doctrine of separate spheres, Monlau would also impose what is a middle and upper-class ideal onto lower-class

---

[40] Monlau, p. 164. José López Piñero calls Monlau "...the most important contemporary Spanish hygienist" ("...el más importante higienista español contemporáneo"). And he goes on to say, "During more than half a century, Spanish physicians were taught from the many editions of his works on public and private hygiene." ("En las sucesivas ediciones de sus tratados de higiene pública y privada se educaron los médicos españoles durante más de medio siglo..."). "El testimonio de los médicos españoles del siglo xix acerca de su tiempo," in *Medicina y sociedad en la España del siglo xix* (Madrid: Sociedad de Estudios y Publicaciones, 1964), p. 131.

[41] Monlau, p. 33.

and working women as well: "...a woman should be a woman, she should be a true *mother*, and not a worker." ("...que la mujer sea una mujer, que sea una verdadera *madre* y no una obrera.")[42]

The scientific explanation elaborated in the second half of the nineteenth century to explain women's supposedly greater emotional sensitivity – which in turn provides the justification for the belief that women lack emotional control – rests on the "fact" that the female nervous system is weaker and more vulnerable than the male because it is linked somehow to her reproductive organs:

> Maternity is a woman's main function, and causes conditions which predispose her to a state of nervousness. The appearance of menstruation, pregnancy, childbirth, and nursing... lead her to this state.
>
> (La maternidad, que es la función principal de las mujeres, determina en ellas condiciones predisponentes del estado nervioso. La aparición del flujo menstrual, la preñez, el parto y la lactancia... la conducen a este estado.)[43]

The idea that certain physical types were predisposed to insanity had wide circulation in Spain, and throughout Western Europe during this period,[44] and it naturally followed that women, with their congenitally inferior nervous system, must exist in a condition of habitual nervousness, or neurasthenia,[45] a state which bordered on madness. In a long article printed in *La Guirnalda*, the author underlines the precariousness of women's emotional stability and again reminds the reader that women are not unique individuals, but rather a single genre:

---

[42] Monlau, p. 579.

[43] Juan Drumen, *Tratado elemental de patología médica*, vol. 2 (Madrid, 1850), p. 385. See also Pulido, p. 335.

[44] On Drumen, see Trino Peraza de Ayala, *La psiquiatría española en el siglo XIX* (Madrid: Consejo Superior de Investigaciones Científicas, 1947), pp. 80-87. For an important contemporary source see Pedro Mata Fontanet, *Tratado de medicina y cirugía*, 5th ed., vol. 2 (Tetuán de Chamartín, 1874), p. 289.

[45] The term *neurasthenia* does not come into use until the latter part of the 19th century. It refers to what was previously called a nervous condition, *"un estado nervioso"*: one of hypersensitivity, exhaustion, irritability, depression, fits of crying and insomnia. See Peraza de Ayala, p. 3. See also Ilza Veith, *Hysteria: The History of a Disease* (Chicago: University of Chicago Press, 1965), pp. 242-43, for a chart of symptoms.

> Finally, the hysterical condition is embodied in the woman's organization, it is normal to her; it is a result of the highly developed emotional element of her nervous system, and it [the hysterical condition] has existed since woman was woman, in every level of civilization, and in every kind of physical and mental variety. She is in continual danger of exploding unrestrainedly and unexpectedly into paroxysms produced by the slightest event... This hysterical condition could be compared to a package of dynamite: inoffensive as long as the particles remain in equilibrium, terrible when they are disturbed.
>
> (Por último, existe encarnada en la organización de la mujer la condición histérica, que es normal en ella; es resultado del alto desarrollo de lo emocional en su sistema nervioso, y ha existido desde que la mujer fue mujer, en todos los grados de civilización, y en todas sus variedades físicas y mentales. Está en continuo peligro de estallar desenfrenada e inesperadamente en paroxismos producidos por el menor acontecimiento... Esta condición histérica puede compararse a un paquete de dinamita: inofensivo mientras sus partículas están en equilibrio, terrible cuando se conmueve.)[46]

The statement that women are by nature hysterics may seem merely a crude manifestation of male prejudice, but the overwhelming appearance of real hysterical symptoms among the women of the Victorian Era – partial paralysis, temporary loss of sight, hearing or other senses, and especially the presence of the choking contraction of the throat muscles known as the *globus histericus* – explains in part such an assumption.[47] Ilsa Veith links the presence of hysteria and the form it takes to the social mores of a given period:

> ...The manifestation of this disease tended to change from era to era quite as much as did the beliefs as to etiology and the methods of the treatment. The symptoms, it seems, were conditioned by social expectancy, tastes, mores and religion, and were further shaped by the state of medicine in general and the knowledge of the public about medical matters,... Furthermore,

---

[46] "La mujer y la política," *La Guirnalda* (20 agosto 1883), pp. 125-6.

[47] The most comprehensive and accessible historical treatment of the subject for the lay person is still the work of Ilza Veith cited in n. 44. The more recent work by George Frederick Drinka, M.D. *The Birth of Neurosis: Myth, Malady, and the Victorians* (New York: Simon & Schuster, Inc., 1984) is also very useful and readable.

throughout history the symptoms were modified by the prevailing concept of the feminine ideal. In the 19th century, especially, young women and girls were expected to be delicate and vulnerable both physically and emotionally, and this image was reflected in their disposition to hysteria and the nature of the symptoms.[48]

The reified image of the hysterical female as a potentially harmful weapon, "a package of dynamite" capable of killing and maiming, clearly expresses a fear of women. But what did men have to fear from the gentle sex? Certainly there exists a wide-felt presentiment on the part of the traditionalists that both working-class movements and the push for women's rights constitute real obstacles to the future maintenance of the status quo, the state of order and harmony to which the ascendant Spanish bourgeoisie aspires in order to more efficiently exert its power. But male fear of losing control over women also stems in part from the empirical evidence of a female sexuality completely divorced from the glorified function of childbearing. So entrenched is the belief that the decent woman does not experience sexual desire that indecorous manifestations to the contrary were often recorded as symptoms of insanity, i.e., of nymphomania. The theory of a hyper-sensitive nervous system is extrapolated to include greater sensitivity of the female sexual organs. The disease of *furor uterinus* is something so unseemly and repulsive that its presence can only be explained by categorizing it as a mental (moral) aberration.[49]

> In nymphomaniacs, one ordinarily observes a kind of discomfort in the epigastrium, a sensitivity of the uterus, anxiety and fearfulness, an engaging show of affection, tender and expressive glances, every kind of solicitation, insinuating attitudes, unexpected familiarities, pleas and lascivious caresses, lecherous postures, finally arriving at a complete and uninhibited nudity, and *furor uterinus* declares its presence with unseemly grimaces and cries, which reveal the tremendous excitation of the genital organs. If there is satisfaction through copulation or its supplements, a state of calm will be attained without however extinguishing the desire itself, but at the first opportunity, the erotic

---
[48] Veith, p. 209.
[49] Veith, p. 172. See also Fabre y D'Huc, pp. 403-24, for a nineteenth-century discussion of hysteria versus nymphomania.

paroxysm reappears and demands new acts and the subject gives herself up to new excesses, without ever achieving satisfaction. When chastity and modesty do not restrain women, the venereal pleasures manifest themselves much more stridently.... If a woman loses modesty's constraint, which so greatly enhances her beauty, there is no one capable of witnessing the lecherous and obscene acts to which she is driven by her greater sexual sensitivity.

(En las ninfomaníacas se observa de ordinario una especie de incomodidad, arrumacos graciosos, miradas muy tiernas y expresivas, solicitaciones bajo todas las formas, actitudes provocadoras, familiaridades insólitas, ruegos y caricias lascivas, posturas lúbricas, viendo a parar al fin a una desnudez completa y sin rodeos, y el furor uterino se declara con gestos y gritos desordenados, que revelan la grande exaltación de los órganos genitales. Si hay satisfacción con la cópula o sus suplementos sobreviene la calma, sin apagarse los mismos deseos, pero a la primera ocasión se reproduce el paroxismo erótico, y exige nuevos actos, y se entrega el sujeto a nuevos excesos, sin que se satisfaga jamás. Cuando la castidad y el pudor no enfrenan a la mujer, los placeres venéreos son en ella mucho más estrepitosos.... Si la mujer llega a perder el freno del pudor que tanto la embellece, nadie es capaz de presentar los actos lúbricos y obscenos a que la arrastra su mayor sensibilidad sexual.) [50]

What is of particular interest to us, following on our discussion of the concept of modesty, is the lack of specificity in what is apparently a list of identifiable medical symptoms of mental illness. The image of the nymphomanic is painted in a crescendo of accumulated details, beginning with manifestations of unease ("anxiety and fearfulness"), symptoms which would certainly be socially acceptable under ordinary circumstances, but which become contaminated by their insertion into the total picture. If we separate out the nouns from their qualifying adjectives, the nouns per se: glances, solicitation, attitude, pleas, caresses, postures, expressions *(gestos)*, cries — provide no information regarding mental or physical health. The burden of defining and describing *"el furor uterino"* rests solely upon a series of adjectives: provocative, unexpected, lascivious, lecherous, unruly *(desordenado)*, strident or noisy *(estrepitoso)* — which in turn

---

[50] Mata Fontanet, p. 373.

are judgements or evaluations ruled not by the laws of medical science but rather by nineteenth-century canons of decorum. Only the first symptom, discomfort of the epigastrium falls into the category of physiological disorder. Even the apparent objectivity of "a complete and uninhibited nudity" could conceivably signify, given the standard of modest dress for women during this period, no more than the removal of the outer garments or the appearance of a woman in her night dress.

While it comes as no surprise to learn of the author's disgust for the disease of nymphomania (leprosy, syphilis and smallpox also provoked fear and disgust), it is important to understand why the categorization of female sexual desire as mental illness does not protect the sufferer of this disease from a disapproval that implies a more than limited degree of guilt – indeed, of responsibility – for the disease.

The work of Pinel, *Traité medico-philosophique sur l'aliénation mentale* (1809), introduces the possibility that hitherto incurable mental disorders, now perceived as having a functional rather than an organic etiology, could be at least controlled, if not completely cured by means of a "moral" therapy or treatment.[51] The classification of mental illness as a moral disturbance (Veith points out that "moral" is used in the nineteenth century as the equivalent of the modern term "functional") reflects the belief that the etiology of non-organic mental disorders lay in the emotional excesses provoked by some factor in the patient's environment. Thus we have the constant strictures against certain stimulants, spices or meats; forbidden books; hot climates or cold; soft beds or sedentary occupations.[52] But this concept of mental illness went hand in hand with the belief in the inherited predisposition to insanity of certain physical types. *All* women belonged to this category because of an organic capacity for excessive emotion as well as a latent susceptibility to factors in the environment which provoked emotional excesses. Women were vulnerable, women were weak. Men could not control women, and they concluded that women were incapable of controlling themselves.

In 1792, Josefa Amar y Borbón sounded the warning note for women of succeeding generations: "Lately women are accused of

---

[51] Veith, pp. 174-79.
[52] Fabre y D'Huc, pp. 420-21.

being extreme in their emotions, be it love or hatred, anger, wrath, their way of thinking, etc." ("Últimamente se reprende a las mujeres de que son extremadas en todos sus afectos, ya de amor, ya de aborrecimiento, de enojo, de ira, de pensar, etc.")[53] Excessive emotion, then, translates into passion, and Dr. Ángel Pulido, in *Bosquejos médico-sociales para la mujer* reflects the prevalent abhorrence of passion as excess when he states: "I look upon passion as a transition state between sanity and insanity. In my opinion, the extremely passionate individual has one foot in the former and another in the latter condition." ("Yo miro el estado de la pasión como una transición entre la cordura y la locura. Para mí, el individuo muy apasionado tiene un pie en un campo y el otro en otro.")[54]

The problem of determining what is excessive or unacceptable social behavior stumbles over the inevitable subjectivity involved in defining standards of feminine comportment and even men of science express themselves in unselfconscious and uncritical tautologies:

> We have said that women are more inclined to a nervous condition than are men, and because they are more impressionable, all their physical and moral actions should be more moderate, because otherwise, they would be excessive.
>
> (Dijimos que la mujer está más sujeta al estado nervioso que el hombre, y como más impresionable, todas sus acciones físicas y morales deben ser para ella más moderadas, pues de otro modo serían excesivas.)[55]

Although it may seem obvious that the medical description of the female nervous system as weaker and more fragile than the male is merely a particularized version of the general belief that women are morally and physically defective, the importance of the role that medical scientists play in giving new credence to old prejudices cannot be overestimated. The scientific arguments that provided a spurious materialist explanation for women's different and supposedly inadequate physiology are cited again and again to justify women's confinement to the domestic sphere, while their radius of influence is radically abridged by their supposed incapacity to func-

---

[53] Amar y Borbón, p. 240.
[54] Pulido, p. 338.
[55] Drumen, pp. 394-95.

tion with any degree of physical and emotional stability. As one doctor exclaims, in an essay entitled "Carácter moral de la mujer": "*Everything* exercises a powerful influence upon such a fragile and delicate organization, upon such weak and profoundly irritable fibers..." (*"Todo* ejerce un influjo poderoso sobre organización tan frágil y delicada, sobre fibras tan débiles y profundamente irritables...")[56] This statement is a total negation of the possibility that women could exert influence in any situation whatsoever. They are perceived here as raw, skinless material, completely at the mercy of their environment. Their capacity to act as subject rather than as object is nonexistent.

Idealization implies control within the imagination over the desired object. The idealization of another human being demands the transformation of the human subject into object in order to achieve this imaginary control. The reification of the female subject is nowhere more evident than in the physician's prescription for proper bedroom behavior. Monlau's advice to the newly wedded husband reads as follows: "Do not abuse your new possession, as all too frequently happens,..." ("Que no abuse de su reciente posesión, como harto generalmente sucede,...") In his customary aseptic style, he explains the role of women in sexual intercourse: "The role of women in copulation is virtually limited to allowing the mechanical insertion of the masculine copulative organ." ("El oficio de la mujer en la copulación casi está limitado a sufrir la intromisión mecánica del órgano copulador masculino.")[57] This physical description is obviously a totally dehumanized vision of what is generally thought of as a human activity, but even when the expression of sexual desire is infused with the degree of emotion permissible to women, the restraint of decorum prescribes definite limits to her active participation. The following warning is given to the readers of *La Guirnalda* in 1876:

> A woman can, must love her husband tenderly; but there are limits beyond which she should never go. Her title of wife, of mother, her personal dignity, the need to command respect should never be absent.

---

[56] Justo Jiménez de Pedro, *Carácter moral de la mujer* (Madrid, 1854), p. 112.
[57] Monlau, p. 209.

> (La mujer puede, debe amar tiernamente a su marido; pero hay límites de que no debe nunca pasar. Su título de esposa, de madre, su dignidad personal, la necesidad de hacerse respetar no deben nunca abandonarla.)[58]

Tenderness but not passion is the normative standard for the modest wife, passion or lust being associated with the sexual activity which takes place between a man and his mistress or a prostitute.

But one passion, that of a mother's love for her child, is not only allowed but sanctified: "Maternal love is, then, the only inexhaustible one, the only one that never grows old..." ("El amor materno es pues el único inagotable, el solo que nunca envejece...")[59] writes Dr. Jiménez. The exaltation of maternal love by the physicians is partially a result of their need to rationalize the contradiction between the negation of sexual desire in the pure woman, and evidence of disorders brought about by frustrated sexual needs. But when Dr. Pulido says that "The main source of love is the instinct for reproduction" ("La fuente principal del amor es el instinto de la reproducción"),[60] he is not speaking euphemistically of the desire to experience sexual intercourse. Rather women are seen as literally satisfying whatever sexual needs they may have through pregnancy and childbirth. Thus the need to bear children becomes one of the few legitimate passions allowed to women. In his opening chapter entitled "El árbol sin fruto" ("The Tree without Fruit"), Dr. Pulido relates with compassion the heart-rending story of a young woman of the Lisbon aristocracy whom he visited in the insane asylum of Rilafolles:

> She suffers from a strange monomania. She thinks that all the children she sees are her own. It has been necessary to bring her here, because she would kiss them all and wanted to take them with her, suffering horribly when she was separated from them.
>
> (Padece una monomanía extraña. Cree hijos suyos cuantos niños ve. Se ha hecho necesario traerla aquí, porque a todos los besaba y quería llevar consigo, sufriendo horriblemente cuando se los separaba de ella.)[61]

---

[58] Condesa Dash, "De la castidad conyugal," *La Guirnalda* (29 marzo, 1876).
[59] Jiménez de Pedro, p. 26.
[60] Pulido, p. 221.
[61] Pulido, pp. 2-3.

Given the fact that middle-class women were made to feel non-existent, or at best, *de trop*, until they married and bore a child, it is quite conceivable that some women would be obssessed with this idea to the point of madness. It is also possible to theorize, in light of the restraints on physical intimacy with her husband which the modest wife felt obliged to exercise, that women frequently turned to their children in order to enjoy a less inhibited relationship of affection and closeness; certainly during this period, the moral sanctions against kissing and caressing children have been removed. Amar y Borbón, arguing against the traditional parental severity, insists that a more benign attitude with children facilitates a correct moral upbringing. [62] But her image of filial piety, a blend of respect, love and the necessary fear of authority is still many steps removed from the caressing angel-mother of the nineteenth century. In *El Museo de las Familias* we read:

> From the moment we are born, Nature entrusts us to a mother's love and caresses. Her beautiful shape, her pleasant voice naturally make our existence serene. Resting in her lap, she guides us by her loving gaze, and instructs us with her tenderness.
>
> (La naturaleza nos confía desde que nacemos al amor y a las caricias de una madre. Sus formas hermosas, su voz grata, hacen desde luego plácida nuestra existencia. Reposando entre su regazo, nos guía con su mirada cariñosa, y nos instruye con su ternura.) [63]

We have selected this passage, first, as an example of the typical style which relies on an enumeration of virtually synonymous and interchangeable series of nouns and adjectives: love-loving, beautiful, tender, pleasant, serene — words which themselves have a generic and dispassionate quality. And secondly, because this particular passage highlights the extent to which the creators of the image of the angel-mother identify with the product of their fantasy. The point of view is not that of the father observing the mother with his own child upon her lap, but that of the man-child himself, gazing up into the eyes of his mother.

This same phenomenon, the identification of the adult male with the role of the child rather than that of the father, is found in an

---

[62] Amar y Borbón, pp. 252-54.
[63] A. P. (cf. note 5), p. 126.

exceptionally beautiful and sensual passage in Fray Luis, when he attempts to persuade the perfect wife of her obligation to nurse:

> Because, is there any labor for which the child does not compensate his mother, when she holds him naked in her lap, when he plays with her breast, when he hits her with his little hand, when he looks at her in laughter, when he gurgles? And then when he winds himself around her neck and kisses her, it seems to me that it is she who is obligated to him.
>
> (Porque, ¿qué trabajo no paga el niño a la madre, quando ella le tiene en el regazo desnudo, quando él juega con la teta, quando la hiere con la manezilla, quando la mira con risa, quando gorgea? Pues quando se le anuda al cuello y la besa, paréceme, que aun la dexa obligada.)[64]

What is completely foreign to the nineteenth-century image of mother and child is the sensual quality of Fray Luis' description. This erotic overtone emphasizes the fact that it is a male child – the passage would make no sense if the baby were a little girl – that kisses a mother who is also a woman possessed of her own sexuality and capable of responding to the male infant.

In the nineteenth century, although nursing was acclaimed by both moralists and physicians to be the mother's sacred duty to her child, our general impression is that working-class women nursed not only their own but the majority of upper-class infants as well. In an article entitled "Amas de cría" ("Wet Nurses"), the author protests the fact that many middle-class women and almost all those of the upper-class refused to nurse because it would ruin their beauty. Whether a middle-class woman nursed or not, according to this author, would seem to have depended entirely on her financial and social status, on having the resources to imitate the customs set by the bourgeoisie who in turn imitated the ladies of the aristocracy.[65] As a result, the criticism leveled against women who employed a wet nurse became, in part, a criticism of the vain and frivolous mores of the upper-class women who preferred the seductions of a *té-dansant* to those of their own offspring. The antagonism expressed toward the aristocracy is paralleled by an enumeration of

---

[64] Luis de León, p. 106.
[65] Carlos Frontaura, "Las amas de cría," *El Museo Universal* (1 febrero, 1863), p. 39.

the vices of lower-class women employed as wet nurses: drunkenness, sexual promiscuity, greed and slovenly personal habits. Thus, we see that the insistence that "women" nurse their children represents a rejection of both the moneyed and the working classes; that is to say, a reaffirmation of the author's own middle-class status.

It would appear that while ideally the mother should nurse, feminine weakness was considered an acceptable excuse. The repressive attitudes toward sexuality may have made nursing seem too onerous a burden to demand of so spiritual a creature. Certainly Dr. Pulido, who insists that "the breasts are not organs of adornment" ("los pechos no son órganos de adorno"), backs off from any physical contact in his description of the mother and child:

> The chaste matron who watches by the side of the crib the fruit which heaven has granted her, who lulls him to sleep with sweet song and gentle rocking, and who deposits upon his white forehead a loving kiss [osculation],... is the image of Jesus Christ...
>
> (La casta matrona que vela al lado de la cuna por el fruto que el cielo la ha concedido, que le adormece con dulces cantos y suaves balanceos, y que deposita sobre su blanca frente un amoroso ósculo,... representa a Jesucristo...)[66]

We will let this final image of the ideal mother speak our concluding remarks. It is an image entirely devoid of sensuality, almost inert. The woman, faceless, without any identifying physical characteristics, hovers over the crib like the guardian angels in the penny Holy Cards of the period. And like them, she can safely be put away and forgotten.

---

[66] Pulido, p. 30.

CHAPTER THREE

EL LUJO: THE PROBLEM OF CONSPICUOUS CONSUMPTION

> *El lujo:* Excess in ostentation and comfort
> *Diccionario de Autoridades*
>
> *La Luxuria:* The unruly appetite or excessive use of sensuality or carnality
> *Diccionario de Autoridades*
>
> *Luxus:* (Latin), Excess, licenciousness
> *Diccionario crítico etimológico de la lengua castellana*

Although the word luxury, *"luxo"* or *"lujo,"* is absent from Covarrubias' early seventeenth-century dictionary, the concept of luxury as defined by the eighteenth-century Royal Academy of the Language's *Diccionario de Autoridades:* "excess in ostentation and comfort" ("exceso y demasía en la pompa y regalo"), is certainly in evidence long before the first recorded usage of the word by the religious and political thinker, Saavedra y Fajardo in 1640.[1] The key word in this definition is excess. Excess, within the moral framework of Catholic Counter-Reformation thought, is placed in opposition, not to plenitude but to abstinence. The moral tension between Christian abstinence and pagan self-indulgence – the catchword was "oriental luxury" ("el lujo oriental") – between God and Mammon, between

---

[1] See J. Corominas, *Diccionario crítico etimológico de la lengua castellana* (Madrid: Gredos, 1954). *"Luxo"* or *"lujo"* is derived from the Latin *luxus:* Excess, libertinism *(exceso, libertinaje)*. According to Corominas, the word *lujo* does not appear in any of the works of either Cervantes or Góngora.

the sacred and the profane, structures Fray Luis de León's definition of the perfect wife.

It is worth noting that Fray Luis dedicates the longest single passage of *La perfecta casada* to the subject of female finery.[2] The amount of attention dedicated to this subject is not disproportionate if we remember that *La perfecta casada* is, above all, a treatise on domestic economy, the domestic economy of the landowning Spanish gentry of the late sixteenth century in a time of galloping inflation, of increased cost of labor and a pattern of conspicuous consumption among the aristocracy.[3] Fray Luis concentrates on dress and make-up because these articles materially embody the moral and economical sin of conspicuous female waste, that is, the nonproductive expenditure of male labor. Underlying the critique is a belief in the parasitical existence of the upper-class lady who consumes her husband's wealth and produces nothing in return. Fray Luis does not distinguish between productive consumption, that is, the outlay of capital investment, and non-productive consumption, but he does make a distinction between the objects of consumption of men and women:

> ...men, when they decide to spend their money, usually decide to do so on things which, even though they are not necessary, are longlasting and honorable, or are in some way useful or advantageous, like those [men] who construct splendid buildings, or those who maintain many servants, or, for example, those who like to keep a large stable of horses: but the expenditure of women is completely frivolous: the expense is enormous and that which is purchased is neither valuable nor worthy of display.

> (...los hombres si les acontece ser gastadores, las más vezes lo son en cosas, aunque no necesarias, pero duraderas, o honrosas, o que tienen alguna parte de utilidad y provecho, como los que edifican suntuosamente, y los que mantienen grande familia, o, como los que gustan de tener muchos cavallos: mas el gasto de las mugeres es todo en el ayre: el gasto muy grande, y aquello en que se gasta, ni vale; ni luze.)[4]

This passage is inevitably colored by Fray Luis' perception of all women's unworthiness, so that by extension all activities and

---

[2] Luis de León, pp. 60-88, of an edition which consists of 116 pages.
[3] See *supra*, Ch. 1.
[4] Luis de León, p. 26.

objects associated with women become frivolous. But he is particularly affronted by what he considers to be the artificial manners of the overbred lady:

> Silk is too rough for them, and roses too harsh and they can't bear to stay on their feet, and they faint with the least gust of wind, and to say a complete sentence wearies them, and even the words that come out of their mouth are only half spoken, and the sight of the sun exhausts them, and they are all of them affected and putrid and disgusting,...

> (Que la seda les es áspera, y la rosa dura, y les quebrante el tenerse en los pies, y del ayre que suena se desmayan, y el dezir la palabra entera las cansa, y aun hasta lo que dizen lo abortan, y no las ha de mirar el sol, y todas ellas son un melindre y un lizo, y un asco,...)[5]

Although he criticizes the feminine upper-class style, the expenditures of the patriarch — houses, horses and numerous servants (*grande familia*) — are perceived as increasing the gentleman's patrimony and consequently are justifiable and even honorable expenses.[6] Fray Luis' critique of the customs of the wealthy gentry is a qualified one that is directed specifically at the participation of upper-class women in a general increase in consumption. His comments underline the limited areas of the domestic economy over which women would be likely to exercise a degree of control: their personal wardrobe and nonessential household furnishings, knick-knacks or *cachivaches*.

Fray Luis is very aware that a style of conspicuous consumption will find ready defenders. His polemical tone derives in part from the necessity of rebutting contemporary arguments which justified the consumption of luxury goods. The first and most important defense is based on the right to private property. To the question, "Do I not have the right to make use of my own things?" ("¿No tengo de usar de mis cosas?"), Fray Luis answers that the world is ruled by God's laws, not by man's.[7] It is God who sets the fashion of the day:

---

[5] Luis de León, p. 50.
[6] See Thorstein Veblen, *The Theory of the Leisure Class* (New York: Mentor Books, 1953), pp. 52-59, for a discussion of domestic servants and social status.
[7] Luis de León, pp. 82-83.

...this suit should not be cut to fit one's fancy, nor to conform to a fashion that is worldly and disgraceful, but in accordance to what is demanded by decency and modesty. So that in this case, God is indicating that clothing should be sacred in order to condemn that which is profane.

(...este traje no se ha de cortar a la medida del antojo, o del uso vituperable y mundano, sino conforme a lo que pide la honestidad y la vergüenza. Assí que señala aquí Dios vestido sancto, para condenar lo profano.)[8]

Another justification for the consumption of luxury goods was the familiar argument that one's station in life demanded conformity to a set standard of expenditure. The upper class could sin in the opposite direction, that of avarice, of storing up treasure on earth "for one's coffers and for the moths" ("para el arca y para la polilla"),[9] but avarice – a *male* sin, since not spending for a woman is the virtue of thrift *(economía)* – is not of primary concern when weighed against the more prevalent evil of the idolotrous worship of rare and expensive commodities.

Fray Luis distinguishes between the use value of raw materials such as gold and silver and the value added as a result of the scarcity of the materials and the skilled workmanship of the finished product. The total value of the product, the exchange value, is measured in money, and it is a high exchange value, the expensiveness *(lo costoso)* of a commodity, which attracts women:

Scarcity is added to fine workmanship in order to set the price, and this price in turn gives birth to the evil cupidity which women have towards these things: they ruin themselves in their desire for precious and expensive goods.

(Juntóse con el ser raro la delicadez del artificio y de allí nasció el precio, y del precio la mala codicia que dello las mugeres tienen: las cuales se pierden por lo precioso y costoso.)[10]

The fact that women are attracted by what is expensive, by an item's exchange value rather than its use value, is an aspect of their fetishistic and essentially frivolous or superficial nature, because

---

[8] Luis de León, p. 61.
[9] Luis de León, p. 54.
[10] Luis de León, p. 83.

they worship the appearance of value measured by money, rather than the substance of the item, which is the use which can be derived from it.

The argument that it is necessary to conform to a level of expenditure commensurate with one's social status is difficult for Fray Luis to refute because he himself believes in the sacredness of the social hierarchy and in the lack of distinction between virtue and the appearance of virtue. He agrees that one should dress "as one's status requires and in conformity with one's social level, in both everyday and extraordinary circumstances." ("en la manera que su estado lo pide, y trayéndose conforme a su qualidad, assí en lo ordinario como en lo extraordinario también.")[11] But the difficulty of defining the limits which determine legitimate expenditure are as problematic in the sixteenth century as they will be in the nineteenth. Fray Luis laments that "...there is great excess, even in women who are, in every other way, virtuous." ("...ay grande excesso, aun en las mugeres que en lo demás son honestas.")[12] Like the nineteenth-century conservatives, Fray Luis is critical of the economic laws of the market-place which permit the prostitute to dress herself in the same fashion as the lady. And like all traditionalists he seeks solace in an ephemeral Golden Age – possibly that of Spain under Roman Law – when virtue and vice were immediately recognized by their vestments. One more manifestation of "the ever-increasing evil of this century" ("la maldad de este siglo que siempre cresce") is the impossibility of distinguishing between a virtuous housewife and a whore, for dress has made them equal.[13]

The nexus between luxury and prostitution is money, the nexus of exchange. Women's innate desire for expensive goods leads them directly to evaluating themselves as exchange: "How easy it is to see how close ostentatious display is to lewdness, and how distant it is from the rules of propriety..." ("Que fácil es de ver quan junta anda essa pompa con la lascivia, y quan apartada de las reglas honestas...")[14] Although the causal relationship between luxury and lust is not *always* clear, they are always intertwined. Women dress to attract men, but it is also their attraction to finery which causes

---

[11] Luis de León, p. 61.
[12] Luis de León, p. 62.
[13] Luis de León, p. 85.
[14] Luis de León, p. 81.

them to sell themselves or to pilfer their husband's estate in order to satisfy their insatiable vanity.

It is vanity, not lust, which is ultimately the cardinal female sin. Women's desire for attention and praise causes them to paint their faces and adorn their bodies, to emphasize and underscore their physical presence in the world. This need to be seen, to be complimented and commented upon is condemned by Fray Luis as a disgusting act of self-assertion on the part of the vainglorious weaker sex. His furious diatribe against the use of make-up bears a strong resemblance to the nineteenth-century medical discourse on female sexuality. In answer to the question why do women use make-up, he exclaims:

> ...the reason why is the most uncontrolled egoism, an insatiable appetite for vainglorious display: ugly greed, a heart filled with treachery, adultery, harlotry, never-ending sinfulness.
>
> (...la respuesta de aquel, Para que, es amor propio desordenadissimo, appetito insaciable de vana excellencia: cobdicia fea: deshonestidad arraygada en el coraçón! adulterio, ramería, delicto que jamás cessa.)[15]

Women and their disorderly and insatiable appetite for finery lay siege not only to men's pocket books but also to their immortal souls. Not even the chastity of pure and temperate men is proof against the designs of the temptress:

> Even when men have reached their quiet years, and have arrived safely in the port of temperance, the finery of rich and showy dresses drive them wild and disturb their grave and sober maturity with sinful desires...
>
> (Aun a las edades quietas ya, y metidas en el puerto de la templanza, las galas de los vestidos luzidos y ricos las sacan de sus casillas, e inquietan con ruynes desseos su madurez grave y severa...)[16]

For Fray Luis, there is no distinction between prostitution and adultery. The line of demarcation is drawn between legitimate sex

---

[15] Luis de León, p. 67. See Ch. 2, "....unruly cries... the subject gives herself up to new excesses, without ever being satisfied." ("...gritos desordenados... se entrega el sujeto a nuevos excesos, sin que se satisfaga jamás.")

[16] Luis de León, p. 82.

– the monogamous, heterosexual activity of the married couple – and all other sexual activity, which is illegitimate or sinful. The married woman who commits adultery is a whore. Her desire for finery indicates whorish thoughts because the virtuous woman, *"la mujer honesta,"* desires nothing, neither finery nor love nor sexual satisfaction, for herself.

Fray Antonio Arbiol, in a book entitled *Estragos de la luxuria, y sus remedios, conforme a las Divinas Escrituras, y Santos Padres de la Iglesia*, also associates male lust with the provocation of female dress: "If a man's spirit is filled with lust, even the touch of female vestments can be lustful..." ("Si el ánimo del hombre está manchado de luxuria, aun el tocamiento de las vestiduras de la mujer puede ser luxurioso...")[17] But Arbiol makes it very clear that the real object of desire is the female body: "The neck, throat, nape [cervix], shoulders and naked backs, provoke lust,..." ("El cuello, garganta, cerviz, hombros y espaldas desnudas, dan voces de luxuria,...")[18] His fear of women is directly linked to the "ravages of lust" ("los estragos de la luxuria"), that is, the consequences of venereal disease visited upon the sinner and his innocent progeny.[19] Control of lust must be achieved by controlling, not he who lusts, but the object of lust; thus we have his insistence upon a style of dress for the virtuous woman which would cover her "...in such a way, that she reveals only her face and hands... even her feet should be concealed." ("...de tal modo, que sólo se la descubran las manos y cara... hasta los pies se deben cubrir.")[20] His censure logically extends to the new fashions in entertainment among the leisure class, which have begun to undermine the traditional system of sexual apartheid in the home:

> Many are sacrificed in this regrettable century which has introduced this disorder of banquets, *saraos*[21] [dances], *meriendas* [af-

---

[17] Antonio Arbiol, *Estragos de la luxuria, y sus remedios, conforme a las Divinas Escrituras, y Santos Padres de la Iglesia*, written in 1725 and published posthumously (Zaragoza, 1786), p. 10.
[18] Arbiol, *Estragos...*, p. 24.
[19] Arbiol, *Estragos...*, pp. 92-93.
[20] Arbiol, *Estragos...*, p. 33.
[21] Corominas documents an early use of *"sarau"* in Catalan used in 1537 with the sense of "evening dance (informal)" ("baile nocturno (popular)." Covarrubias includes *"serao"*: "A gathering of ladies and their escorts in a formal party by invitation only, especially in the palaces of royalty and great lords,... and because

ternoon snacks or picnics], and games, to which every age and sex are invited,... as a result of which we have flattery, flirting and misconduct, all to the detriment and endangerment of our youth's virtue and moral habits.

(Muchos sacrificios se deben ofrecer en este lamentable siglo en el cual se halla introducido este desorden de convites, saraos, meriendas, y juegos, en que occurren de todas edades, y sexos,... de donde resulten galanteos, y desmanes, con detrimento de la honestidad, buenas costumbres, y riesgo de la juventud.)[22]

The picture which Arbiol paints, of frivolity run wild, of food and drink, of music and dancing and games, and the promiscuous intermingling of men and women, young and old, can only be appreciated if we place it within the traditional model of domestic life molded to the Spanish style of pompous gravity and a rigid preservation of the honors and rituals accorded to the gerontocracy. The isolation of upper-class women in the home, until the seventeenth century the solution for preserving female virtue and male honor, became irrelevant when the door of the home opened, not to permit women to go out into society, but to allow society to enter in.

By the end of the eighteenth century, this radical change, the use of the private home as a locus of leisure activity, permits upper-class women to win what novelist and historian C. Martín Gaite calls "the right to luxury" ("el derecho al lujo").[23] Entertainment in the home resulted in a whole new spectrum of necessary female expenditure beyond that of personal dress: expenses such as household furnishings, food and drink and the proper means of serving them. The luxurious atmosphere of intimate sensuality and refinement, hitherto relegated to the petit-maisons of the courtesans, was grad-

---

one dances to the sound of many musical instruments, and there are also usually singers." ("La junta de damas y galanes en fiesta principal y acordada, particularmente en los palacios de reyes y grandes señores,... y porque se dança al son de muchos instrumentos músicos, y también suele aver música de cantores." The definition of the *Diccionario de Autoridades* suggests that the *"sarao"* was not limited to the houses of the aristocracy or *grandes señores:* "Assembly of persons of reputation and category, for the purpose of celebrating with musical instruments, and with formal dancing." ("Junta de personas de estimación y gerarchía, para festejarse con instrumentos, y bailes cortesanos.") *Diccionario de Autoridades,* first published in 1737, ed. (Madrid: Gredos, 1969).

[22] Arbiol, *Estragos...*, p. 195.
[23] Martín Gaite, p. 27.

ually legitimized, along with the right of the married woman to maintain at her side, if she could, her *cortejo*[24] (suitor or personal companion).

In his book, *Luxury and Capitalism,* Werner Sombart underlines the dialectic between the increase in the consumption of luxury items by the legitimate wife and the style of the courtesan. "The elevation of the elegant courtesan helped to form the tastes of the virtuous woman," and he concludes: "If the virtuous woman in society didn't wish to be completely eliminated, she was forced to enter into competition with the *cocotte.*"[25]

The direct relationship between the prevalence of a style of conspicuous consumption among the ladies of the upper class and an increase in the practice of adultery is a difficult question to investigate. Martín Gaite maintains that "the fact is undeniable that between the reign of Carlos III and that of Carlos IV, the transformation of the *cortejo* into an adulterous relationship was rapid." ("es indudable que entre el reinado de Carlos III y el de Carlos IV se aceleró la metamorfosis del cortejo en adulterio.")[26] And the Spanish Enlightenment's most eloquent defender of conspicuous consumption, J. Sempere y Guarino, has no hesitation in attributing "our century's corruption" ("la corrupción de nuestro siglo") to women's infidelity.[27] Both Fray Luis in 1583 and Fray Arbiol in 1725 emphasize a direct causal relationship between consumption run wild, *el lujo,* and *lujuria,* uncontrolled sexual desire. The curtailment of luxury is only one aspect of a general ascetic punishment of the flesh which had as its main purpose the subjugation of those sexual impulses which would result in illegitimate sexual activity. Arbiol exclaims:

> What else are these *saraos*... but: useless laughter, the devil's pomp, a drain on one's wealth, an unnecessary waste of time,

---

[24] The most complete documentation of the etymology, usage and social customs implied in the word *cortejo* is C. Martín Gaite's monograph previously cited.

[25] Werner Sombart, *Lujo y capitalismo,* trad. Luis Isabel from the original German, *Luxus und Kapitalismus* (Madrid: Alianza, 1979): "El encumbramiento de la cortesana elegante contribuye a la formación del gusto en la mujer honesta. [...] La señora honesta de la sociedad, si no quiere ser totalmente eliminada, ha de entrar en competencia con la *cocotte.*" p. 61.

[26] Martín Gaite, p. 121.

[27] Juan Sempere y Guarino, *Historia del luxo y de las leyes suntuarias de España,* vol. II (Madrid, 1788), p. 183.

> incitement to concupiscence, contemplation of adultery, the hall of fornication, school of gluttony, inducement to turpitude, an example of sinfulness,...?
>
> (¿Qué otra cosa son estos saraos... sino: inútil risa, pompa del demonio, efusión de la hacienda, superflua perdición de los días, inducción de la concupiscencia, meditación del adulterio, aula de la fornicación, escuela de la gula, exortación de la torpeza, exemplo de la deshonestidad,...?)[28]

This passage, taken from Fray Arbiol's *Los estragos de la luxuria*, synthesizes the traditional Catholic arguments against luxury defined as excessive or wasteful expenditure: 1) it depletes wealth; 2) it is associated with idleness or sloth, *el ocio;* 3) it is the cause of adultery and fornication. In order for Sempere y Guarino to defend the aristocratic style of conspicuous consumption in 1788, he must either tacitly approve the illegitimate sexual activity which has always been linked to the consumption of luxury goods, or he must somehow disassociate adultery and prostitution from conspicuous consumption. His own strong sense of traditional morality precludes any approbation of sexual license. He therefore offers a solution to the problem of female infidelity which will restore order in the home, but will not necessarily interfere with the level of consumption:

> The slightest offense in the delicate question of one's honor used to be cleansed with blood or with the total deprivation of freedom. When female licentiousness was restrained thus severely, marriages were more united...
>
> (La más leve ofensa en la delicada materia del honor se lavaba con sangre o la privación absoluta de la libertad. Refrenada con esta severidad la licencia mujeril, estaban los matrimonios más unidos...)[29]

His call for a revival of absolute patriarchal authority in the family, of the Calderonian honor code of duels and blood-cleansings is an anachronism by the end of the eighteenth century, and reveals the ideological confusion of Enlightenment thinkers who analyze production and consumption according to the laws of the market

---

[28] Arbiol, *Estragos...*, p. 195.
[29] Sempere y Guarino, p. 183.

but insist on maintaining the feudal relationship of female servitude in return for male protection within the institution of the family.

Sempere y Guarino does not dwell long on this subject, because he is ultimately a political economist and the business at hand is the nation's economy. His defense of consumption derives from an analysis of the nation's wealth which is radically different from that of Fray Luis, who based his analysis on the economy of the individual landlord, for whom an increase in wealth is an automatic result of thrift, or *economía*. If one does not spend, "wealth increases" ("la hacienda cresce"). [30] Sempere y Guarino, on the other hand, is analyzing the national, rather than the private, economy. The source of national wealth is not land, or gold, but industry; that is, the production of commodities, and especially, of luxury goods. Fray Luis' utopian vision of abundance is one in which the needs of food and shelter are satisfied. Sempere y Guarino translates the concept of abundance into surplus production on a national scale which is then consumed by a minority class: "...luxury is usually the effect of abundance, and of wealth, and its unequal distribution." ("...el lujo es, por lo general, efecto de la abundancia, y de las riquezas, y de su desigual distribución.") [31]

By defining the leisure of the aristocracy as an economic necessity which benefits the urban workers and artisans by redistributing wealth through the creation of employment, Sempere y Guarino not only seeks to vindicate their style of consumption, but also to provide the aristocracy with a social *raison d'être* which will replace their now obsolete function of exemplar for the community.

The formula of "Spending equals waste equals penury (loss of landed property)" is rewritten as "Spending equals consumption equals wealth (increased national production)." Consequently, the leisure of the upper classes becomes the basis for the work of the "laboring poor," the artisan and the urban wage-laborer. Luxury, now defined not as waste but as consumption, is at worst a necessary evil, and at best, a benefit to the national economy. [32]

The main target of Sempere y Guarino's critique is the Sumptuary Laws which attempted to control public morality by legisla-

---

[30] Luis de León, p. 9.
[31] Sempere y Guarino, p. 176.
[32] Sempere y Guarino, p. 205. See also Richard Herr, *The Eighteenth Century Revolution in Spain* (New Jersey: Princeton University Press, 1969), pp. 51-54.

tion against individual consumption. These laws can no longer be allowed to enchain domestic production: "Spain, free from the chain which tied her for many years to foreigners, would produce for herself all the commodities she consumes..." ("España, libre de la cadena que la sujetó por muchos años a los estranjeros, cultivaría por sí misma todos los objetos de su consumo...")[33] This indictment of the Sumptuary Laws is one of the more coherent manifestations of the bourgeois mentality that must separate the question of moral values out from the analysis of economic laws. The introduction of the ideas of Adam Smith into Spain during the reign of Carlos III served to legitimate the economic upheavals brought about by the gradual accumulation of capital in the hands of the bourgeoisie as a manifestation of the necessary principle of *laissez faire*. According to Richard Herr, among Enlightenment thinkers, "economics was already the unchallenged arbiter of social relations and justice it was to become in the nineteenth-century industrial states."[34] The sacred right to private property – the untrammelled right of the individual to accumulate and exploit capital – is the keystone of the "Rights of Man" and will henceforth define and shape public policy.

Another important element of Spanish Enlightenment philosophy that is in direct contradiction to the principle of Christian asceticism and its teleology of ultraterrestrialism is the revolutionary belief in the right to material happiness. Sempere y Guarino's statement that "Vice does not lie in the things that man uses: rather it lies in the uncontrolled use of these things." ("No está el vicio en las cosas de que usa el hombre: sino en el uso desordenado de ellas.")[35] speaks directly to the Catholic theologians who urged their flock to flee from earthly temptations of food, drink, and women. If the Devil's work, evil, is embodied in the object of desire, it is the object itself which must be shunned. The absolutism of a morality which says shun *all* evil and defines evil within the object itself, is now replaced by a relative morality which defines evil according to utilitarian principles.[36] Evil resides not in the object, but in the abuse of the object by its user. The object itself is

---

[33] Sempere y Guarino, p. 189.
[34] Herr, p. 57. See also José Luis L. Aranguren, *Moral y Sociedad* (Madrid: Cuadernos para el Diálogo, S. A., 1967), pp. 11-12.
[35] Sempere y Guarino, pp. 195-96.
[36] See Aranguren, p. 66, on Utilitarianism in Spain.

redefined in neutral economic terms as a commodity, *los consumos*. Luxury goods – like the upper class which consumes them – are thus morally rehabilitated into everyday life as a necessary and integral part of the national economy.

LUXURY AND LUST IN THE NINETEENTH CENTURY

Moral relativism underlies every discussion of luxury that appears in the family and fashion magazines in Spain from the mid-1840s and throughout the rest of the century. Before analyzing the specific dialectic between women and conspicuous consumption, it will be helpful to survey the wider context in which the subject of women and consumption takes place.

Luxury is the topic of one of the *Conferencias Dominicales* (Sunday Lectures), a series of talks for women organized by Fernando de Castro and other Krausists in 1860, lectures which later evolved into the Escuela de Institutrices and the Asociación para la Enseñanza de la Mujer.[37] The author, economist Antonio María Segovia, begins with the following definition: "[Luxury is]... superfluous and non-productive spending, for the purpose of mere ostentation, or in disproportion to the resources of the spender." ("[El lujo es] ... gasto superfluo e improductivo, sostenido por mera ostentación, o desproporcionado a los recursos de quien le costea.")[38] The concept of *non-productive* consumption is clarified by defining its opposite, *productive* consumption. After a series of pedantic asides – Segovia quarrels with the use of the French word *confortable* – he begins his argument with the detailed description of a luxurious Madrid café. The essence of his argument follows: the luxury of the café's appointments – the marble tables and thick rugs – are a necessary capital investment by the proprietor in order to attract a clientele with the money to consume his product, which is not only a cup of coffee, but a cup of coffee taken in a certain ambience of wealth and refinement. In turn, the consumer of this ease and elegance does not commit the sin of *el lujo*, of excess consumption, if his private economy extends to such an expenditure, after the

---

[37] Scanlon, pp. 31-35.
[38] Antonio María Segovia, "Del lujo" (14 marzo 1869), p. 4, included in *Conferencias dominicales sobre la educación de la mujer* (Madrid, 1869).

basic requirements of subsistence are met. Concludes Segovia: "The concept of luxury is strictly relative." ("La idea del lujo es puramente relativa.") [39]

The morality of productive consumption, that is, of capital investment, is found at the bottom line of the ledger where profits and debits are read. The morality of non-productive or use consumption is more problematic. But what is important to underline is that women enter into the economic picture only as non-productive consumers. The arguments against "women's luxury" ("el lujo de la mujer") are consequently focussed on the impact of female consumption on the private economy of the family. Excess, now defined precisely as "beyond one's means," is a direct function of economic power, that is to say, of one's class origin.

In an economy in which private consumption is not yet dependent on systems of credit, to spend more than one has on hand is perceived as a crime against society. We read in *La Familia*, a magazine which attempted to popularize the conservative ideology of *La Defensa de la Sociedad*, the following:

> To spend more than one earns, wracking one's brain in order to do it, is a serious crime, just as serious as that which one commits by appropriating another's goods...
>
> (Gastar más de lo que se gana, poniendo la imaginación en tortura para llevarlo a efecto, es un delito grave, tan grave como el que se comete al apropiarse los bienes agenos...)

And the perpetrators of this crime come from every class:

> And it is not only those of modest position who wish to place themselves alongside those of a superior rank. These people also have others whom they wish to imitate, and instead of the different social classes forming one continuous chain which joins everyone together from the humble worker to the powerful magnate, everyone wants to weld themselves into just one link, and to aspire to that which will never be anything but a myth: social equality.
>
> (Y no son exclusivamente las personas de modesta posición las que quieren colocarse a la altura de las de superior jerarquía.

---

[39] Segovia, p. 10.

> Éstas, a su vez, tienen otras a quienes imitar, y en vez de ser las diferentes clases sociales una cadena que enlace desde el humilde obrero hasta el poderoso magnate, todos quieren refundirse en un solo eslabón y aspirar a lo que nunca pasará de ser un mito: a la nivelación social.)[40]

The argument that excessive consumption wreaks havoc among the lower and middle classes, and is a personal affront to the social status of the bourgeoisie, "the powerful magnates," does not explain why the crime of *el lujo*, or conspicuous consumption should be categorized as specifically feminine. Yet the belief that luxury consumption is a woman's sin is argued by no less an authority than the ruling magnate of the Catholic Church, Pope Pius IX. His encyclical "Concerning Women and Luxury" ("Sobre el lujo de las mujeres") appeared in various magazines in 1875, among them *La Familia*. Pius IX repeats the traditional arguments outlined by Fray Luis de León and Fray Antonio Arbiol that excessive spending is a sin related to the sin of sloth or idleness *(el ocio)*, and that luxury spending robs the sons of their inheritance:

> Luxury is a provacation in elegant gatherings, in the public concourses and other spectacles, because it motivates one to promenade from house to house, under the pretext of necessary social obligations to pay and hence to give oneself up to idleness, to curiosity and to indiscreeet conversations. It [luxury] foments evil desires, it consumes the property which should be kept for the sons and used to help the poor.
>
> (El lujo es provocativo en las reuniones brillantes, en paseos públicos y otros espectáculos, porque enseña andar de casa en casa, bajo el pretexto de atenciones de cumplir y allí entregarse a la ociosidad, a la curiosidad y a las conversaciones indiscretas. Él es el que sirve de alimento a malos deseos, el que consume la hacienda que se debía guardar para los hijos y para socorrer a los pobres.)

But another complaint has been added to the list of charges against frivolous women. Because of women's penchant for luxury, the men refuse to marry. And, the encyclical affirms: "experience shows that this drawing back from matrimony is a new cause of disorder."

---

[40] Alfredo, "El lujo," *La Familia*, II, 22 (agosto 1876), p. 253.

("la experiencia demuestra que este alejamiento del matrimonio es un nuevo alimento para el desorden.")[41]

The term "social or public disorder" generally evokes a panorama of riots or strikes, of interference in the functioning of government or of labor and production. Pius IX's reference to "these calamities that surround us everywhere today" ("estas calamidades que hoy día nos rodean de todas partes") is certainly meant to include such events as the rise of the Paris Commune in 1871 and the growing strength of the socialist movement in Europe among the urban proletariat. But the specific social disorder linked to a decline in marriage must be understood in relation to the purpose of the marriage institution within the development of a society based on industrial capitalism. Marriage perpetuates the class structure through its control over private sexual behavior: marriage among the working class results in the reproduction and the maintenance of labor power; marriage among the wealthy preserves the power of the ruling class through the transmission of its property from father to male heir.

Michel Foucault points out in his introductory volume of *The History of Sexuality* that demography, the science of population control which emerges at the end of the eighteenth century, incorporates the private realm of human sexuality into the public sphere of political economy:

> It was essential that the state know what was happening with its citizens' sex, and the use they made of it, but also that each individual be capable of controlling the use he made of it. Between the state and the individual, sex became a public issue no less; a whole web of discourses, special knowledge, analyses, and injunctions settled upon it.[42]

Foucault then sets out to show that the discourses produced by the agents of social control — the educators, the physicians, the politicians — are not directed toward married, heterosexual activity (defined by Church and State as legitimate), but toward all other sexual activities, of children, of criminals and prostitutes, the promiscuous

---

[41] Breve de su Santidad Pío IX a María de Gentelles, "Sobre el lujo de las mujeres," *La Familia* (30 octubre 1875), p. 171.

[42] Michel Foucault, *The History of Sexuality: Volume I, An Introduction*, trans. R. Hurley (New York: Pantheon Books, 1978), p. 26.

and the insane. The world of illegitimate sex, hitherto given little attention, becomes the laboratory subject of scientists. Deviance from the social norm of heterosexual, monogamous marriage is defined as the pathology of sexual perversion.[43] Illegitimate sexual activity no longer merely results in a social disease (syphilis, for example), it *is* a disease. Foucault's argument is very convincing and we have seen this logic demonstrated in our discussion of female sexuality and the ready classification of overt female sexual desire as the disease of nymphomania.[44]

The focus of our discussion, however, is not the area of illegitimate sex, but rather the relationship between luxury, or conspicuous consumption, and the supposedly asexual, legitimate wife. The audience to whom Segovia directs his Sunday lecture, and the readers of Pius IX's pastoral letter, consist of Ángel Pulido's "chaste matrons," the respectable women of the community who uphold the standards of decency. These women have been judged by medical science to be completely devoid of lustful impulses, yet they sit and listen quietly while Segovia ascribes to them an uncontrollable instinct for luxury:

> ...in those of your sex, the cases of a hydropical frenzy for luxury are more frequent. And I would dare to say even more: women, and only women, are the ones who spread this disastrous contagion, just as they are also the only ones who can contain the onslaught of such a pernicious licentiousness.
>
> (...son más frecuentes en las personas de vuestro sexo los casos del hidrópico frenesí del lujo. Y me atrevo a decir más todavía: las mujeres, y solamente las mujeres, son las que propagan ese funesto contagio, así como también son ellas las únicas que pueden contener el torrente de tan pernicioso desenfreno.)[45]

An anonymous writer appearing in the feminist journal *La Mujer* in 1852 writes that the principal defect of women is their "fatal passion for luxury" ("funesta pasión por el lujo").[46] It is the *"furor del lujo,"* a frenetic need for luxury rather than *"el furor uterino"* or sexual desire that drives women from their homes and into the

---

[43] Foucault, pp. 27-48.
[44] See *supra*, Chapter 2.
[45] Segovia, p. 12.
[46] No author, no title, *La Mujer*, I, 52 (25 julio 1852).

world of fashion and society in search of satisfaction.[47] María Pilar Sinués de Marco, founder of the magazine *El Ángel del Hogar*, a *literata* and a novelist, exclaims:

> ...luxury is the cancer of our sex, because of it, the modest working girl is ruined, because of it, the diligent shopman who can no longer support with his wages his wife's and his children's luxurious habits, becomes involved in business transactions: nobody is happy with what they have, because everyone wants to possess much more...
>
> (...el lujo es el cáncer de nuestro sexo, por él se pierde la modesta obrera; por él emprende negocios el laborioso empleado que ya no puede atender con su sueldo al lujo de su mujer y de sus hijos: nadie se contenta con lo que tiene, porque todos aspiran a poseer mucho más...)[48]

These commentaries are both explicit and allusive. Women suffer from frequent attacks of a dropsy-like disease, a kind of swelling edema that fills them with a frenzy, a furor of desire. This desire is a cancer, which spreads throughout the body and is contagious. As Susan Sontag points out, the cancer metaphor is one of space and not of time.[49] This woman's disease is contagious, a plague, thus a social disease. The space that is being contaminated is social space, and the body, the body politic. Women are literally polluting *mankind*.

At this point it becomes obvious that we are hearing a familiar song. The question is, is it the same song that was sung by Fray Luis? We are immediately struck by the similarity in tone and language between the diatribes against feminine luxury and the equally vitriolic condemnations of female sexuality. The vocabulary is the same: irresistible, insatiable, licentiousness, furor, and especially, instinct and passion. One could theorize that the discourse on luxury is in reality a sublimated discussion of female sexuality. The "instinct" for luxury is perceived as acting upon women in the same way that the sexual instinct acts upon the male organism: it is a desire that comes from within the organism and that is constant-

---

[47] No author, no title, *La Mujer*, I, 38 (18 abril 1852).
[48] María Pilar Sinués de Marco, "Contra el lujo," *El Correo de la Moda* (2 septiembre 1883), p. 258.
[49] Susan Sontag, *Illness as Metaphor* (New York: Vintage Books, 1979), p. 14.

ly renewed, never completely satisfied or only temporarily satisfied. The desire for luxury is an instinct which, if not rigidly controlled, cut off at the first sign of arousal, ends by controlling the individual. It is a destructive force, and it is greatly feared. Like syphilis, "luxury" is contagious.

Yet if the instinct for luxury was thought to be the female equivalent of the sexual instinct, one might very well expect Sinués de Marco to claim that "luxury is the syphilis (rather than the cancer) of our [the female] sex." However, there is more at stake than a possibly inappropriate metaphor, or the habitual nineteenth-century sense of propriety.[50] The use of the cancer metaphor speaks to the general lack of understanding of the market laws that govern the distribution (availability) and the consumption of commodities. Luxury spending could never be described as the "syphilis of our time" or the "syphilis of our sex" because the cause and effect between venereal disease and sexual activity was a known quantity. The presence of the human sexual instinct, although terrifying because of its power over the individual, is not a presence which mystifies. On the contrary, sexual desire is an old and familiar enemy, fought off by the abstemious nuns and monks in their cells, subjugated within the confines of Holy Matrimony, wept over and pardoned in the confessional box. The source of satisfaction of the (male) sexual instinct is also a familiar and specific entity: the female body, asexual and chaste or clean within marriage, filthy and contaminated but somehow overwhelmingly attractive outside of marriage. The market place where supply meets with sexual demand is a carefully circumscribed area: the streets and brothels for black-market sex, and the dances or *soirées* where marriageable daughters are placed on display.

On the other hand, the relation between a supposed female instinct for conspicuous consumption and the objects which would satisfy this "instinct" is an uncharted terrain. The relationship between women and luxury horrifies precisely because, unlike sexual desire, it is not understood. The main characteristic of the diatribes

---

[50] Although the all-pervasive fear of venereal disease does exist as a sub-text in the discussions of *"el lujo"* that link it to prostitution, specific discussions on venereal disease are relegated to the medical and public hygiene textbooks and journals and do not appear in the family and fashion magazines. Prostitution is discussed in these magazines in either self-righteous or romanticized terms, but venereal disease is not discussed.

against "the frenzy for luxury" is the lack of understanding of supply and demand of this "fatal passion." Segovia recoils in horror from "the hydropical thirst for the easy life and material pleasures" ("la sed hidrópica de la molicie y de los goces materiales") and Sinués de Marco is dismayed because nobody is content anymore and everyone wants more. An instinct which is satisfied by the pleasure of possessing material goods is perceived as completely open-ended, unquantifiable and truly insatiable, unlike sexual desire, which is necessarily limited by the physical capacity for orgasm.

The dialectic between a demand (or an "instinct") for luxury goods and their supply differs in two essential ways from the demands of sexual desire and the means of satisfying them. First, in this period before Freud and any theory of sublimation, the satisfaction of a desire for material possessions was thought to be an asexual activity limited to the relation between the purchaser and the commodity consumer. In particular, the virtuous wife can now legitimately satisfy her drive for pleasure in a way which disassociates her completely from her husband and his drive for sexual satisfaction. Second, unlike sexual activity, the morality of commodity consumption is now, in the nineteenth century, posited strictly in economic terms: one spends according to one's means. Since buying new hats and laces is not immoral *per se*, the traditional authority which the husband exercised over his wife's sexual activity cannot be applied with equal force to her spending orgies. He cannot shoot her when she is caught *in flagrante* in the ribbon store, he cannot challenge the shopkeeper to a duel.

Thus we see that an important distinction exists between Sempere y Guarino's judgement that female infidelity is the source of "this century's corruption" and his proposed solution – a revival of absolute patriarchal authority in the home –; and Segovia's conclusion that women's passion for finery will bring about the downfall of modern Christian civilization if it is not controlled: "On this point, women provide the standard, and like many other proverbs, they justify the well-known one that men make the laws and women the customs." ("La mujer da en este punto la pauta, y justifica, como en otros muchos, aquel sabido apotegma de que los hombres hacen las leyes, y las mujeres las costumbres.")[51] Morality has become a private affair, and a woman's affair to the degree that she will

---

[51] Segovia, p. 12.

inevitably be held responsible for the decline of Western civilization. But more important is Segovia's implicit statement that women have somehow slipped through men's fingers and are definitively beyond their control. The Spanish code of honor, the subject of the great Calderonian tragedies, becomes irrelevant when honor is defined according to economic power and the capacity to maintain an appearance of decency, an appearance which can be purchased.

THE FASHION OF FEMININITY

In order to know what constituted popular thought on the subject of women's nature and femininity, it is necessary to attempt to ascertain to what extent the self-proclaimed moralists and social commentators of the nineteenth century believed their own words. What was their point of departure for the axiom that women were born with an instinct or passion for adornment? The basic principle which underlies all discussion of the so-called innate female characteristics is the belief that women were created by God to give pleasure to men. This axiom informs Fray Luis' analysis of the perfect wife's obligation to submit to her husband's authority. There is, however, an important and qualitative distinction between Fray Luis' discussion of feminine vanity and that of Jean-Jacques Rousseau, the modern philosopher most responsible for formulating the concept of femininity in circulation during the nineteenth century.[52] For Fray Luis, vanity, like gluttony or lust, is a human sin. Women, because they are morally and physically weaker than or inferior to men, fall prey more easily to these *human* temptations, and especially to the sin of vanity. Rousseau, on the other hand, bases his description of innate female and male characteristics on the premise that all human instincts are good. He observes that little girls love dress, and that their behavior, unlike that of little boys, is easily molded

---

[52] The influence of J.-J. Rousseau in the Spanish Enlightenment has been thoroughly documented by J. R. Spell, *Rousseau in the Spanish World Before 1833: A Study in Franco-Spanish Literary Relations* (New York: Octogan Books, 1969). The popular press from 1840-1900 is permeated with Rousseauian concepts on education, child-care and especially, femininity. For a more general discussion on Rousseau's influence within the European intellectual history on the subject of women and the family, see S. M. Okin, *Women in Western Political Thought* (New Jersey: Princeton University Press, 1979) and Eva Figes, *Patriarchal Attitudes* (New York: Stein and Day, 1970).

by others' opinions of them. Women are *essentially* different from men, and must be judged according to a different criterion. What might be faults in men may become virtues in women.[53] Rousseau goes on to comment on the female child's desire to dress her doll, and later, on the adult woman's instinct to adorn herself: "she awaits the moment when she shall be her own doll."[54] This typical feminine behavior fits into a rational cosmovision based on separate spheres of activity. Little girls adorn themselves to please others, thus demonstrating that they know that their purpose in life is to give pleasure. Female vanity is therefore a moral good; and male vanity does not exist.

Nevertheless, instinct for adornment defined as a charming manifestation of women's innate desire to please men is not the same thing as the disgusting instinct for luxury decried by Segovia *et al.* The difference between these two instincts is mainly teleological, centering on the purpose or motivation which impels women into a pattern of conspicuous consumption. Ultimately, what pleases men is women's desire to please them, while what so disgusts the nineteenth-century moralists is women's perceived desire to give pleasure to themselves. Henri Lefebvre, in *Everyday Life in the Modern World*, states:

> ...the ideology of femininity, or of happiness by and in femininity, is only another form of the ideology of consumption (happiness through consuming) and the ideology of technicality (women possessing the technique of happiness!) but with something more appealing.[55]

From the point of view of the male consumer, different styles of femininity package different products. In the nineteenth century, the male consumer of happiness through the purchase of Rousseau's grown-up doll, may choose from among several models. There is the sweet submissive *"ángel del hogar"* guaranteed to obey your slightest command; there is the luxury model, the new and improved *"mujer instruida"* who appears at night in the *tertulias*, and

---

[53] J.-J. Rousseau, *Emile or On Education*, intro. and trans. Allan Bloom (New York: Basic Books, Inc., 1979), p. 365.
[54] Rousseau, p. 367.
[55] Henri Lefebvre, *Everyday Life in the Modern World*, trans. S. Rabinavitch (New York: Harper Torchbooks, 1971), p. 96.

like her French cousin, the *femme savante,* not only walks but talks; the slightly shop-worn Courtesan is a big seller; and of course, the bargain basement Streetwalker.

Femininity is a fashion, a style. But the consumers of fashion are also women. In fact, the world of fashion, of *la moda,* is considered by definition a woman's world. In *El Museo de las Familias,* one of the earliest nineteenth-century Spanish magazines designed to provide "entertainment and moral instruction" to a broad middle-class audience, we read in 1844:

> What has especially struck my attention is the name [of fashion] *(la moda),* because since it is derived from the Latin word *modus,* and since the word itself *[la moda]* signifies the manner *[el modo]* of dressing, eating, building houses, walking, etc., according to the latest usage, it might just as well have retained its masculine gender, but... it was desirable to give this word a feminine gender, because the feminine expresses all of the fickleness, the coquetery and the imagination which it *[la moda]* encompasses,...
>
> (Lo que más particularmente ha llamado mi atención es el nombre [la moda], porque siendo derivado de la palabra latina *modus,* y significando ella misma el modo de vestirse, comer, edificar, andar, etc: según el uso últimamente introducido, pudiera muy bien habérsele conservado masculino, pero... quiso darle el género femenino, porque comprendió toda la veleidad, coquetería e imaginación que ella encierra,...) [56]

Fashion is seen as embodying one of women's defining characteristics: fickleness *(veleidad),* with its connotations of capriciousness, inconstancy, mutability, a lack of stability, reliability or permanence. Fernand Braudel, in *Capitalism and Material Life,* reminds us that the imposition of fashion as constant change was not the rule until the eighteenth century. Prior to this period, "the general rule was changelessness." [57]

Occasionally it is possible to read a reference to the fact that constant change in fashion results from the need to foment consumption in order to insure a profitable return on capital invest-

---

[56] J. de Quevedo, "Estudios morales: la moda," *El Museo de las Familias,* 1-2 (1844), pp. 288-91.

[57] Fernand Braudel, *Capitalism and Material Life,* trans. M. Kochon (New York: Harper Torchbooks, 1974), p. 231.

ment. Like Communism, atheism and the decadent custom of wet-nursing, fashion comes from Paris:

> ...thanks to the efforts of French industrialism, which in order to survive must be constantly changing its frivolous products and inventing and devising a million worthless baubles that, under the name of the newest fad, are used to exploit the family.
>
> (...merced a los esfuerzos del industrialismo francés, que para vivir necesita estar variando perpetuamente sus frívolos productos e ingeniando y discurriendo cada mes mil y mil fruslerías insustanciales que, con el nombre de *novedades,* sirven para explotar a las familias.)⁵⁸

The depiction of fashion as a woman's world reflects the reality that changes in style of dress are directed primarily at female consumers in the nineteenth century. Kathryn Weibel, in her excellent study of the image of women in popular culture, emphasizes the stability of male dress in comparison to the fluctuation of the female costume:

> Before the nineteenth century, men's fashions had all the characteristics attributed to women's fashions of the nineteenth and twentieth century. They were cyclical; they depicted the status of the wearer; and they were used for sex display... In the early nineteenth century, however, men's clothing, especially the "business suit," became the standardized, tailored, and reasonably comfortable uniform it has remained ever since. Only in the second half of the twentieth century, has women's clothing taken on these characteristics. ⁵⁹

Although the world of fashion is identified as a woman's world, unlike the private enclave of domestic life it is located in the geography of the prohibited public sphere. The description of the public sphere as a space which contains a series of autonomous and isolated worlds – the world of commerce *(negocios),* the world of politics and the world of fashion – that exist on a plane parallel to but closed off from the private sphere (and from each other), functions to hide the interdependency of production and consump-

---

[58] No author, "La familia y la moda," *La Guirnalda* (16 octubre 1875), p. 154.
[59] K. Weibel, *Mirror, Mirror* (New York: Anchor Books, 1977), p. 176.

tion and to mask the class nature of fashionable society, in reality accessible only to an economically privileged minority. The middle-class Spanish woman, confined within the rigid circumference of victorian [60] respectability as she was within the steel hoops of her crinolines, [61] could only enter the public sphere through the door of fashionable society, a journey of upward mobility, precarious and at times dangerous for the woman of limited means. [62]

The relation between conspicuous consumption, social status and the dynamics of class mobility has been analyzed in depth by Thorstein Veblen in his classic study of nineteenth-century New England society, first published in 1899:

> In modern civilized communities the lines of demarcation between social classes have grown vague and transient, and wherever this happens the norms of reputability imposed by the upper class extends its coercive influence with but the slightest hindrance down through the social structure to the lowest strata. The result is that the members of each strata accept as their ideal of decency the scheme in life in vogue in the next higher stratum, and bend their energies to live up to that idea. [63]

---

[60] I use the word "victorian" according to Webster's second definition: "showing the middle-class respectability, prudery, bigotry, etc. generally attributed to the Victorians." *Webster's New Twentieth Century Dictionary of the English Language*, unabridged, second edition (Collins World, 1978).

[61] See Alison Gernsheim, *Fashion and Reality* (London: Faber and Faber, 1963), pp. 25-29, for a history of the crinoline. See also Weibel, pp. 181-88 for a concise description of the development of the crinoline into the crinolette in the 1880s.

[62] Concepción Arenal makes a veiled reference to the prostitution of middle-class wives for the purpose of maintaining a standard of "decent" consumption. "[This] is often observed in the case of women who unwittingly advise reprobatory actions to their husbands and children, blinded as they are by the selfish emotion of the family's well-being, the only thing that concerns them and that they desire and understand, and for which they are disposed to sacrifice dignity, their finer sentiments, and even their honor." ("Así puede observarse muy a menudo, en mujeres que aconsejan a sus maridos e hijos acciones reprobables, que no se lo parecen, cegadas por el sentimiento egoísta del provecho de la familia, único de que se ocupan, comprenden y desean, y al cual están dispuestas a sacrificar dignidad, delicadeza, y hasta el honor.") *La mujer de su casa*, written in 1881 (Madrid: Biblioteca Júcar, 1974), p. 212. For a documentation of the prostitution of married women from the point of view of the public health and medical institutions, see Philip Hauser, *Madrid bajo el punto de vista médico-social*, first published in 1902, ed. Carmen del Moral, vol. 2 (Madrid: Editora Nacional, 1979), pp. 145-55.

[63] Thorstein Veblen, *The Theory of the Leisure Class*, first published in 1899 (New York: Mentor Edition, 1960), p. 70.

Decency, defined as conformity to the standard of consumption of one's class, is the moral justification which legitimates conspicuous consumption as a socially necessary activity. The feminine readers of the popular women's magazines are warned against excess (*el lujo*) but they are also consistently reassured that a certain level of consumption is part of their social obligations as a result of their middle-class status.

> Do not be afraid that you will sin against morality, or offend religion, because just as we have demonstrated, man is obliged to be well-groomed, decent and proper and to conform to the standards of the society in which he lives.
>
> (No tema faltar a la moral, y ofender a la religión, porque según hemos demonstrado, el hombre tiene la obligación de ser curioso, decente, y decoroso, y de conformarse con los usos de la sociedad en que vive.)[64]

But as Veblen demonstrates, standards of decency are based on conformity to a style of expenditure just out of reach of one's pecuniary power. Decency is a standard which is "indefinitely extensible...."[65] Middle-class Spanish women, as consumers of the various styles of femininity, must be persuaded to purchase the only model they can "decently" afford, that of the "ángel del hogar." In effect, they must be persuaded to buy middle-class consciousness. They must internalize the ideology of the middle-class and their role as women in it: the values of industriousness and thrift, as well as sexual repression reinforced by the long tradition of submission to patriarchal authority in the home. They must know themselves to be what they are:

> Luxury, gone to extremes in the matter of dress, is not truly authorized, except if one possesses great wealth:... The difficult art of how to dress consists in knowing oneself and adopting only those styles which are suitable for one's age, figure, and social position.
>
> (El lujo, llevado demasiado en el traje, no está verdaderamente autorizado, sino contando con una gran fortuna:... El arte difícil

---

[64] J. de Quevedo, p. 291.
[65] Veblin, p. 81.

de vestir consiste en conocerse y no adoptar más que las modas que convienen a la edad, a la figura y a la posición social.)[66]

The tone of admonition and coercion which permeates the discourse on conspicuous consumption is a clear sign that the ideology of femininity and self-denial was not being marketed with complete success. Women needed to be reminded that freedom of choice in the market place was not an absolute right:

> The day in which the decent woman of the middle class, her head turned by certain pernicious doctrines, believes that appearances make everything equal, she will aspire unfortunately to blend in with the aristocratic lady, receiving a proud rebuke and making herself ridiculous by leaving her modest sphere, and perhaps, perhaps, because she wants to make a place for herself in society [*el gran mundo*], she may forget her sacred duties to the family.
>
> (El día en que la honrada mujer de la clase media, alucinada con ciertas doctrinas perniciosas crea que las apariencias lo nivelen todo, aspirará a confundirse lastimosamente con la dama aristocrática, recibiendo un orgulloso desprecio y poniéndose en ridículo por salirse de su modesta esfera, y quizás, quizás por figurar en el gran mundo olvide los santos deberes de la familia.)[67]

This quote, taken from *La Familia* in 1875, demonstrates clearly how the ideology of domesticity, personified in the *ángel del hogar* is utilized to truncate the desire of middle-class women for upward mobility. The Angel is threatened with censure and ridicule, she will be derided as out of fashion, out-moded, an imitator, an upstart, *cursi*[68] – if she attempts to set foot in the rarefied terrain of those who demonstrate their participation in fashion's power by their

---

[66] M. P. Sinués de Marco, "El arte de vestir," *La Guirnalda*, XVI, 24 (1882), p. 190.

[67] M. Martínez Giniesta, "La educación de la mujer," *La Familia*, 30 (mayo 1875), p. 44. This quote demonstrates clearly that the term "modest sphere" used as a synonym for family life, is defined by class origin rather than by gender, since the "modest sphere" pertains specifically to the "respectable woman of the middle class" ("honrada mujer de la clase media") and is placed in opposition to the "aristocratic lady" ("la dama aristocrática").

[68] See Enrique Tierno Galván, "Aparición y desarrollo de nuevas perspectivas de valoración social en el siglo XIX: 'Lo cursi,'" in *Desde el espectáculo a la trivialización* (Madrid: Taurus, 1961), pp. 79-108.

ability to anticipate, and even precede change. The social space reserved for the middle class lies within the time frame of the quotidian. As Henri Lefebvre explains, fashion, on the other hand, is the antithesis of everyday life:

> Fashion governs everyday life by excluding it, for everyday life cannot be fashionable and therefore is not; the demigods have not (or are supposed to have not) an everyday life; their life passes every day from wonder to wonder in the sphere of fashion and yet everyday life is there, perpetually excluded. [69]

In the minds of Spanish Restoration moralists, Fashion, like Don Juan, is endowed with a fatal seductive power, capable of scaling the barricade of bourgeois domesticity and penetrating into its inner-most core which is located, and it comes as no surprise, in the bedroom. Faustina Sáez de Melgar, a well-known *literata* and editor of *La Mujer* writes: "Fashion, that tyrant of the home and domestic fortunes, has also poked its magic wand into the private habits of the family, and it has begun by dividing the marriage bed." ("La moda, esa tirana del hogar y de la ventura doméstica, ha entrometido también su varita mágica en las íntimas costumbres de la familia, empezando por dividir el lecho nupcial.") She does not attack the immorality of separate beds or bedrooms in economic terms as excess expenditure, however, but in terms of the husband's right to absolute authority over his wife's will and body: "When wills and bodies are divided, two souls cannot become one, feelings and affections cannot be one and the same." ("Cuando las voluntades y los cuerpos están separados, no puede formarse un alma de dos, no pueden ser unos mismos sus afectos y sentimientos.") [70]

The siren call of fashion's delights, anathemized as a socially disruptive element which produces envy and dissatisfaction among the working class is also seen as a quasi-supernatural force which threatens patriarchal authority in the home. But although fashion's influence upon women is described as mysterious, fashion does have one visible face which can be targeted and attacked. In 1875, *La Guirnalda* feels obliged to insist that it is not a fashion magazine: "...it is a publication of healthy Christian morals, of domestic labors,

---

[69] Lefebvre, p. 165.
[70] Faustina Sáez del Melgar, "Deberes de la mujer," *La Mujer* (16 agosto 1871), pp. 3-4.

of sobriety, of elegance, of the industrious and educated family." ("...es el periódico de la sana moral cristiana, del trabajo doméstico, de la sobriedad, de la delicadeza, de la familia laboriosa y culta.")[71]

The motto of these magazines and their justification for existence is the formula of elegance *by means* of economy. In order to consolidate their position as spokesman for the middle class, they use as their foil the ultra-right position of neo-Catholics and the Carlist royalists against any manifestation of "materialism." *Beatería* or exaggerated and ostentatious piety as a model for femininity is old-fashioned and not in good taste:

> ...nor do we want them [women] to be overly pius *[beatas]*, like the Carlists, dressed in a nun's habit and thonged belt; all extremes are evil, and that is why we would look for a middle ground; we will give our subscribers, therefore, sufficent patterns for them to dress themselves with elegance, not just in order that they might occupy their time with them, but that they might cumply with the demanding obligation of appearing well in public, without waste, without luxury, without spending all their time on the capricious fads that the dressmakers, who dedicate their lives to this business, seek to impose upon us.
>
> (...ni a manera de los carlistas las querremos beatas, vestidas con el hábito y la correa; todos los estremos son viciosos, y esta es la razón de que busquemos un término medio; daremos, pues, a nuestras suscritoras los figurines suficientes para que se vistan elegantemente, no para que sólo se ocupen de ellos, sino para que atiendan a la necesidad imperiosa de presentarse bien, sin dispilfarro, sin lujo, sin gastar todo su tiempo en las caprichosas variaciones que quieren imponernos las modistas que consagran su vida a este comercio.)[72]

The author's attempt to lay the blame for "materialism" on *las modistas*, the working-class women who supply the material needs of the Lady is typical of the general attitude of distrust and antagonism felt towards servants, wet-nurses and those whose livelihood consisted in waiting upon the wealthy and the comfortable middle-class. But what stands out in this quote is the manner in which women's fashion magazines have appropriated moral authority over

---

[71] "La familia y la moda," *La Guirnalda* (16 octubre 1875), p. 154.
[72] "Advertencia al público," *La Mujer* (8 junio 1871), p. 2.

their clientele, prescribing and defining the content of that moral abstraction "the golden mean" (Fray Luis' *justo medio*) as "elegance without excess."

This attitude of firm albeit restrained support for the world of fashion represents a clear rejection of those who would turn away completely from the world of fashion, a rejection of *beatería* as a style of femininity which is not only outmoded but also hypocritical, not credible. Religion cannot be used as a pretext for avoiding one's obligations to society:

> Unfortunately, it has been thought that in order to avoid the mistakes of fashion, to comply with religion in that which pertains to dress, it was necessary to go to ridiculous extremes... [God] desires that we cleanse and anoint ourselves and not go about like hypocrites covered in a cloak of woe. How much better it is to conform to fashion, as long as it is not done to excess!

> (Por desgracia se ha creído que para evitar los defectos de la moda, para cumplir con la religión en lo relativo al trage, era necesario caer en el ridículo... [Dios] nos manda lavarnos y ungirnos y no aparecer como hipócritas en el trage de la tristeza... ¡Cuánto mejor es conformarse con la moda, con tal que no sea con exceso!)[73]

The rhetorical separation between a secular public world and the spiritualization of the home is contradicted by the general affirmation of the middle-class woman's right and even obligation to pursue the lights of fashion, within the limits of what was considered 'proper and economical.' We can be sure that the daily life of the *ángel del hogar*, although lived out within the walls of her middle-class sanctuary, included at the very least a window and more likely a door opened to the sins of the secular world.

---

[73] "La familia y la moda," p. 154.

CHAPTER FOUR

LA FAMILIA DE LEÓN ROCH: DOMESTICITY AND DIVORCE IN SPAIN

In 1878, Benito Pérez Galdós publishes the novel that opens the gate to his series of Contemporary Novels which will establish his reputation as a novelist of European stature.[1] Although Galdós did not consider *La familia de León Roch* to be one of the Contemporary Novels, in effect, it is a blueprint for the different themes he will enlarge upon throughout the 1880s: 1) the self-righteous hypocrisy of middle- and upper-class respectability; 2) the lack of a bourgeois work ethic; 3) the moral and economic destructiveness of conspicuous consumption *(el lujo)* and its use to define class status; 4) the economic decline and amorality of the aristocracy; 5) the negative effect of financial speculation and a parasitical government burocracy on a national economy that is undercapitalized and industrially underdeveloped; and finally, 6) the emotional poverty of middle- and upper-class family life.

La familia de León Roch demonstrates many of the defects of a novel in transition: frequently analyzing conflicts and problems rather than narrating them. Nevertheless, Galdós' treatment of the ideology of domesticity is of particular interest because the battle between secular scientific Spain and Catholic reactionary Spain, the subject of two previous novels, *Doña Perfecta* and *Gloria*, is here located within the parameters of the family institution. This change in focus from the so-called thesis novels to a concentration on the drama of everyday life also constitutes a shift from the problematiza-

---

[1] José F. Montesinos, *Galdós*, I (Madrid: Castalia, 1969), p. 286.

tion of contemporary Spanish history in terms of adverse ideological and political forces, to a consideration of the effect of the conflict between liberals and reactionaries upon the personal life of the individual. At the same time, one of the novel's most serious defects is an almost mechanical transfer of the ideological struggle from the broad canvas to the reduced framework of daily family life. The result is an awkward and fragmented plot that, at the same time, reproduces the broken fragments that are the remains of León Roch's lost dream of domestic bliss.

The protagonist's bride, María Egipcíaca, with her enticing sexuality, is one piece of the complete design, but her sexuality acts as a barrier that ultimately prevents León Roch from recognizing that his true "companion-wife" is Pepa Fúcar. The ideal marriage needs children, but the adored little girl, Monina, is another man's child. And when finally the protagonist understands that Pepa and Monina constitute his ideal family, it is too late. They are separated from him by the dual barriers of God's law and of man's. By reconstructing León Roch's fragmented ideal, we can piece together Galdós' formula for domestic happiness and compare it with the ideal of bourgeois domesticity that glowed in the pages of *La Familia, La Guirnalda* and other magazines of the period directed towards a growing middle-class readership.

The primary building blocks that Galdós will employ to construct his own model of ideal married life are four: first, compatibility of temperament and intellect; second, children and the development of a parent-child bond that includes the father; third, social legitimacy defined as conformity to both the civil and religious marriage laws of Spanish society; and fourth, mutual sexual attraction. The element in Galdós' formula that veers radically away from the chaste recipe for marital bliss promulgated by moralists and social commentators is evident. Sexual compatability between husband and wife is a concept that is completely extraneous to the formula for domestic happiness in nineteenth-century Catholic Spain where the wife's compliance to her husband's sexual demands was still considered the "cross" that married women were forced to bear in return for the joy and privilege of maternity.[2] Not until seven years later, when Galdós writes the love story of Camila and Constantino Miquis in *Lo prohibido*, will he reunite the four elements

---

[2] See *supra*, Chapter 2.

that together make up his personal ideal of the perfect marriage. Galdós uses *La familia de León Roch* to weigh the importance of each separate element and to study their relationship to each other. It is an analytical method which enables both author and reader to diagnose the health of the upper-class family institution, and to ascertain some of the factors that impede the realization of the ideal bourgeois family.

León Roch and the Limits of Liberalism

In spite of the fact that León Roch is "a product of the University, the Atheneum [a private club for writers and intellectuals still in existence] and the School of Mining" ("un producto de la universidad, el Ateneo y la Escuela de Minas") [p. 174],[3] as well as a self-proclaimed rationalist who publishes scientific articles in liberal magazines, he formulates his vision of domesticity in the most conventional terms:

> ...a beautiful ideal, the Christian family, center of all peace, the foundation of virtue, the ladder to moral perfection, the crucible in which all that we possess of every order is purified. It [the family] educates us, it obliges us to be better than we are, it smooths the rough edges of our character, it provides us with our most useful lesson, putting into our hands the men of the future, so that we may bring them up from the cradle to the age of reason.
>
> (...un ideal hermoso, la familia cristiana, centro de toda paz, fundamento de la virtud, escala de la perfección moral, crisol donde cuanto tenemos, en uno y otro orden, se purifica. Ella nos educa, nos obliga a ser mejores de lo que somos, nos quita las asperezas de nuestro carácter, nos da la más provechosa de las lecciones, poniendo en nuestras manos a los hombres futuros, para que desde la cuna los llevemos a la edad de la razón.) [pp. 974-75]

The contradiction between León Roch's need to ultilize married life as a kind of purifying flame that will temper and mold moral

---

[3] Benito Pérez Galdós, *La familia de León Roch* (Madrid: Aguilar, 1973). All quotes from Galdós' novels will be taken from this edition and page numbers will be cited in the text.

character, and his infatuation with a petty ignorant woman, is one that undermines the reader's confidence in the protagonist's common sense, and consequently reduces the potential for dramatic tension that relies on the possible identification with a protagonist who is more or less in control of his destiny. When we look over his shoulder as León Roch reads a love letter from his future wife, we can read between the lines the disaster that awaits this incompatible pair. His fiancée shows herself to be jealous, insecure and dependent on her mother's approval. In spite of the family's poverty, she is a snob, full of the self-importance of her class. Her character defects are hidden from León Roch, who sees only her beauty and outward piety. His moral blindness is further demonstrated by his inability to recognize the sincere love of his childhood sweetheart, Pepa Fúcar – a fact that is made evident to the reader in the famous rose-spitting scene that so horrified the eminent Krausist, D. Giner de los Ríos.[4] Thus, from the very beginning, we are aware that this union encompasses many risks, and we can only sit back and wait for the inevitable to happen.

In the novel of domestic interiors, character development depends on the interaction of the family members within the context of familial situations. What brings the realist genre to life is the narrative continuity that enlivens the series of domestic vignettes and unites them into a comprehensible whole, for the mere accumulation of arbitrary domestic detail bereft of any narrative context is the formula of *costumbrismo*, Spain's literary equivalent of genre painting. In *La familia de León Roch*, the family scenes of anguish and exhilaration that will highlight Galdós' future novels are generally absent. In fact, the locus of the home is replaced by the characters' peripatetic frenzy as they rush from their townhouses to train stations to vacation spas, stopping only to pack a suitcase and lecture the reader on the virtues and vices of their family and acquaintances.

This rhythm of frenetic activity may well be a faithful depiction of nineteenth-century Madrid high society, but the result is a defocussing of the central conflict, the struggle between the married couple for moral authority in the home. Rather than participating in this struggle, we are told what happens: that after a year of marriage, León Roch tires of his wife, and that she, in turn, seeks

---

[4] Montesinos, p. 279.

emotional satisfaction in the rituals of the Church. But we learn about their marital problems as if we were listening over the fence to the neighbor's gossip, seldom are we permitted to be present.

The tabloid structure of *costumbrista* vignettes and the lack of narrative continuity forces Galdós to have recourse to a series of arbitrary plot interventions to impell the novel towards a definitive conclusion. Galdós relies on a series of death-bed scenes – the death of María Egipcíaca's saintly brother Luis, the fortuitous death of María Egipcíaca herself that frees León Roch from his marriage bonds, and the near death of the child Monina from diphtheria. It would seem that the intensity of death was necessary to act as leaven upon a plot that stagnates because of the protagonist's passivity.

The fragmentation of Galdós' domestic ideal into its components: compatability of character, children, social legitimacy and mutual sexual attraction, is an approach that allows Galdós to weigh the value of each element separately, but that also tends to distort his analysis of sexual compatability, the one component which distinguishes Galdós' formula from the traditional recipe for domestic happiness. León Roch's decision not to live "outside the law" ("fuera de la ley") [p. 975] with Pepa and Monina is a decision that places the welfare of the child above the satisfaction of sexual desire and the couple's own need for companionship. Galdós emphasizes the woman's point of view in his description of Pepa's suffering which becomes an eloquent statement that women do need something more than a maternal bond with their children or fraternal companionship. He also breaks with the conventional romance by having Pepa, rather than the timid León, make the case for violating society's constraints.

Nevertheless, these scenes form part of the dénouement, while the more obvious treatment of female sexuality, the portrayal of María Egipcíaca, conforms completely to the literary convention of Eve, the seductress. María Egipcíaca's sensuality and the fact that she derives pleasure from the marriage bed is linked to her spiritual poverty and her religious superstition. The description of her sexual attractiveness fits into the misoginistic literary tradition exemplified by Galdós' contemporary, the Catholic writer Pedro de Alarcón whose bad women undulate provocatively, hissing like serpents through the pages of *El escándalo:* for example, in *León Roch* we read, "After wriggling around in front of the mirror, María went into her bedroom." ("Después de culebrear en derredor del espejo, María entró en su alcoba.") [p. 821] Her strong sensuality is not a virtue, but rather the cause of León Roch's fall from grace, the loss of his capacity to reason.

The sterility of a marriage that shares nothing more than sexual pleasure is underscored by the novel's structure. Only a few paragraphs are alloted to the honeymoon atmosphere of the first year; the novel proceeds immediately to the terrain of León Roch's discontent, his failure to force María Egipcíaca to place herself under his moral tutelage. Sexual pleasure is a barrier to the real purpose of marriage, moral regeneration – of his wife, since he never questions his own moral attributes. After ten months, we find the frustrated husband muttering to himself:

> This will all come to an end: it must end as a matter of course. When it does end, I will approach the awesome question resolutely, and I will begin to mold – he used with great frequency the terminology of sculpture – María's character.
>
> (Esto va pasando: necesariamente tiene que pasar. Cuando pase, yo abordaré resueltamente la temida cuestión, y empezaré a modelar – empleaba con mucha frecuencia este término de escultura – el carácter de María.) [p. 798]

But after two years of marriage, León Roch still feels "the irresistible effect of her face and figure's perfect beauty" ("el efecto irresistible de belleza tan acabada en rostro y figura") [p. 821]. It is at this point that Galdós must bring into the narrative María Egipcíaca's brother Luis, an aspiring mystic who has been living an ascetic life in a Jesuit community in France. Joaquín Casalduero sees this intervention in the plot as a means of reinforcing the theme of religious conflict in the family,[5] but it is more than a question of reinforcement. The battle over who would exert moral authority over María Egipcíaca's "infantile conscience" [p. 820], her husband or María herself, had reached a stalemate. The astuteness of María Egipcíaca's confessor, the Italian priest Father Paoletti, had helped to prevent a final break between the couple. This society priest knows how to advise his spiritual daughters so that neither they nor he risk losing the economic support of their husbands. He had always insisted that a wife has the obligation to submit to her husband's sexual demands

---

[5] J. Casalduero, *Vida y obra de Galdós* (Madrid: Gredos, 1974), p. 64.

[p. 948]. There is no question of the priest exercising any authority in the conjugal bedroom. Not until María Egipcíaca begins to follow her brother's advice, to dress in sackcloth and especially, to deny her husband sexual access, does León Roch take the step towards separation.

With the creation of León Roch – pompous, conventional, and passive – Galdós calls into question the popular concept of moral regeneration through education, and especially the Krausist belief in education through example. The theme of Krausism has been studied by J. López-Morillas, who concludes that:

> ...*León Roch's Family* is the arena in which, disguised as an imaginary fable, the eighteenth-century position of optimistic rationalism held by Krause's disciples takes up swords against the pessimistic determinism which Galdós, more in tune with the times, accepts. Without a doubt, he accepts this position in spite of himself, for there always remains in Galdós a core of eighteenth-century perfectibility.
>
> (...*La familia de León Roch* es el palenque donde, bajo el disfraz de una fábula novelesca, rompen lanzas el racionalismo optimista, muy siglo XVIII, de los discípulos de Krause y el determinismo pesimista que, más acorde con los tiempos, acepta Galdós. No cabe duda de que lo acepta muy a pesar suyo, pues en Galdós queda siempre un trasfondo de perfectibilismo dieciochista.)[6]

The struggle between man and wife unmasks the terms moral authority and education. What lies behind the euphemism of "education" is a desire for power, for control over each other's will and in both cases, moral and intellectual intolerance.

"MAN MOLDS THE WOMAN?" OR... "WOMAN MAKES THE MAN?"[7]

The institutionalization of patriarchal authority in Spain in the domestic sphere was spelled out in the articles of the Napoleonic

---

[6] J. López-Morillas, *Hacia el 98* (Barcelona: Ariel, 1973), p. 102.

[7] See *supra*, Chapter 2, for a discussion of the idea that the man molded the character of his wife, "hace a la mujer." This idea has its corollary in the belief in "the woman behind the man," the popular expression of a sense of woman's growing importance in society as a result of her socializing influence in the home. For example, see "La influencia de la mujer en la vida del hombre," *La Familia*

Code which granted the husband control over his wife's property, place of residence, possibility of employment, and afforded him complete and permanent custody of the children after the age of three, the so-called right of *patria potestas*.[8] Cultural expectations changed with the cult of domesticity and the belief that one of the wife's duties was to provide her husband with the companionship that he had previously sought in the café or casino among his male associates. But the model for this new marital relationship was not derived from the give and take of political discussions recreated by Galdós in *La Fontana de Oro*. The intellectual companionship which men were taught to expect from their wives, and from women in general, never changes in the nineteenth century from the model of feminine intellect canonized by Rousseau in his creation of Sophie, Emile's ideal partner:

> Sophie has a mind that is agreeable without being brilliant, and solid without being profound – a mind about which people do not say anything, because they never find in it anything more or less than what they find in their own minds.[9]

This image of symbiotic absorption is clearly not the expression of an egalitarian relationship between two individuals, but rather the reduction of two points of view into one. The question, of course, is whose?

In general, Galdós critics agree that the theme of this novel is, in the words of Montesinos, "the problem of marriage and religion" ("el problema religión-matrimonio").[10] J. López-Morillas, acting as León Roch's advocate, places the blame for the couple's marital problems squarely on the head of the recalcitrant wife: "...the real

---

(21 julio 1875), p. 83: "Women are capable of creating scholars, poets, warriors and artists, and in those instances in which men, driven by genius, penetrate the outer reaches of infinity in order to tear from fame's grasp a crown of glory, if they have no woman to make immortal, *they must invent her.*" ("La mujer puede hacer sabios, poetas, guerreros y artistas, y en esos momentos en que el hombre, impulsado por el genio, se lanza a las regiones de lo infinito para arrancar de manos de la fama una corona de gloria, si no tiene una mujer a quien inmortalizar, *necesita inventarla.*")

[8] See Scanlon, *La polémica feminista en la España contemporánea (1868-1974)* (Madrid: Siglo Veintiuno, 1976), pp. 122-37, 141.

[9] J.-J. Rousseau, *Emile or On Education*, trans. and intro. by A. Bloom (New York: Basic Books, 1979), pp. 395-96.

[10] Montesinos, p. 256. See also, Casalduero, p. 64.

cause of the separation is María's irreligiosity, her false mysticism, her unmerciful fanaticism, which is certainly the equivalent of a moral crime." ("...la verdadera causa de la separación es la irreligiosidad de María, su falso misticismo, su fanatismo inmisericorde, lo que equivale ciertamente a un crimen moral.")[11]

We would like to suggest a more sympathetic interpretation of María Egipcíaca's challenge to her husband's authority, she tells him: "I, with my love, which is greater than anyone's judgement upon me, aspire to conquer your mind, making you into my image and likeness." ("Yo, con mi amor, que es más grande que todos los juicios, aspiro a conquistar el juicio tuyo, haciéndote a mi imagen y semejanza.") [p. 802]. Her language uses the same vocabulary of power and domination employed by León Roch: "I will be able to mold her in my image and likeness" ("Podré hacerla a mi imagen y semejanza") [p. 796], which is also the language of hierarchy and patriarchal authority used by the Catholic Church. Thus, if we question the intentions of the woman, Galdós forces us to also question the validity of the man's pedagogical goals, for both express themselves identically.

María Egipcíaca is portrayed as a genuine Sophie, limited to reflecting the ideas of others, incapable of any original thought. Her goal is the missionary's: to compel her husband to join the rank and file of the faithful and to submit to the authority she herself worships. León Roch, imbued with the Krausist belief that each individual must respond to his own conscience, has appropriated the moral authority of the Church. He is his own priest, his own spiritual director, a kind of lay priest who will ultimately be satisfied with a small congregation, a parish of one, his wife.

León Roch's belief that his wife has been alienated away from him by the influence of Father Paoletti is predicated upon his conviction that his wife has no will of her own, since will is a function of the capacity to reason, and he has judged his wife to be irrational. The reader is excluded from participating in the husband's attempts at pedagogy. We arrive at the moment of moral divorce, without ever knowing his methods or his curriculum. Like unwilling marriage counselors, we can only listen as the couple read off their long list of grievances:

---

[11] López-Morillas, p. 115.

> He: I have struggled firmly with you; I have employed every means, arguments based on reason and on sentiment; I have even used force, all was useless.
>
> She: Oh! You cannot deny that the freedom which you granted me was mixed with disdain. You had such a smile when I talked to you of my beliefs!... You used to smile, you would smile so, oh how you did smile!
>
> (Él): (He luchado tenazmente contigo; he empleado todos los medios, argumentos de razón, de sentimientos, hasta de fuerza, todo ha sido inútil.)
>
> (Ella): (¡Ah! no puedes negarme que en la libertad que me dabas había cierto desprecio. ¡Sonreías de un modo cuando yo te hablaba de mis devociones!... Tú te sonreías, te sonreías, ¡cómo te sonreías!...) [p. 853]

In this cry of hurt pride lies the key to María Egipcíaca's revolt against her husband's authority. Like Fortunata, she has an "idea" that is essentially a plan designed to recuperate her damaged self-esteem, for she does agree with her mother and her husband that he is, in every way but one, her superior. She tells him: "I, only a weak woman, inferior to you in many ways, and mainly in knowledge and experience, will win a victory that your proud superiority can never achieve." ("Yo, mujer débil, inferior a ti en muchas cosas, y principalmente en saber y experiencia, lograré un triunfo que jamás alcanzará tu orgullosa superioridad.") [pp. 801-2]. Her idea, to protect her social status as the perfect Christian wife through her husband's conversion, is firmly rooted in the Catholic arguments of the period which credited Christianity and the sacrament of Holy Matrimony with raising women from the mire of their own irredeemable sexuality. In an article significantly entitled "El magisterio de la mujer" ("Women as Teachers") and published in *La Defensa de la Sociedad* in 1872, women's debt to Christianity and their role in the great nineteenth-century project of the rehabilitation of society is made specific:

> She owes everything to the religion of He who was Crucified: Dignity, respect, every consideration; it is only just that she responds gratefully to His request, hastening to help in the work of social regeneration, the betterment of customs, and to spread the gospel by the example of her virtue.

(Ella se debe todo a la religión del Crucificado: dignidad, respeto, consideraciones; justo es que corresponda agradecida a su solicitud, concurriendo a la obra de la regeneración social, a la mejora de las costumbres, a difundir con la virtud el Evangelio.) [12]

It is unlikely that María Egipcíaca spent her time reading *La Defensa de la Sociedad,* but clearly she has read the popular literature which reinforced Catholic ideology through the guise of sentimental female stereotypes portrayed as man's guardian angels and long-suffering Penelopes. [13] She tells her husband: "Yes, there are cases that seem incredible, cases of evil men who have converted..., and you aren't evil..." ("Sí, hay casos que parecen increíbles, casos de hombres malvados que se han convertido..., y tú no eres malvado...") [p. 821]. León Roch's refusal to convert to Catholicism becomes, in her eyes, a testimony which necessarily casts doubt upon her own virtue and explains her religious scruples, for which she must seek constant reassurance from the only person who gives her "respect and consideration," Father Paoletti.

If we accept León Roch's interpretation of his wife as a candorous woman under the control of nefarious influences, then the struggle for power should take place between the husband and his adversary, the priest. One critic has even gone so far as to claim that *La familia de León Roch* is a fictionalized gloss of J. Michelet's *Le Prêtre, la famille et la femme.* [14] But Paoletti's role as spiritual advisor to the upper class is to teach María Egipcíaca how to fulfill her obligations to God *and* mammon. He cannot afford to alienate the wealthy parishioners upon whom he depends for a livelihood. He encourages her to take part in the social functions disguised as philanthropy that had come into vogue during the '50s and '60s. [15] And as long as her piety does not cross over the line into *beatería,* the ostentatious religiosity of the women who lived on bended knee before the Eucharist, her pious sentiments can be classified as one of the fashionable categories of femininity. She is, according to the narrator: "Lady Pious *à la mode*" ("la dama piadosa a la moda") [p. 823].

---

[12] Ramón Losada, "El magisterio de la mujer," *La Defensa de la Sociedad,* II (1872), p. 391.

[13] See A. Andreu, *Galdós y la literatura popular* (Madrid: SGEL, 1982).

[14] Alfred Rodríguez, "Algunos aspectos de la elaboración literaria de *La familia de León Roch,*" *PMLA,* 82 (1967), pp. 121-27.

[15] José Luis L. Aranguren, *Moral y sociedad* (Madrid: Cuadernos para el Diálogo, 1967), pp. 115-16.

The true villain in this domestic battle is not fanatical religiosity, but the social mores of the upper class which prevent the creation of the privatized intimacy and the emotional bonds of family life predicated upon a withdrawal from society. The frenzied social activities of the aristocratic Tellerías family and their rampant egoism, manifested crudely when they abandon the dying Luis, is a reflection of the irreconcilable antagonism between León Roch's ideal of domesticity and the perpetuation of social status within the upper class. Montesinos points this out when he comments:

> If *La familia de León Roch* were a better focussed novel, it would be the story of how a frivolous and irresponsible society, gratuitously fanatical, vents its fury blindly on someone who for some reason is perceived as not being one of them, and it could be a terrifying story.
>
> (Si *La familia de León Roch* fuese una novela mejor enfocada, sería más bien la historia de cómo una sociedad frívola e irresponsable, fanática sin causa, se ensaña estúpidamente en un individuo que por alguna razón no considera afín de ella misma, y podría ser una historia estremecedora.)[16]

This lack of focus is less obvious in the second half of the novel, however, when Galdós returns to his most credible character, the endearing Pepa Fúcar.

PEPA AND MONINA: THE CHILD IN DOMESTIC SOCIETY

The disappearance of Pepa Fúcar from the first half of the novel makes her reappearance, and what she comes to represent, that much more tantalizing. Her Dulcinea-like elusiveness is further reinforced by framing the plot with the painful trauma of separation. As a result of this framing, the idyllic home of Pepa and her little daughter Monina in Carabanchel is defined by a pervasive sentiment of imminent loss, which is heightened rather than tenuated by León Roch's physical proximity.

Galdós' description of their country residence is a deliberate exercise in contrasts: natural sunlight and the innocent spontaneity of the child and her playmates are played off against the constricting

---

[16] Montesinos, p. 268.

atmosphere of artificial manners and malicious gossip in the fashionable Madrid salons. The most telling contrast is, however, that which exists between the two principal actors in the scene, Pepa Fúcar and León Roch himself.

Pepa Fúcar is Galdós' first attempt at creating his own personal feminine ideal. In her footsteps will follow Camila and Fortunata. Jacinta's sweetness will be spiced with a similar although greatly reduced capacity for rebellion. Eloísa's reckless ambition and Isidora's foolhardiness will be tempered by the same loyalty to their lovers. Unlike the prissy manners of the stylish *señorita*, Galdós' ideal woman is a little wild, spontaneous and strong-willed. While she does not bore with the intellectual pretensions of the blue-stocking, she possesses a natural wit and liveliness that enhances an unpretentious and generally unadorned beauty. Galdós' ideal woman is sexually passionate and her generosity of spirit is rewarded with fertility.

León Roch is the mirror opposite of the courage and energy which defines Pepa Fúcar. He is essentially timid, conventional and, above all, a passive man, like José María Bueno de Guzmán or Juanito Santa Cruz, who plays at living but turns to his mother for a bride and to his father for solutions to his problems. The relationship between Pepa Fúcar and León Roch sets a pattern for the failed love relationships of future novels: the woman will offer passion, tenderness and an almost indestructible loyalty while the man, egocentric pleasure seeker, consumes and discards or, in the case of León Roch, fails to respond until it is too late.

In spite of the bifurcation between the sensuality and sterility of León Roch's marriage and the chaste fecundity of the female household in Carabanchel, Galdós' formula for bourgeois domesticity does not exclude sexuality. León Roch's movement towards the mother and child meets a response in Pepa's frustrated passion for her childhood sweetheart. Montesinos has interpreted Pepa's rage upon losing León to his pious bride as frustration of the maternal instinct,[17] an interpretation very much in agreement with popular nineteenth-century notions concerning female sexuality. But by separating sexual desire from maternal love, Galdós refutes the belief that women's sexual desire was satisfied through reproduction.[18]

---

[17] Montesinos, p. 273.
[18] See *supra*, Chapter 2.

Even though María Egipcíaca does not bear children, she blossoms during the first period of sexual fulfillment [p. 798]. And in contrast, we learn at the end of the novel that Pepa Fúcar continues to live with her daughter, but "Very sad, very alone, and in indifferent health." ("Muy triste, muy sola, con mediana salud") [p. 979].

By releasing female sexuality from the bond of reproduction, Galdós also breaks the hegemony exercised by women over the so-called maternal instinct and allows the male characters to express a need for and appreciation of children's society. Both Pepa Fúcar's husband, the amoral Federico Cimarra, and León Roch are men who have been in some way defrauded by the attainment of quintessentially male goals: adventure, wealth, beautiful women and intellectual activity. León Roch's most scarring experience is his disillusionment with sexual passion. His boredom with his wife's society does much to explain his fascination with the child Monina and his decision to sacrifice a possible sexual liaison with Pepa to the rules of social convention.

In Monina's company, León Roch seeks the freedom of intimacy unburdened by sexual obligation, an intimacy which cannot exist between two adults in a society which cannot conceive of male-female friendship without a sexual component. The missing element in his marriage – the tenderness, spontaneity and mutual creativity born of "that sweet likeness of spirit that even simple people find" ("ese dulce parentesco del espíritu que descubren hasta los tontos") [p. 816] – finally materializes in an image of collaboration when Monina and her playmates take upon themselves the task of improving León Roch's scientific research with their scribbles. The reconciliation scene between Roch and Monina – tears, kisses, and the crime is forgiven and forgotten – contrasts vividly with the acrimonious adult relationships devoid of any possibility of resolution and emotional catharsis.

Thus it is the child, Monina, who comes to embody the essence of domesticity. Home is where the heart is, and the heart of the home is the child. Monina humanizes León Roch by teaching him tolerance for imperfection, for a child is loved not in spite of but because of its inevitable incompleteness and vulnerability. Galdós would seem to imply that the altruism inevitably inherent in a non-exploitive adult-child relationship must be the model for the emotional bond between two adults. María Egipcíaca's sterility is also a symbolic representation of her inability to respond to her husband's need for comfort and solace, to the child in every adult: "He was like a hungry child who holds out his arms to his mother's breast only to find that his mother's breast is made of cardboard..." ("Parecía un niño hambriento que extiende los brazos hacia el seno de su madre, y se encuentra con que el seno de su madre es de cartón...") [p. 951], María Egipcíaca tells the reader during her interminable death-bed scene. León Roch's decision to sacrifice an illegitimate union with Pepa Fúcar to the welfare of her child is portrayed as the voice of reason that transcends Pepa's "law of love." And Pepa, in her submission to his judgement, shows herself to be the perfect wife of his imagination: "You know that my only life's pleasure is to obey you." ("Ya sabes que obedecerte es el único placer de mi vida") [p. 922].

But was separation their only alternative? The dénouement analyzes the possible alternatives to this seemingly insoluble situation, and a subject that Galdós critics have avoided, the question of divorce in nineteenth-century Catholic Spain.

CIVIL DIVORCE AND THE SEPARATION OF CHURCH AND STATE

Until the publication of Carmen de Burgos' opinion poll on divorce in 1904,[19] public statements on the subject in Spain were intermittent and restrained. But this popular reticence did not preclude a fierce debate that was taking place between the advocates of Church power, on the one hand, and on the other, the proponents of "modernism" or "naturalism"; that is, of universal male suffrage, the sovereignty of the new nation-states, and in general, those nineteenth-century political and legal reforms that would complete the process of secularization and democratization of the bourgeois state. In an article on marriage and divorce that appeared in the *Revista de España* in 1873, the author comments upon and contributes himself to the bitter tone of the polemic:

> ...today more than ever, a veritable storm has broken out in the areas of law and philosophy, one that is increasing day by day, one that rages and imposes its terrible presence; and black and sinister it threatens to destroy with its violent whirlwinds the most sacred of social institutions.

---

[19] Carmen de Burgos Seguí (Columbine), *El divorcio en España* (Madrid, 1904).

(...ha estallado hoy más que nunca en las regiones del derecho y de la filosofía, una verdadera tormenta que de día en día crece, se enfurece, se presenta terrible e imponente, y negra y aciaga amenaza destruir con sus violentos torbellinos la más sagrada de las instituciones sociales.) [20]

In Spain, secularization of the state was advanced by the nationalization of Church property under Mendizábal in 1836-37,[21] and its legitimation through the Concordat of 1851, whereby the Church accepted as indemnification the state's agreement to pay the clergy a modest salary.[22] But with the rising tide of democratic nationalism in Western Europe in the decades of the '50s, '60s, and '70s, and Italy's push towards unification during the years 1858-1870,[23] culminating in the reduction of the Catholic Church's empire to the present-day territorial limits of the Vatican State, the Catholic hierarchy in Rome was compelled to take what amounted to a final stand.

The papal gauntlet thrown down in 1864 took the form of the encyclical *Quanta Cura,* followed by the *Syllabus: A Catalogue of Modern Errors* in 1865. Together they constituted, in the words of the Krausist Gumersindo de Azcárate, "an undisguised negation of every principle upon which modern civilization is predicated." ("una negación manifiesta de todos los principios que inspiran la civilización moderna.")[24] With these documents, the Catholic Church officially lay claim to a legislative jurisdiction over daily life which would, according to Azcárate, return to it the power it had held in the Middle Ages when its influence extended "like a net that covered everything and reached into every corner." ("como una red que todo lo cubría y a todas partes alcanzaba.")[25]

The debate on divorce in Spain must therefore be placed within this wider context of a battle between the Catholic traditionalists with the neo-Catholic movement as their vanguard[26] and the parti-

---

[20] Joaquín Sánchez de Toca, "El matrimonio," *Revista de España,* 34 (1873), p. 173.
[21] See Raymond Carr, *España (1808-1939)* (Barcelona: Ariel, 1969), pp. 174-179.
[22] Carr, pp. 233-34.
[23] See E. J. Hobsbawm, *The Age of Capital* (New York: Mentor Books, 1979), pp. 87-96.
[24] Gumersindo de Azcárate, *Estudios filosóficos y políticos* (Madrid, 1877), p. 276.
[25] Azcárate, p. 273.
[26] See Carr, pp. 279-80. See also, Aranguren, pp. 171-72.

sans of a civil and democratic state: prominent Krausists such as Azcárate, Urbano González Serrano, Fernando de Castro and Francisco Giner de los Ríos, as well as the architects of the first Spanish Republic, men like Emilio Castelar and Francisco Pi y Margall. It was a battle for political power that took on the bitterness and violence of a death struggle, and the bunker atmosphere may well have been due in part to the fact that the struggle was fought to a large degree over control of the intimate arena of the marriage bed. Although the question of Church control over primary and secondary education was also a point of controversy, the separation between civil and ecclesiastical courts and legislation was by then almost complete and only the institution of marriage and its correlatives – annulment, separation and divorce – remained under the jurisdiction of the Church.

In Spain, the arguments against divorce in the nineteenth century avoid the real issue of the separation of Church and state, and the interference of the Vatican in the exercise of Spain's national sovereignty. Instead, there were lengthy discussions of divine versus human or natural law. Marriage was a sacrament, rather than a civil contract, divinely instituted and therefore eternal. Other arguments in support of the indissolubility of marriage tended to exploit the insecurities of an economically precarious middle class. Women were threatened with abandonment, public scorn and penury. Older women (over forty) were seen as especially vulnerable, so much so that even those who favored divorce discussed the possibility of making it unavailable for women beyond that age.

It is not surprising that the majority of women would have been against divorce, in spite of the fact that upon marrying they could no longer sell their property, hold employment, sign contracts or change their place of residence without their husband's permission.[27] Divorce, with its implication of sexual promiscuity, was perceived as a threat to women's new status as "angels." The new attitude towards the family and the glorification of women's influence in the family and thus in society was seen by many women themselves as a kind of victory after centuries of misogyny and abuse: "Do not destroy the throne to which feudalism elevated us and with it all of its consequences...," ("No derrumbes el trono que

---

[27] See Scanlon, pp. 141-43.

a sus consecuencias nos alzó el feudalismo...,") warns the author of "Carta a María sobre la emancipación de la mujer" to her readers.[28]

From the viewpoint of the male, secure in his right to maintain extramarital liaisons, if he could afford it and as long as he obeyed the social conventions, divorce struck at the heart of his authority over his wife, an authority that was based on his right to control her sexual activity. The option of divorce signified an end to feminine submission.

Galdós' critique of marriage and divorce in *La familia de León Roch* might seem limited by the fact that both León Roch and Pepa Fúcar are rich and can consider the alternatives available to the upper class, expensive lawyers and a Church annulment which Catholics could frequently purchase through the Vatican. Nevertheless, although the novel's ending is obviously contrived for didactic purposes, there is a careful attempt to penetrate behind the mystifying abstractions of Law and Justice to the source of their power. The absence of divorce in Spain is shown to be, in part, a result of a concerted social pact among those who have internalized the politics and the rhetoric of the neo-Catholics and believe that sexual repression is indeed necessary for social control. The exercise of individual sexuality, especially female sexuality, must come under some form of institutionalized control, and marriage enforces the standard of monogamous heterosexual behavior. Even the theoretical division of social space into the private sphere of the home and the public sphere of production does not eliminate the presence of a social watchdog within the home. The "purification" of human nature through the repression of individual sexual behavior by state or Church can take place only with the collaboration of women *inside the home:*

> The authority over conjugal society is embodied in the woman in accordance with her relationship to the interior of the domestic home; while the social power which directs her is embodied in the male in accordance with his external social relationships.
>
> (En la mujer está personificada la autoridad de la sociedad conyugal según sus relaciones con el interior del hogar doméstico; y en el hombre, el poder social que la dirige según sus externas relaciones sociales.)[29]

---

[28] Dolores Gómez de Cádiz, "Carta a María sobre la emancipación de la mujer," *El Museo Universal*, 6, 24 (1862), p. 187.

[29] Sánchez de Toca, 34 (1873), p. 55.

Thus we find María Egipcíaca acting out the role of society's moral guardian when she arrives to claim her husband from Pepa Fúcar: "Prisoner!... I am the police!" ("¡Presidiario!... yo soy la policía!") [p. 904], she screams.

Pepa Fúcar and León Roch have three possible alternatives: 1) the implementation of the honor code, i.e., a blood solution; 2) flight into exile; 3) the modern solution of recourse to the law. The fact that Roch is bored with his wife does not justify murder, nevertheless he gives some wistful consideration to this alternative: "If she had committed adultery, I would have killed her" ("Si hubiera sido adúltera, la habría matado") [p. 882]. Although this statement may be shocking to our twentieth-century mentality and we may even be inclined to think that he is not serious, the right of the husband to take murderous revenge on an unfaithful wife was still being debated. [30] But this is not a viable option for a man of reason, and pages later, when Pepa insists that she must break her marriage bonds with Cimarra, Roch tells her that a break would require someone's murder [p. 962], and he is not capable. Nor is flight an option, for the welfare of the child includes protecting her from public scandal.

Galdós analyzes in detail Cimarra's right of *patria potestas* over his daughter Monina. Cimarra's accusation of adultery against Pepa Fúcar is sufficient to award him total custody of Monina, once she reaches the age of three [pp. 958-59]. What interests Galdós is the application of justice in a society in which, although the Calderonian solution of the sword is no longer viable, the modern solution of the law is not yet developed in regard to marital conflict. Pepa Fúcar has hoarded evidence of her husband's business malfeasance and she plans to use this evidence so that she may keep her child. León Roch assures her that with her father's protection, Cimarra's guilt

---

[30] See U. González Serrano, "Una cuestión de la actualidad," *Revista de España*, 31, 29-30 (1872-1873), pp. 84-95, 340-52, 191-205. Serrano concludes: "When the intimate bond of marriage has been broken... the husband who has faithfully and with dignity fulfilled all his obligation has the right, not to kill... but to expell from the temple of the home she who should have been the priestess that honored and dignified the sacred rites of the family, and instead contaminates and vilifies with every shameless breath, love's holy refuge." ("Cuando en el matrimonio ha quedado roto el vínculo interior... tiene el hombre, que ha cumplido leal y dignamente todos sus deberes, el derecho, no de matar... sino de arrojar del templo de su hogar aquella, que debiendo ser la sacerdotisa que honrara y dignificara el culto de la familia, mancha y envilece con su aliento impúdico el santo albergue del amor.") [p. 195].

will be easy to prove [p. 962]. But the father who should protect her has pacted with her husband. The trial, judgement and sentence are carried out, not in a public court of law, but in the Marqués de Fúcar's private study. The future of the mother and her child are decided in Pepa's presence but without her participation. The evidence against her husband implicates her father as well, and the men have agreed privately not to expose each other. Both Roch and Cimarra will give up any claim to Pepa, and the woman and her child will be returned, like war booty, to the father. The scandal that must be avoided is not the acceptable scandal of adultery but any attack on the Marqués' reputation as an honorable business man. Pepa, powerless in spite of her wealth, is reduced to the status of a child whose only recourse is to hide her head on her father's shoulder and weep [p. 976].

In Galdós' novels of the next decade, the question of divorce appears as an absence that shapes the marriage institution. Adultery, prostitution, and the institutionalization of the mistress are some of the unsatisfactory solutions to the problem of sexual repression. The women turn to their children, to compulsive consumption of finery and, like the men, to adulterous affairs to compensate for the sterility of their marriages. The four remaining novels that we will discuss, *Tormento, La de Bringas, Lo prohibido,* and *Tristana,* share one important element: Galdós' disillusionment with the idea of romantic love, and especially with its main tenet that true love is unique and eternal.

Tormento and *Lo prohibido* are both concerned with the way in which the ideal of romantic love for the perfect woman becomes an impediment that distants the man from an understanding of his real emotions and desires. The idealization of the family and of the wife-mother as an angel, a sexless submissive creature without individual personality, is harmful because it imposes upon both men and women the burden of distorting their emotions and their sexuality to fit an abstraction. Galdós' concern with ideological rhetoric reflects his interest in the way in which powerful discourses shape mentalities. At the end of *La familia de León Roch,* he shows that it is impossible to escape the use of clichés but that worn-out rhetorical phrases can be revitalized if they are infused with sincerity and spontaneity. Pepa Fúcar turns to her lover and repeats to him the same words that he had spoken to his wife: "We're the mirror image of each other" ("Somos espejo el uno del otro") [p. 961]. But they see in each other's faces more than an abstract and undefinable love. They see the sickly pallor of fear and exhaustion, the physiological manifestation of their shared emotion.

Galdós' narration of his personal ideal of domesticity will bring into play many material factors: money, the lack of education of both men and women, the interesting vagaries of human sexuality. As his novels become more immersed in concrete details of daily life, Galdós will continue to analyze the importance of the ideology of the family in the shaping of a middle-class mentality in Spain, that middle class which is, according to the author's own words: "The foundation of social order: through its initiative and by means of its intelligence, it appropriates national sovereignty, from it comes XIX century man..." ("la base del orden social: ella asume por su iniciativa y por su inteligencia la soberanía de las naciones, y en ella está el hombre del siglo XIX...").[31]

---

[31] B. Pérez Galdós, "Observaciones sobre la novela contemporánea en España," first published in *Revista de España* in 1870, collected in *Ensayos de crítica literaria*, intro. L. Bonet (Barcelona: Ediciones Península, 1972), p. 122.

CHAPTER FIVE

TORMENTO: BOURGEOIS MORALITY AND THE PRIVATIZATION OF VIRTUE

In 1881, Galdós publishes *La desheredada* and in 1882, *El amigo Manso,* both novels in the tradition of the *bildungsroman,* in which the protagonist, through a process of trial and error in society's laboratory, learns to adjust his personal definition of reality to the collective norms of the society in which he is forced to live. Galdós continues to develop the theme of the social education of the individual, using the structure of the *bildungsroman* in *El doctor Centeno* (1883), a novel which introduces many of the characters which will appear later in *Tormento* (1884), which in turn will be followed by a sequel, *La de Bringas,* in May of the same year.

The *bildungsroman* has always served as a mode which permits the author to analyze, criticize and evaluate society – one thinks of *Candide,* and especially, Flaubert's *Sentimental Education.* The protagonist of the *bildungsroman* is not only the character around whom the plot is structured, he or she also functions as a witness whose testimony transcends the events of his personal history. What permits the protagonist to survive in a hostile environment is his hard-earned knowledge of the mechanisms that govern the society in which he lives. This knowledge, the ability to read the social blueprint and to explain it to himself (and consequently to the reader) becomes, in a sense, autonomous. That is to say, the critique of society's laws becomes the true protagonist of the novel mediated by the viewpoint of the hero-protagonist, whose individual story is lived in relation to his function to give testimony to the inadequacies and contradictions of the social conventions.

Galdós' experimentation with the structure of the *bildungsroman* and the double function of protagonist and witness in *El doctor Centeno* paves the way for several innovations which will find their way into *Tormento*. In *El doctor Centeno*, the structuring of plot and point of view around a single protagonist, Felipe Centeno, is broken down. By de-emphasizing Centeno's adventures, Galdós is able to bring the social institutions into the foreground. Thus the school becomes one of several analytic perspectives, along with that of the priesthood and the theatre. Felipe Centeno functions primarily as a witness (rather than protagonist), pulling together the bifurcated plot, which centers alternately on the priest Pedro Polo, a hero of Heathcliffian proportions, and the playwright, Alejandro Miquis, who embodies the decadence of Spanish romanticism.[1]

This experimentation with the dual functions of protagonist and witness in *El doctor Centeno* teaches Galdós two things. First, the use of a character as witness and commentator eliminates the necessity of relying solely upon the omniscient third-person narrator to interpret the novel's events to the reader. And second, if witness and protagonist(s) are separated, several critical perspectives can be introduced simultaneously.

In *Tormento*, Galdós discards the basic structure of the *bildungsroman* which restricts the point of view to one main protagonist, but he retains the function of witness and commentator in one of his more endearing characters, Don José Ido del Sagrario. José Ido, who first appears in *El doctor Centeno* as a teacher of calligraphy in the Dickensian school of the priest, Pedro Polo de Cortés, is, in *Tormento*, a minor character. If he were removed from the novel the dynamics of the plot would remain unchanged. This fact enables us to see clearly that José Ido's importance to the structure of *Tormento* lies in his role as witness to the actors in the love triangle: the helpless Amparo, and her two suitors, Agustín Caballero and Pedro Polo.

Galdós' innovation consists not only of incorporating a minor character who will act as "reality's" interpreter; in addition, he does not impose upon him the burden of objectivity. José Ido does not

---

[1] For an excellent study see G. M. Scanlon, *"El doctor Centeno:* a study in obsolescent values," *Bulletin of Hispanic Studies*, 55 (1978), pp. 245-53. Scanlon makes the point that the thematic unity of the novel – the inadequacy of romantic idealism and outmoded pedagogical institutions for solving Spain's basic economic and social problems – belies the apparent diffusion of the plot.

personify the realist author who supposedly writes from a position of ideological neutrality. On the contrary, Don José, a member of Isabeline society who lives and supports his numerous family by writing sentimental fiction, is a commentator with a specific ideology. In fact, what enables José Ido to be a successful author of romantic dime novels – one who specializes in endings – is his belief in the moral and social values which are the raw material of the commodity he produces.

By relieving his character of the obligation to be objective, Galdós avoids the trap of creating a fictional voice which would inevitably be cast in the role of authoritative voice, in both the sense of author (Galdós) and of privileged interpreter of the text. And by endowing his witness not only with a carefully delineated ideological viewpoint, but also one that is materially incorporated into the social relations of the economy, the novel's structure allows the reader to perceive and evaluate for himself the dialectical relationship between the production of ideology – in this case, the sentimental piety of Don José's romances – and the limited possibilities for class mobility in the impoverished Spanish economy during the years preceding the Revolution of 1868.

Until *Tormento*, the contradiction between the pious rhetoric of the conservatives and neo-Catholics and their cynical manipulation of this rhetoric in order to maintain oligarchic power within the framework of Altar-Throne-Family has generally been personified in a single character: Doña Perfecta, for example, or in *La familia de León Roch*, Federico Cimarra and his strategy of social reintegration through "moral regeneration." These novels, like the novel *Gloria*, are structured upon a scheme in which society is divided into two camps (the two Spains). There is a coincidence between political-economic alignments and their ideological banners, and the characters tend to fall neatly into one or the other camp.

In *Tormento*, however, Galdós backs away from a tendentious frontal attack on religious hypocrisy in order to analyze the popular dissemination of sentimental Catholic piety and its incorporation into middle-class Spanish consciousness and manners. The object under the author's microscope is the ethos of petty bourgeois respectability. Rather than analyze the contradiction between an individual ideological position – definably liberal or conservative – and its social practice, we are given a hegemonic ideal posited as an apolitical moral standard for the community, but an ideal which only materializes in the pages of Don José's *folletines*.

In Galdós' construction of this new dialectic between society and popular literature, it is important that José Ido, whose job as a hack commercial writer makes him the conduit for the values of a sentimentalized Catholicism, is himself not a sinister man. He cannot become a personal target for any quarrel we may have with the content of the literature he produces. His own probity is, in fact, partly responsible for his creativity, for Don José believes in his product. The real key to his success, however, lies in his knowledge of the consumer market. In a word, he is able to give the public what it wants to buy: "something with a lot of feeling, that makes people cry and is chock-full of morality" ("una obra de mucho sentimiento, que haga llorar a la gente y que esté bien cargada de moralidad") [p. 12]

Alicia Andreu's study of the Virtuous Woman as literary archetype in popular nineteenth-century Spanish literature includes a penetrating comment on how this kind of literature worked to promote social integration and the passivity of its readers:

> ...the romantic exaltation of the individual as such becomes in popular literature a passive acceptance of the surrounding reality. The note of protest which characterizes many of the romantic heros is lacking; in its place there is an attitude of resignation and of obedience to established modes of conduct.
>
> (...la exaltación romántica del individuo como tal ha pasado a ser en la obra popular una aceptación pasiva de la realidad circundante. Falta en la segunda la nota de protesta que caracteriza a muchos de los héroes románticos, estableciéndose en su lugar una actitud de resignación y de obediencia a los cánones establecidos.)[2]

Virtue is defined as Christian submission to an inevitable and meritorious destiny of poverty and suffering. A euphoric Ido exclaims: "Where does honor lie? In the poor man, in the worker, in the beggar. Where do you find the rascals? It's the rich man, the noble, the ministers, the generals, the courtiers..." ("¿Dónde está la

---

[2] A. Andreu, *Galdós y la literatura popular* (Madrid: SGEL, 1982), pp. 47-48.

honradez? En el pobre, en el obrero, en el mendigo. ¿Dónde está la picardía? En el rico, en el noble, en el ministro, en el general, en el cortesano...") [p. 12].[3]

We are reading here the forging of the myth of the "noble worker," a myth that idealizes the working class and the disenfranchized and absolves them from the responsibilities – the white man's burden – and, of course, from the priviliges of the ruling Spanish oligarchy.[4] A corollary of the myth of the "noble worker" that functions to rationalize and maintain the status quo of the urban "working poor" is the idea of the innate virtue of rural simplicity. The idea of the virtuousness of rural life or that of the "noble savage" functions to displace the presence of virtue itself from the urban centers to a safe distance, where the worker (or the Indian or the Black) can be idealized *in absentia*, simultaneously creating a rhetorical space that can include the condemnation of the urban poor (or immigrants or colonized people) as filthy degenerate lazy and subversive. The impossibility of locating an identifiable or real "noble worker" can then be explained by the fact that virtue resides elsewhere: in the innocence of bucolic life, in the uncorrupted primitive colonies of the Empire, or in the case of women, in the home, rather than in the factory, the university or any other sector of public life. So by definition, the poor, if they aspire to class mobility – or merely to resist the inevitability of their social condition – cease to be virtuous, for they can remain virtuous only by remaining poor.[5]

---

[3] José Ido's list of villains reflects a popular mentality that is turned toward the past and is unaware of Spain's lag in industrialization and capitalist development in comparison to the rest of Western Europe. His villains, the "courtier," the "noble" and even the unspecified "rich" are primarily aristocratic ones. Absent from his list are such bourgeois "rascals" as the banker or the exploitative factory owner, all targets for satire or condemnation in the English novel, and of course, in many of Galdós' as well, for example, the unscrupulous banker, the Marqués de Fúcar.

[4] See *infra*, Chapter 6 for a discussion of the myth of the noble worker in the context of Civilization versus Barbarism.

[5] Caballero expresses the appeal of Amparo's feminine submissiveness when he praises "that pleasing conformity with her humble condition, which so dignifies her." ("Aquella graciosa conformidad con su estado pobre, que tanto la enaltece") [p. 35].

Amparo: The Genesis of an Angel

Within the canon of popular sentimental fiction, the young virtuous female occupied a special place. Her chastity symbolized the strength of virtue over worldly temptation and her body, young, beautiful and chaste, became an icon. In the creation of Amparo, Galdós analyzes the components of the feminine ideal: beauty, vulnerability, humility and sexual purity. Amparo's Cinderella story becomes Galdós' strongest indictment of both the ideal itself, and its effect on the women who aspired to live as an *ángel del hogar* in the absence of adequate material resources.

Galdós' presentation of Amparo to the reader is carefully calculated to establish the central problem of the novel. Amparo's ambiguous role in the Bringas household is a reflection of her tenuous foothold in the middle class.[6] She is poor, but still "respectable." The problem of class definition, that is, the process by which social class is defined and maintained, and especially, the immerging class-consciousness of Spain's middle class, is the theme which ties together *Tormento* and *La de Bringas*.

Like the smile of the Cheshire Cat, Amparo comes slowly into focus, already eclipsed by the detailed and vigorous portrait of Rosalía Bringas. She is a pair of hands scrubbing pots, ears to hear the orders of her "friend" and mistress, and feet to obey them. Finally, she is a voice: "Don Francisco, the ends of these nails are all bent" ("Don Francisco, que a estos clavos se les han torcido las puntas") [p. 18]. The fury of the domestic storm, dust flying, water sloshing over tiles, sleeves rolled up and bare female arms plunged into soapy water is a scene in which Galdós takes evident pleasure. He will repeat it again in Chapter XV, when Amparo visits her former lover, Pedro Polo, and in a frenzy of cleaning, shopping and cooking, reestablishes domestic order.

---

[6] The term middle class rather than bourgeoisie, although more fluid and imprecise, permits the inclusion of the petty-bourgeoisie, the spectrum of functionaries, professionals and others who constitute the *"materia novelable,"* the basis of Galdós' novels. Obviously, an awareness of class, or 'class consciousness' follows upon the development of a class society. For a brief theoretical discussion of the development of the European bourgeoisie *qua* class from their roots in the European oligarchy see E. J. Hobsbawm, *The Age of Capital (1848-1939)* (New York: Mentor, 1979), pp. 266-76. See also, Raymond Carr, *España 1808-1939* (Barcelona: Ariel, 1969), pp. 272-84, for a description of Spain's oligarchy, the "five-hundred families."

Amparo's evident capacity to take control in the business of housewifery stands in sharp contrast to her inability to confront and control the exploitive relationships that define her daily existence. Her sister Refugio will not recognize her authority as older sister, and sells her meager possessions, thus undermining Amparo's feeble attempts to create her own private domestic life away from the surveillance of her self-styled protectors. In the Bringas household, her status as friend and distant relative affords her the dubious privilege of dining on occasion with the family, an indication of equal social status. But in order to sustain this illusion of equality, Amparo must forfeit any right to demand a wage for her services. Payment for her work is dependent on her benefactors' goodwill and capricious charitable instincts.

If the reader is guided by the narrator, Amparo's lamb-like submissiveness will be read as a moral weakness. She is repeatedly described as a person with a weak character. Montesinos' use of the word unhealthy or morbid ("enfermizo")[7] is not without justification, for Amparo acts, or rather reacts, in the manner of a defenseless animal, paralyzed by the light of the hunter. But Amparo's submission has its roots in her own personal history. The quintessentially female virtue of self-abnegation is revealed early on to be the desperate strategy of a woman for whom self-assertion means self-exposure of "the worst mistake and the only sin of her life" ("el mayor tropiezo y la única mancha de su vida") [p. 53], her brief affair with the renegade priest, Pedro Polo de Cortés. The possibility of salvation – economic security through marriage with Caballero – also sets in motion the social mechanisms that will result in exposure, since her engagement propels her from her safe obscurity, her state of *anomie*, and into the public arena and the merciless scrutiny of the public eye.

Galdós gives us few clues to the past love affair of Amparo and Pedro Polo. Their story constitutes the missing first volume in what should have been a typical "three decker" trilogy so popular in the nineteenth-century publishing world. Amparo's orphanhood and Polo's brooding dissatisfaction with the role of cleric evidently played a part. The key element, however, and one which is still in force as their story continues, is the inability of either one to satisfy their needs, whether economic, emotional or sexual, within the

---

[7] José F. Montesinos, *Galdós*, II (Madrid: Castalia, 1969), p. 106.

canons of bourgeois respectability. Father Nones' solution for the frustrated priest — that he purify his body and mind in the hygienic environment of a rural town — would feed the body but not the spirit: "I'll end up a healthy idiot" ("Saldré sano, pero idiota") [p. 79], Polo writes to Amparo. Equally illusory is Rosalía Bringas' suggestion that Amparo enter a convent. She could never accumulate the necessary dowry and her loving nature is obviously not suited for the emotional deprivation of a life dedicated to a mystical husband.[8]

The climax of the novel, the final confrontation scene between Pedro Polo and "Tormento" reveals clearly that moral salvation for Amparo must include a recuperation of at least a limited autonomy. "I'm not called Tormento anymore, I have my name back now" ("Ya no me llamo Tormento, ya recobro mi nombre") [p. 75], she exclaimed after her first visit with her former lover. But the euphoria produced by this momentary sense of control smashes into the real limits of any possibility of change. The locked room in which the final struggle with the priest takes place becomes a physical representation of the couple's mutual lack of social mobility, but it also defines the relationship of power between the two, for the key to the door belongs to Pedro Polo and it is he who has locked it.

For the reader who has been frustrated by Amparo's inability to defend herself against Rosalía's scorn or Polo's harrassment, this scene introduces the tantalizing hope of a decisive victory, the possibility of freedom from the priest's blackmail. But the tactics of both conquest and resistance have already been determined by the power relationship between the two adversaries. Isolated from any outside intervention, the struggle is reduced to that of superior masculine strength against devious feminine wiles. In her terror, Amparo denies any love for Caballero, only to see her lie utilized by her persecutor as a justification for continuing the affair after her marriage. When she rebels against this suggestion, she is told bluntly the rules of the game, rules that force her to move within the parameters of socially prescribed "feminine" behavior. "You already know that you won't get anything out of me by behaving badly. If you're nice to me, I'll give you anything you want..."

---

[8] See G. M. Scanlon, *La polémica feminista en la España contemporánea* (Madrid: Siglo XXI, 1976), pp. 113-14, for a discussion of the asylum afforded "fallen women" by religious orders, including the Comunidad de Adoratrices Esclavas del Santísimo Sacramento, founded in 1845 by Micaela Demaisières.

("Ya sabes que de mí no consigues nada por malas. Por buenas, todo lo que tú quieras...") [p. 92]. And Amparo responds with "a woman's weapons."[9] She weeps, "like a child when he is being beaten" ("como un niño cuando le pegan") [p. 92]. Again, she attempts to flee. Vanquished, she hides her head in the pillows of the sofa.

This is the crucial moment in this very long and painful scene. Open rebellion has failed, escape is shut off. It is a momentary victory for Polo and he reinforces Amparo's feminine strategy of conciliation and appeasment by again warning her that aggressive resistance will only provoke him to utilize his superior strength: "You think you can treat me like a stray dog, and that's not right... Even if I try to contain myself, I won't be able to avoid losing control and I'll do something horrible" ("Quieres tratarme como perro forastero, y eso no es justo... Aunque procure contenerme, no podré evitar un arrebato y haré cualquier barbaridad") [p. 93]. The veiled threat of rape forces Amparo to act. Employing the defense prescribed for her by her conquerer, she attempts to reason with him, speaking to him sweetly.

The resolution of this scene is a statement in support of active rebellion against tyranny, and consequently, a strong criticism of the lies and subterfuges that constituted Amparo's defense against society's censure. Goaded finally into a choice between honor and, if not death, a very likely beating, Amparo refuses to spend the night with the priest: "no, a thousand times, no..." ("No, no mil veces...") [p. 96]. How satisfying is her fury for the reader! And how apparently logical the defeat of the savage beast: "You can leave whenever you want" ("Puedes salir cuando quieras") [p. 96].

And yet, this cathartic resolution, the seemingly inevitable climax of tension meticulously structured, is full of ambiguities, not the least of which is the presence of Celedonia, the aged servant who lies dying in the adjacent room. She is the real reason for Amparo's victory, since her presence provides the young woman with the option of seeking sanctuary – one that she exercises at a critical moment in the struggle. Polo's careful nursing of the old woman also gives the lie to his threat to "lose control," and enables us to see exactly how he uses his superior strength to manipulate and control the frightened woman.

---

[9] The phrase, "las armas de la mujer" (a woman's weapons) was a cliché of the period: these weapons were her "tears and smiles" ("lágrimas y sonrisas").

But Celedonia's presence is not gratuitous. It is the direct result of a consistent pattern of charitable acts on the part of the priest. Polo's interaction with Celedonia, although incongruous in this violent scene, is not out of character, at least it appears to agree with other actions described to us by the narrator. Because of this knowledge, the reader is prevented from taking easy satisfaction in a cliché, the triumph of Virtue over Lust. Such an ending would only be appropriate in the *folletines* of Don José, Galdós' parodic alter-ego. Nor is Polo's bitter exclamation unconvincing: "Even so, even so, I am worth more than you, and will reach heights to which you can never aspire." ("Todavía, todavía, sé valer más que tú, y ponerme donde tú no te pondrás nunca") [p. 97]. Unlike Amparo, Polo had dreamed of total rebellion, of fleeing with his love from the society that holds them both in bondage, while Amparo's moment of revolt against her tormentor has come too late perhaps to fully rehabilitate her in our eyes.

The reason for the ambiguous nature of Amparo's victory over Pedro Polo does not lie only in the moral complexity of the priest, however. Galdós makes clear through his careful depiction of Polo's bullying tactics that the satisfaction of sexual desire through the use of force is evil. The ambiguity lies rather in the fact that the reader's perspective at this moment has been narrowed to encompass only the personal problems of two unequal personalities. The reader, locked into the room with the characters, locked also into this metaphor of society, experiences a kind of tunnel vision which reduces the conflict to male against female, to strong against weak. Without the social context which has created the personal conflict, it is reduced melodramatically to a question of biology.

Yet it is not the man Pedro Polo who has deprived Amparo of her autonomy and human dignity, even though he exploits her situation of weakness. Amparo's economic dependency and consequent precarious social status is the source of the abject fear that defines her character. This fear, which is the fear of downward class mobility, of losing the protection of the domestic interior that rightfully belongs to the respectable middle-class women, motivates her actions, or rather, her passivity. Her sister Refugio has had the courage (or the foolhardiness) needed to free herself from the strictures of a middle-class status that insists upon propriety but provides no financial compensation in return. Amparo, on the other hand, seeks security through her identity with and acceptance by the middle class. Given the impossibility of divorce in Spain, her marriage to Caballero would afford her a permanent social refuge, a true *amparo*, which a life of concubinage could never provide.

Marcelina Polo: Guardian at the Gate of Public Morals

Pedro Polo and Amparo's personal conflict is abruptly reinserted into the social context that has shaped the trajectories of their individual destinies with the entrance on the scene of the priest's sister, the terrifying Marcelina Polo. Throughout the novel, the factor that consistently defines Amparo's situation and influences her choices is her condition of *desamparo*, her state of abandonment or social orphanhood. Marcelina Polo, moral guardian of the middle class, is the incarnation of Amparo's deepest fears. She is a merciless woman incapable of pardoning any transgression. Her arrival brings into play the repressive forces that are perverting both the woman and the man: Polo laments to himself: "I am a despicable weakling, bound up in the muscles of a Hercules." ("Soy un muñeco indigno, forrado en la musculatura de un Hércules") [p. 94]. The need to confront a common enemy makes these two antagonists temporary allies: "They sat down face to face in the living room, each one as crestfallen and dejected as the other." ("En la sala sentáronse el uno frente al otro, igualmente desalentados y abatidos") [p. 101]. Padre Nones arrives, and discreetly avoids any question to Amparo concerning her presence in the priest's apartment, in evident contrast to Marcelina Polo, whose insistent cry of "I want to know, I want to know, I want to know..." ("Quiero saber, quiero saber, quiero saber...") [p. 100], proclaims her arrogant sense of a right to involve herself in other's affairs. Amparo leaves the apartment under her furious gaze but protected by the Church – Padre Nones –, and Marcelina Polo is forced to step aside and let them pass.

Marcelina Polo belongs to the coterie of religious hypocrites, the self-righteous and arrogant Lady Perfects who are a special target of Galdós' pen. Both Marcelina Polo and Doña Perfecta reflect a long tradition in which the public's right to be informed concerning individual sexual behavior (especially the female's) was accepted because a rigid standard of female chastity was the basis for the marriage contract that perpetuated and legitimized patriarchal economic power. Marcelina Polo is Doña Perfecta's doppelganger removed from the autarchic structure which enabled the *cacique* or local strong-man to exert total social-economic control. In the earlier novel *Doña Perfecta,* the ostracism of the three orphaned sisters – who are here reproduced in an urban context as Amparo and Refugio – demonstrates the power of a rural oligarchy to exert hegemony over all aspects of social existence. Doña Perfecta's condemnation affects the inhabitants of Orbajosa not only socially, but economically as well. But this model of rural *caciquismo,* which depends for its existence on the political and geographical isolation of the small town, Orbajosa, cannot be transferred to an urban metropolis where political power is based not only on landed property but also on capital investment that is dispersed among powerful families such as the Fúcars and the Salamancas. Doña Perfecta, metamorphosed into Marcelina Polo, is reduced to the role of gossip-monger for the sake of personal satisfaction. In other words, Marcelina Polo, standbearer for bourgeois respectability, has ceased to be a political force.

Nineteenth-century ideology employed a topographical metaphor that divided the social landscape into public and private spheres. The frequent use of the word "sphere" underlines the metaphoric rather than empirical sense in which social space is imagined: the public sphere is defined as the province of the male – that of production, finance and politics. The women's private sphere of consumption was organized around the institution of the bourgeois family. This apparently clear-cut division: public/private, production/consumption, male/female distorts the reality of the private ownership of the means of production which takes place in the so-called "public" sphere: for example, the private ownership of factories, banks, businesses, and supporting institutions such as hospitals and even post offices. This privatization also extended into the "sphere" of cultural production and consumption with the privatization of learning institutions, the press, lending libraries and clubs for the intelligentsia. The privatization of virtue is, therefore, only one aspect of the general privatization of social existence that occurs with the developmemt of the bourgeois state and the gradual implementation of industrial capitalism as the dominant mode of production.

The privatization of virtue entails various aspects: first, the appropriation of all "virtue" and its redefinition by the bourgeoisie as decorum or respectability; second, the social arbitration of this standard of decorum only in the sphere of consumption; third, the absence of any concept of honor, virtue or respectability that might serve to control the accumulation and expansion of capital; and finally, the rise of the idea of the *right* to privacy of the individual. With the rise of the bourgeois state, a distinction will gradually be made between social contracts agreed upon in the public sphere where privacy does not exist, and the organization of one's existence outside the realm of capital and labor relations. It is the social division between Work and Family.

Amparo is vulnerable to Marcelina Polo's attack on her privacy because her contract with society is not based on her labor power but rather on her good character or reputation which is, in turn, dependent on conserving a state of virginity. She will be protected socially as a member of the Bringas family, that is, of the middle class, only for so long as that condition is maintained. For women, then, the intersection between the private and public spheres comes precisely at this point where a certain prescribed standard of sexual conduct is required as a *precondition* for the selling of their labor power whether as servant or as mistress of a household.

Amparo's lack of a moral right to enter into a marriage contract with Caballero without informing him of her blemished past is not in debate. Amparo herself, her confessor, Caballero – who tells her "you don't deserve me, admit that you don't deserve me" ("No me mereces, reconoce que no me mereces") [p. 121] – and public opinion all agree that their engagement constitutes a felony [p. 73], the crime of selling defective goods. But Marcelina Polo's feverish cry of "I want to know" raises the issue of Amparo's right to conduct her personal affairs privately, or rather, the question of what exactly is or is not public business and who is entitled to the luxury of bourgeois privacy.

Galdós avoids a direct confrontation with this issue by permitting the social mechanisms to grind out an apparently inevitable conclusion. The sanctuary provided Amparo by Padre Nones is temporary, dependent on the good will of an exceptional individual, not on the institution he represents. The private lives of the lower class are still lived out in the public eye. Marcelina Polo will not be satisfied until she has made Amparo's secret public knowledge. The specter of "what people will say" ("el qué dirán") moves in to take control over those individuals who both willingly and unwillingly pay it homage.

The exposure of Amparo's past deprives her of the last opportunity to take control over her future, either by confessing the truth to Caballero or by persisting in her deception. And it was this possibility of action, of exerting a limited autonomy, that provided Amparo with a human dimension. During the rest of the novel, when even suicide is denied her, she will gradually be reduced to the pretty mechanical doll we see waving goodbye in the train station. Caballero tells himself: "I get so furious when I think that the part of her which is still good will belong to someone else." ("¡Me da más rabia cuando pienso que la parte que aún conserva sana ha de ser para otro!") [p. 119]. For Caballero, she is a difficult toy to discard, and since she is one he can afford, he decides to buy her instead.

Amparo's inability to become the subject of her history is partially a result of her awareness that autonomy might only translate into conditions of exploitation even more cruel than those she had been forced to accept under the protection of the Bringas family and so she clings to her ersatz and precarious respectability. But precisely because of Amparo's ambivalent social status, she cannot be placed in the category of middle-class daughters and wives whose artificial manners Caballero so abhors. Amparo's condition of *anomie* enables Caballero to recreate her in his imagination as the ideal wife, an *ángel del hogar,* the *amparo* or refuge of the warrior. Her beauty provides the raw material for Caballero's fantasy, while her almost pathological submissiveness translates easily into a litany of the traditional domestic virtues: "...she was virtuous, prudent, modest, unpretentious, discreet..." ("...era virtuosa, prudente, modesta, sencilla, discreta...") [p. 35]. They are the same virtues that define the spiritual nature of Fray Luis' perfect wife or the virtuous heroines of José Ido's romances.

When Caballero is forced to acknowledge Amparo's lack of virginity, the entire framework of "virtue" that he had constructed around her comes tumbling down. He had sought her, apparently, for those spiritual qualities which seemed to promise an affinity of personalities and tastes. She would be, above all, his companion: "...his love for her was a tranquil one, his soul drawn more to the delights of domesticity, always loving and occupied, than to the unstable restlessness of passion." ("...la quería con tranquilo amor, puestos los ojos del alma, más en los encantos del vivir casero, siempre ocupado y afectuoso, que en la desigual inquietud de la pasión") [p. 76]. Now, with the public recognition that Amparo is not a virgin, Amparo herself ceases to exist as a legitimate social entity, the fiancée of a gentleman.

The question then becomes, what remains of Amparo? "I picked an apple that I thought was ripe. When I cut it open, I saw it was rotten." ("La manzana que cogí parecióme buena. Ábrese y la veo dañada.") [p. 119]. The portion of this bruised fruit that can still be consumed is Amparo's young and beautiful body. She cannot be his wife and the mother of his children, but she will suit very well as a pliant and grateful mistress. The future relationship between the two is established when Caballero commands her to pack her suitcase. No contract is verbalized. Amparo does not have the power to negotiate. They both realize that she has no other possible future.

This ending becomes a reversal of Bringas' suggested title for the story of Amparo's engagement: "Virtue's Reward" ("El premio de la virtud") [p. 77]. Galdós has written an ironic reversal of Samuel Richardson's novel *Pamela: Virtue Rewarded*. Published in 1739, it is not a novel about female virtue as much as it is an apology for the virtue of the marriage institution, and an insistence that sexual love confined and legitimized within marriage – rather than the exaltation of adulterous love – is the keystone to the order and stability necessary for the development of bourgeois society. The abuses of the aristocracy must be controlled and limited, and even the servant class must emerge from its state of feudal dependency and be permitted to enjoy a limited version of the "rights of man." For its time, *Pamela* was a revolutionary novel and was condemned because of it. More than a hundred years later, in the absence of a true Spanish bourgeois revolution, it is the cynicism of Thackeray, rather than Richardson's rebellion, that wins the day. The theme of vanity fair will be taken up by Galdós in *La de Bringas;* for the moment he is satisfied with awarding Caballero his prize, a seductive young mistress for a wealthy older gentleman.

Agustín Caballero: The Myth of the "Noble Capitalist"

Why it is Caballero who wins the prize, rather than his rival, Pedro Polo, necessitates elaboration. Galdós establishes a parallel between the two men from the beginning. Both are continuously referred to as Caribs (cannibals), Kaffirs (infidels or Blacks) and savages. Indeed, both men recognize in themselves their incapacity to mold either their manners or their values to Madrid upper-class society. They are each portrayed as a kind of noble savage inserted unwillingly into a decadent and effeminate, that is to say, superficial and hypocritical society. Pedro Polo's critique of urban civilization reads like the gloss of a chapter from Rousseau's *Emile:* "A curse on they who in society's artificial labyrinth have destroyed Nature in order to replace her with pedantry." ("Malditos los que en el laberinto artificioso de las sociedades han derrocado la Naturaleza para poner en su lugar la pedantería...") [p. 80].

Unable to act out the priestly role of moral watch dog, "putting on a mask to scare people with" ("poniéndome una máscara para hacer el bu a la gente") [p. 57], Polo has resorted to a life of passive fantasy in order to preserve the vision of a future upon which survival in the present depends: "It was a strained and artificial kind of life, that life, but at least it was a life" ("Aunque forzada y artificial, aquella vida, vida era") [p. 57]. He uses material from Spain's glorious past to recreate himself, discarding the hated priest's habit for the horse and sword of the conquistador. He is Hernán Cortés, Napoleon, a warrior or a general. The essence of his fantasies is the ease with which the battles are won, the swift and felicitous surmounting of obstacles.

Agustín Caballero, unlike Pedro Polo, has created a fortune, not in the silver mines of Potosí, or, like the real Cortés, in the valleys of Oaxaca, but by speculating in food supplies on the Mexican border during the American Civil War. According to the narrator, Caballero's nobility, his *caballerosidad* or knightliness, derives from his participation in the great nineteenth-century project of imposing "civilization" upon the indigenous "savages" of Northern Mexico and Texas. The voice of the narrator, echoing José Ido's melodramatic rendering of history, describes Caballero as bearing "...the mark or insignia of the colonizing apostolate who with the health and lives of so many noble workers, is forging out the powerful civilizations of the Hispano-American world..." ("...la insignia o marca del apostolado colonizador que, con la vida y salud de tantos nobles obreros, labra las potentes civilizaciones del mundo hispanoamericano...") [p. 23]. The narrator's interpretation of the Spanish colonization process, essentially a recounting of the myth of the struggle between Civilization and Barbarism, merges with Pedro Polo's exotic image of imperial expansion as the discovery of a new Eden where "...all is innocence and true equality; lands without history..." ("todo es inocencia de costumbres y verdadera igualdad; tierras sin historia...") [p. 55].

It is Caballero's voice of experience that serves as a corrective to this Rousseauian vision of the New World as a primeval utopia. As he fantasizes his own future Eden of domestic bliss with Amparo, he remembers the dehumanization of a life spent accumulating wealth, when he was nothing more than "a machine of human flesh to coin money..." ("una máquina de carne para acuñar dinero...") [p. 34]. He remembers the fear and harshness of frontier life, the loneliness of the foreigner. Pedro Polo's dream of freedom and equality in a land without the repressive structures of a collective past materializes as the historical moment in which North America is seeking to replace Spain as a colonial force in Latin America. (According to the information provided by the narrator, Caballero goes to Mexico at the age of fifteen. Consequently, he would have lived through the War of 1848 in which Mexico lost the northern half of its territory to the United States.)

Caballero recalls with horror the absence of social hierarchy, of law and order, and the promiscuous blending of races and nationalities in a territory in which national boundaries are being forcibly contested: "Americans, Frenchmen, Indians, Mexicans, men and women of every caste, one on top of the other and all mixed together, usually hating each other, seldom with any respect... The whole thing was a hell..." ("Americanos, franceses, indios, mejicanos, hombres y mujeres de todas castas, envueltos y confundidos, odiándose por lo común, estimándose rara vez,... Aquello era un infierno...") [p. 34]. His return to a "poor and orderly" Spain shuts the door to Pedro Polo's dream of escape, for Caballero himself is fleeing the brutality of the colonization process. There is no land that exists outside history, there is no Eden. The anarchy that Caballero denounces is not the primitive communism of the Utopian Socialists or the iconoclasm of Voltaire but rather the anarchy of capitalist expansion. In the words of E. J. Hobsbawn, this age of "robber barons" is characterized by:

> ...the total absence of any kind of control over business dealings, however ruthless and crooked, and the really spectacular possibilities of corruption both national and local – especially in the Post-Civil War years. There was indeed little that could be called

government in the United States, and the scope for the powerful and unscrupulous rich was virtually unlimited. In fact, the phrase, "robber barons" should carry its accent on the second rather than on the first word, for as in a weak medieval kingdom, men could not look to the law but only to their own strength – and who were stronger in a capitalist society than the rich?[10]

Wealth is the substance of power and power is the measure of nobility. In the public sphere, there is no virtue. The concept of virtue, used primarily to regulate female sexuality, is replaced in the sphere of production with a business ethic of "measure for measure" as a regulatory standard for the commercial activity of men. Caballero is already molded to this ethic, as his friends and business associates have reason to know. He is "That proprietor who had become angry with Mompous for attempting to give him, at the moment of the distribution of shares, somewhat less than what was owed him..." ("Aquel proprietario que se había enojado con Mompous porque éste quiso ponerle, en el reparto de las contribuciones, un poco menos de lo que le correspondía;...") [p. 76]. Unlike the Marqués de Fúcar, who made his fortune selling bad shoe leather to outfit the Spanish soldiers in Cuba and bad Cuban tobacco to unwary consumers in Spain, Caballero is portrayed as a "good" capitalist. As Montesinos points out,[11] Galdós makes clear his position that the future of Western Civilization – and whether Spain will be included or not in this mythical territory is at the heart of the debate – does not lie in the virtue of sexual and social repression but in the dynamics of capitalism controlled by an ethic of fairness, individual accountability and productivity or hard work.

Pedro Polo's mistaken choice of vocation turns out to be a fatal error that locks him irrevocably into an institution which has no place in the productive sphere and is thus essentially removed from the mainstream of history. "Beggars, priests, functionaries; institutionalized and regulated poverty!" ("¡Mendigos, curas, empleados; la pobreza instituida y reglamentada!") [p. 33], Caballero sneers. Without the capitalist's material power, Polo's dream of rebelling against bourgeois respectability is nothing more than the futile histrionics of a failed romantic.

---

[10] E. J. Hobsbawm, p. 157.
[11] Montesinos, p. 158.

But Caballero's wealth does not add up to absolute power. He cannot buy what in Spain has not yet come into existence – the viable bourgeois community about which he had dreamed in the barren desert of Chihuahua. History, like the newspaper in Polo's dream, is being written in English. The respectability of the impoverished and stagnant Spanish middle class is a vicious caricature of Spain's past: pretentious conformity to a standard of conspicuous consumption it cannot afford, and slavish loyalty to archaic institutions historically out-moded. Spain's attempt to insert itself into the flow of modern history – the Revolution of 1868 – is anticipated with horror by the fervent traditionalists. "The revolution is coming" ("La revolución viene"), Bringas cries. "I'm glad" ("Me alegro"), replies Caballero. "The throne is falling... Goodbye property, goodbye family, goodbye religion." ("El trono se tambalea... Adiós propiedad, adiós familia, adiós religión.") "I'm glad" ("Me alegro"), he answers. "Communism will come next, then Atheism, the Goddess of Reason, free love..." ("Vendrá también el Comunismo, el Ateísmo, la diosa Razón, el amor libre...") "I'm glad" ("Me alegro") [p. 118], is Caballero's sacrilegious response to this litany of sorrows. Caballero's dream of domesticity is not possible in pre-revolutionary Spanish society. Exercising the prerogative of wealth, he picks and chooses the materials he will need, and departs to construct in France his own private kingdom.

A comparison between the endings of *Tormento* and *La familia de León Roch* is inevitable. Caballero's defiance of bourgeois respectability is a reversal of León Roch's reluctant decision to sacrifice material happiness on the altar of abstract principle. Both León Roch and Caballero go through a process in which the verbal code of the Catholic traditionalists is exposed as vacuous rhetoric that bears no relationship to the actions and the sentiments of the people who repeat on cue their chorus of God, Family, Religion, the Throne and Private Property. Both men are aware that in the battle to impose a hypocritical code of social convention one of the main weapons is this same rethoric, but they react differently to the reified words of the traditionalist discourse. León Roch, the Krausist intellectual, continues to be bound by the absolutist concepts that oppose something called social order to something called anarchy. Even though he despises this same social order as unjust and tyrannical, his belief in the moral authority of an *ideal* social contract prevents him from transgressing the real one: "Let the bold idea of rebellion remain in the mind and go no further. He who is not capable of transforming the world and uprooting its errors, must live by them." ("Quédese en la mente esta rebelión osada y no salga de ella") [p. 975].

There is an obvious explanation for Caballero's ability to formulate a different solution. His success as an entrepreneur in the New World has provided him not only with the material means to rebel but also, and more important – for León Roch is also independently wealthy – with the sense of a world geography that extends beyond the perimeters of an upper-class Catholic Spain. León Roch fears expatriation: "To leave and take shelter in a foreign land!" ("¡Partir y guarecernos en país extranjero!") [p. 975], but for Caballero it is not a question of exile but of reappropriating territory already conquered. "It's back to the frontier for me" ("Allá voy a mis fronteras") [p. 119], he exclaims, to the great consternation of his cousins. Like León Roch, Caballero realizes that the bourgeois ideal of order, peace and social harmony is false coin, but unlike the tortured intellectual, Caballero reacts like the ethical business man that he is, with absolute indignation at the fraud that has been perpetuated upon him: "Order, politics, Religion, morality, family, pure gibberish..." ("Orden, política, Religión, moral, familia, monsergas...") [p. 118].

It is impossible not to follow Amparo and her knight as they journey to France. Will they be happy? And will he marry her in the end? Perhaps. He can also afford to buy respectability, to transform his mistress into a wife. Galdós, the architect of this fascinating world, evidently could not resist rewriting his own endings, and it is not entirely surprising to learn in *Lo prohibido* [p. 287] that León Roch and Pepa Fúcar have followed the path laid down by the valiant Caballero.

The last paragraph sets the stage for *La de Bringas* and forces the reader to return from a contemplation of extra-marital bliss in France to the business at hand: Galdós' obsession with the pomposity and the sheer stupidity of nineteenth-century Spanish society and its ubiquitous social climbers with their obsessive need (and lack of means) to keep up appearances. As if to deliberately undermine one of his few happy endings, Galdós tacks on an additional paragraph that combines the false note of melodrama with the dialogue form of the theatre, thus evoking – and also giving to him the final word – José Ido and the cape and sword suspense of his serial novels. Any satisfaction that we may take in the ending of *Tormento* – the poor orphan girl protected from poverty and a life on the streets or Rosalía's comeuppance – is given a disquieting twist with this sudden reversion from a realist form to that of melodrama. It is as if Galdós wanted to remind the reader exactly why José Ido, like Galdós a successful novelist, has fared so well. He has learned how to give the public what it wants – an escape from reality through a well-constructed and convincing fantasy.

CHAPTER SIX

LA DE BRINGAS: THE MYTH OF PRIVATE AND PUBLIC SPHERES

La de Bringas (1884) marks another step forward in Galdós' literary project of the Contemporary Novels. In the novels immediately following upon *La familia de León Roch* (1878), he turns his attention to the destructive relation between society and individual protagonists without immediate family ties: Isidora Rufete, in *La desheredada,* Máximo Manso in *El amigo Manso* and Felipe Centeno in *El doctor Centeno.* Until *Tormento,* the basic novelistic schema places a socially naive and idealistic protagonist in struggle with an antagonistic society. And in spite of its title, which gains in irony as the novel proceeds, *La familia de León Roch* is also structured according to this formula. Not until *La de Bringas* does Galdós reintroduce the institution of the family as subject rather than background.

Rosalía Bringas is the first of Galdós' protagonists whose personal ambitions are placed within the context of the marriage institution. *La de Bringas* examines the family institution in its role as mediator between individual and social existence. Galdós investigates not society versus the individual, but the social unit of the middle-class family and its moral and economic ties to society; specifically, to the idiosyncratic world of the government functionary.

In order to understand how Galdós has structured the events that occur in the Bringas' domestic saga, the novel must be read as a continuation of *Tormento,* rather than as a completely separate novel. Thus, the realism of life in the Bringas household unfolds against the absence rather than the presence of the ideal of domesticity, for the remnants of this ideal are – along with Amparo – part of the baggage carried off by Caballero to France. What gives *La de Bringas* its unique tone is the absence of any idealistic perspective. We miss the voice of José Ido, optimist, dream maker, sentimentalist. *La de Bringas* also stands apart as one of only two novels – the other is *El doctor Centeno* – from 1878 through the 1880s, in which there is no love interest.

The search for the perfect other, one's mirror image which will complete the half to make a whole is a concept popularized during this period through the sentimental novel as well as the dissemination of the ideas of Goethe, Rousseau, Michelet, Severo Catalina and other apostles of the companionate marriage.[1] Galdós' most complete elaboration of Goethe's theme of elective affinities is *El amigo Manso*, but the idea also appears as a leit-motif in *La familia de León Roch*, *Tormento* and again in *Lo prohibido*. In *La de Bringas*, however, self-creation through romantic love is replaced by self-definition through class status. Romantic love has vanished completely and in its place stands personal ambition and an impelling need to achieve social recognition. This theme has much in common with Isidora Rufete's history in *La desheredada;* but Isidora, warm loving and passionate, is one of Galdós' innocents. She is much more a sister to Pepa Fúcar or to Fortunata, than to the calculating Rosalía Bringas. José F. Montesinos has commented that what is lacking in the *La de Bringas* is Fortunata,[2] but as the story develops, romantic passion is not missed because the struggle between the married couple over control of the family purse takes on the emotional intensity found in any traditional love triangle. Deception, lies, an unfaithful wife, a wronged husband, all the ingredients are there, but for both protagonists, the beloved is a money box.

---

[1] Sophie, created by Rousseau almost as an afterthought in the final chapter of *Emile*, establishes the basic model for man's ideal companion. Both Rousseau and Michelet are quoted continuously in the popular press from the 1850s on. For the importance of Rousseau in Spain, see José F. Montesinos, *Introducción a una historia de la novela en España en el siglo XIX* (Madrid: Castalia, 1955), pp. 280-81 for a list of translations and editions of Rousseau in Spain up to 1850. Of particular interest is the serialized publication of *Emile* in 1850 by *Las Novedades*. See also, Jefferson R. Spell, *Rousseau in the Spanish World before 1833: A Study in Franco-Spanish Literary Relations* (New York: Octagon Books, 1969). Spell demonstrates convincingly that in spite of official censorship, Rousseau was read throughout the Spanish Enlightenment both in editions smuggled into Spain and in pirated Spanish translations published under pseudonyms.

[2] José F. Montesinos, *Galdós*, II (Madrid: Castalia, 1969), p. 202.

Manuel Pez: The World and the Mind of the Bureaucrat

The opening chapter of *La de Bringas* includes the well-known description of the "hair-painting" ("cuadro de pelos"), a horrendous pastiche of angels, fountains, marble and weeping willows, the epitome of bad taste and maudlin sentimentalism (the different types of hair proceed from various family members) of the Isabeline, and mid-Victorian period. The painting is a striking metaphor of the petty bureaucratic mentality, obssessed with counting paper clips – or their nineteenth-century equivalent – while the grand project is lost through loss of perspective. But the painting also serves as both a symbolic and a real link between the private world of the home and the public world of the palace bureaucracy, for it is intended as a gift to the eminent bureaucrat, Bringas' personal friend, don Manuel Pez [p. 128].

Pez's role as Rosalía Bringas' unctuous suitor is relatively unimportant, but he shines in his role as mentor to her husband, Francisco Bringas. He is the perfect bureaucrat, the yardstick against which the reader will judge the weaknesses and strengths of Bringas, the perfect husband. As we observe the bureaucratic machine, we begin to understand the dialectical relationship between the individual and the system of functionaries that produces a cold-blooded and slippery "fish-like" ("pisciforme") social type such as Manuel "Pez" ("fish"). A system that depends on influence and privilege will always produce a Manuel Pez, because the system itself eliminates those who resist becoming "fishes." Galdós will insist upon the reality of this Darwinian law when out of the ashes of the Glorious Revolution of 1868, crawl a multitude of fish-faces to fill up the empty palace.

The compelling seduction of nineteenth-century ideology that idealized family life, was the promise of a refuge from the hardships and social disruptions brought on by industrialization. Logically this dichotomy between work and family is more acute and the idealization of domesticity more enticing in the work of a novelist like Charles Dickens, writing in the 1830s, 40s and 50s and reacting to the horrors of Manchester and the London slums created by displaced rural workers in search of a livelihood. In Spain, the effects of industrialization are felt principally in the North, in Catalonia and the Basque country.³ In Madrid, however, Galdós studies an entrenched burocracy rather than a system of production, showing us how the relation between family life and the state bureaucracy is shaped by the peculiarities of this social sector. There is a symbiotic relationship between work and homelife, rather than the antagonism that exists between capital and labor in the productive sphere. The socializing which takes place in the office is an extension of social gatherings in the home, or rather, the home becomes a place to fulfill professional commitments made in the office.

The gift of the hair-painting underscores to what extent the daily home life of the Bringas family has been invaded by the social relations of the work place. The work-family dichotomy has been all but erased. Rather than a social geography of distance between a vast and threatening public world and a home tightly secured against the evil that exists outside its door, the palace itself is a private refuge. Inside its walls, the community of functionaries resides in a womb-like existence of blissful ignorance, protected like unhatched eggs by the skirts of her majesty, *"la Señora."*

Even though Galdós focusses in at the beginning of the novel on the labyrinth-like architecture of the palace, it is important to underline that neither its physical structure nor its inhabitants function as a microcosm of the nation, Spain, in the same way that the opening description of Leganés in *La desheredada* (or the jail in Dickens' *Little Dorrit*) do function as metaphors for society and its effect upon the human condition. The protective palace walls are like those of a feudal city, and the relationship of its inhabitants to the Spanish monarchy, their feelings of personal loyalty to the figure of the Queen, their desire to serve and render homage in exchange for her protection, reflect the oligarchy's feudal-like dependency upon the state, a result of their inability to create independent and viable sources of capital. Inside the palace, the exploitive ties between a Master and a Servant class are obscured, for all its residents are members of the same "family" and participate – although certainly to varying degrees – in the domestic (state) treasury. It is a closed city: "where the aristocracy, the middle class and the people all mingle together peacefully, the Monarchs have crowned them-

---

³ Raymond Carr, *España 1808-1939* (Barcelona: Ariel, 1969), pp. 260-72.

selves with a true republic..." ("donde alternan pacíficamente aristocracia, clase media y pueblo, es una real república que los Monarcas se han puesto por corona...") [p. 131].

The eyes of the palace denizens, like those of Rosalía Bringas: "...accustomed to look at the world as if it were all an office and the only way they knew how to make a living was from its budget..." ("...acostumbrados a ver el mundo como si todo él fuera una oficina y no se conocieran otros medios de vivir que los del presupuesto...") [p. 171], do not see the existence of the people who live outside the palace and the Queen's protection. Nor can the palace dwellers understand the resentment of the Spanish subjects against a monarchy which does not represent them. The Spanish state has become the private property of the oligarchy. Symptomatic of this appropriation is Pez's complaint that his friends force him to use his influence to assist them in avoiding the payment of custom fees on luxury items passed through the border at Irún by summer vacationers:

> ...to try to protect the state revenue has become quixotesque. It's the most Spanish thing there is, to see the State as a legal thief, a permanent thief, an historical thief.
>
> (...parece quijotería el mirar por la Renta. Es genuinamente español esto de ver en el Estado el ladrón legal, el ladrón permanente, el ladrón histórico...) [p. 194]

One example follows another: free train tickets, the use of government houses in El Escorial for summer vacations, discarded lumber, reams of paper, bottles of ink, even the queen's cast-off clothing reappears in the wardrobes of the functionaries' wives.

Gradually the reader comes to understand the salient characteristics of the government machinery and the bureaucratic mentality: 1) a conception of work as the management of another's labor; 2) a system of advancement through influence rather than merit; 3) the absence of clear-cut limits between state and private property and the assumption that wages will be supplemented by special privileges; and finally, a child-like sense of dependency upon the state because the bureaucrat, like the child, cannot conceive of survival outside the secure world of his sinecure, his place in the bureaucratic hierarchy that is his family.

In spite of his own adeptness at milking the national treasury, Pez cherishes a plan of reform that would solve Spain's problems of bureaucratic waste and inefficiency:

> His ideal was to set up a perfect administrative system with 80 or 90 separate departments. There would be no aspect of national life that would escape the wise tutelage of the State. That way everything would work right. The country didn't know how to think, the country didn't know how to plan, the country was an idiot. So, then, the State had to think and plan for it, because only the State was intelligent.
>
> (Su ideal era montar un sistema administrativo perfecto, con 80 o 90 direcciones generales. Que no hubiera manifestación alguna de la vida nacional que se escapara a la tutela sabia del Estado. Así andaría todo bien. El país no pensaba, el país no obraba, el país era idiota. Era preciso, pues, que el Estado pensase y obrase por él, porque sólo el Estado era inteligente.) [p. 177]

Pez's conception of the State is paternalistic and authoritarian, a "benevolent" dictatorship closer in spirit to the absolutism of Felipe II than to the enlightened monarchy of Carlos III. The ideal relationship between the people and the state is that of tutelage, of serfs to their Lord, or of children to the father. Pez despises "the people" *(el pueblo)* for the same reasons the traditional patriarch despises his wife, his young children and his servants, for their innate weakness and their incapacity to govern themselves.

Significantly, Pez proposes to resolve the nation's problems not by increasing military power – or by amplifying public education – but by extending the long arm of government burocracy into every facet of national life. Pez's ideal state would increase and further institutionalize the power of his own specific sphere of influence. Whether Pez defends or criticizes the state is ultimately irrelevant because, as a successful bureaucrat, he must continue to play by bureaucracy's rules of influence and privilege. Unlike the shortsighted Bringas, Pez is already cultivating friends among the future "Septembristas" of the 1868 Revolution. At the end of the novel, the moral of the story will read: governments may come and go, but the "fishes" of the world are always with us.

Francisco Bringas: The Perfect Husband

Galdós contrasts the pragmatic opportunism of the bureaucrat, Don Manuel Pez, with Francisco Bringas, who rules his domestic kingdom by "Bringas' Laws" ("los principios Bringuísticos"). Bringas' family budget is a model of economy, of the virtue of frugality advocated by moralists since the time of Fray Luis de León. Always stay within your budget, put something aside for a rainy day, and above all, pay cash on the barrel head. "Bringas' rule was to never buy anything unless he could pay cash for it." ("Bringas tenía por sistema no comprar nada sin el dinero por delante") [p. 144].[4]

The money that Bringas hoards in his strongbox, the result of a lifetime of parsimony and sacrifice, has taken on for him fetishistic properties. It is enjoyed not for what it might purchase, future economic security or consumer goods, but for the pleasure to be derived from any icon – a magical object endowed with the power to release feelings of serenity and peace in the worshiper.

Francisco Bringas fails at being a bureaucrat, for the same reason that he hoards his money; he does not understand the modern principle of capital investment. Wealth, in the form of money, cannot increase, cannot even become capital unless it is placed in circulation. This relation between capital investment and profit is mirrored in the world of bureaucracy as the relation between influence (the bureaucrat's capital) and privilege – an increase in the capacity to generate more bureaucratic power. Like capital, influence reaps a profitable return in ratio to the frequency of its circulation, and like capital, the complete circulation cycle of influence includes not only investment (the granting of favors) but also the realization of profit (acceptance of favors). If the bureaucrat's capital

---

[4] J. E. Varey emphasizes that *La de Bringas* is about "the struggle between two different attitudes towards capital." However, it is not entirely correct to say that Bringas is merely acting out antiquated attitudes towards the hoarding of wealth. What Galdós demonstrates is that there is no room in the Spanish economy to realize Doña Cándida's and Rosalía's eminently petty-bourgeois aspiration to invest their money in such a way that: "It would be a sure thing and give a moderate return" ("Que sea una cosa segura y con un producto moderado") [p. 159]. The two middle-class alternatives are non-productive saving equivalent to hoarding (Bringas) or "robbing" the client through usury (the model is Torquemada). Consequently, the middle class is bound not only by its lack of capital, but also by the lack of means to accumulate capital. See Varey, "Francisco Bringas: nuestro buen Thiers," *Anales Galdosianos*, I (1966), 63-69.

(his influence) is to increase, the circulation cycle must be constantly repeated. Manuel Pez and his cohorts understand this principle, and they possess a mental ledger in which all personal relationships are incorporated into columns of credit and debit. Pez's friend comments:

> I owed him [Pez] some favors; but he owed me some bigger ones. He wanted, then, to put me equally in his debt by taking me in person to visit the head official of the Treasury [Bringas] so that his recommendation would be that much more explicit and effective.
>
> (Yo le debía [a Manuel Pez] algunos favores; pero los que él me debía a mí eran de mayor importancia. Quiso, pues, nivelar mi agradecimiento con el suyo, llevándome en persona a ver al oficial primero del Patrimonio [a Bringas] para que fuera así la recomendación más expresiva y eficaz.) [p. 135]

The bureaucrat whose livelihood depends upon the brokerage of influence must necessarily incorporate the private realm of friendship into the relationships of bureaucratic power. Bringas understands the dynamics of influence-peddling enough to encourage his wife's assiduous attentions to their honored guest, on the frequent occasions of Pez's visits. Nevertheless, he rejects González Bravo's offer of a provincial governorship because he prefers: "his tranquility and the obscure way of life that afforded him such happiness." ("su tranquilidad y aquel vivir obscuro en que era tan feliz.") [p. 152].

Unlike most of Galdós' characters, Bringas demonstrates a rare talent for garnering satisfaction from the fabric of daily existence. More than a refuge, family life is an on-going project in which he participates fully. He is not above taking a hand in the kitchen, his recipe for *gazpacho* is famous. He is the neighborhood Mr. Fix-It, whose motto is "waste not, want not." Like Fray Luis de León's "perfect wife," he is able to find treasure: "...so to speak, from among the sweepings of his doorstep." ("...a manera de dezir, de entre las barreduras de su portal.")[5]

Bringas' ability to enjoy his daughter's society is also revealing. He plays with her because the game of ordering and classifying

---

[5] Luis de León, *La perfecta casada* (Chicago: University of Chicago Press, 1903), p. 38.

ribbons and bottle-tops satisfies both their collector's instincts, but he also plays the role of teacher and parent who has confidence in the values and habits he seeks to impart. This scene, which comes in Chapter XL towards the end of the novel, provides an important dimension because in it, Galdós portrays the unique pleasure to be derived from the intimacy enjoyed in the controlled privacy of the home:

> The two of them... left to themselves, spent the entire afternoon sitting on the floor, taking out objects and classifying them, and then putting them away again very carefully.
>
> (Los dos... sin testigos se pasaron toda la tarde sentados en el suelo, sacando los objetos y clasificándolos, para volver a guardarlos después con mucho cuidado.) [p. 203]

It is significant that the creativity of their play does not depend on material wealth, but rather on the similarity of the players' tastes, the compatability of their characters and their mutual affection. The contented father would seem to have realized, although with his daughter rather than with his wife, Caballero's (and León Roch's)[6] dream of domestic happiness: "intense family sentiment, a desire to seek out comfortable obscurity without fancy trappings, to experience affection and an orderly and legal life." ("el sentimiento intenso de la familia, la ambición de la comodidad obscura y sin aparato, de los afectos y de la vida ordenada y legal") [p. 174]. This scene with father and daughter becomes a tantalizing taste of what might have been – if things had been different. With society's upper-crust removed to the stylish watering-holes of France, the Bringas children are left undisturbed to benefit from an unselfconscious rubbing of elbows with the townspeople on the banks of the Manzanares. The delicate and raquitic Isabelita enjoys a reprieve from the convulsions that threaten her life, and her vigorous little brother "was bursting with health" ("se puso a reventar de sano") [p. 202]. Is it any wonder, then, that Galdós critics have been openly censorious

---

[6] León Roch's dream of domestic bliss is described as "a life that is neither very secluded nor very public, in an attractive hideaway but without hiding, far away from all the noise and bustle, but not inaccessible to select friends." ("vida ni muy apartada ni muy pública, en un dulce retiro sin esquivez, lejos del bullicio, mas no inaccesible a los amigos discretos...") [p. 816].

of the wife who would interject into such a happy home the apple of discord in the form of her own selfish ambition?

The Rebellion of Rosalía Bringas

The critics have tended to interpret *La de Bringas* as a novel about "Rosalía's moral degradation,"[7] even imposing upon her the burden of symbolizing the Isabeline monarchy and by extension, the entire spectrum of Spanish society.[8] Montesinos calls her: "a hateful woman, perhaps the most hateful that Galdós ever invented." ("una mujer odiosa, la más odiosa que quizás inventara Galdós.")[9] And Joaquín Casalduero, although more charitable, maintains that she fails in "...all of her duties as a mother, as a wife." ("...todos sus deberes de madre, de esposa.")[10] Much of this censure results from an unquestioning acceptance of her husband by the critics as a man who embodies the domestic virtues and who is perceived as a victim of his wife's inordinate love for finery and social status. In addition, Rosalía commits the unpardonable sin of cuckolding her husband, not, like the great heroines of Tolstoy and Stendhal, for passion, but for profit.

Nevertheless, if we perceive the husband as his wife's victim, we must also accept uncategorically Francisco Bringas' exercise of authority in the home. The exercise of power between Bringas and his wife mirrors the paternalistic authoritarian model envisaged by Pez as the ideal relation between the state and the people. If it is an exaggeration to say that Rosalía represents all of Madrid society, the Bringas household is indeed a microcosm of bureaucratic proliferation. The mistress of the household lives every moment of family life governed by "...the prodigious quantity of rules which flowed unendingly from that inexhaustable source of domestic legislation" ("...las prolijas reglas que afluían sin cesar de aquel inagotable manantial de legislación doméstica") [p. 174].

---

[7] Nicholas G. Round, "Rosalía Bringas' Children," *Anales Galdosianos*, VI (1971), p. 43.

[8] Chad C. Wright, "Imagery of Light and Darkness in *La de Bringas*," *Anales Galdosianos*, XXIII (1978), p. 5. Also, Peter A. Bly, "The Use of Distance in Galdós' *La de Bringas*," *Modern Language Review*, 69 (1974), p. 89: "...the palace itself is a microcosm of the greater entity, Madrid."

[9] Montesinos, Galdós, II, p. 98.

[10] Joaquín Casalduero, *Vida y obra de Galdós* (Madrid: Gredos, 1974), p. 82.

Bringas is not, however, any exception to a generally more tolerant rule. As the historian Hobsbawm has noted:

> ...the one-family household was both a patriarchal autocracy and a microcosm of the sort of society which the bourgeoisie as a class (or its theoretical spokesman) denounced and destroyed: *a hierarchy of personal dependence.* [11] (my underlining)

Although the rhetoric of the period emphasized the wife's "spiritual" authority in the home, the moral authority of the *ángel del hogar* did not traditionally include any participation in material decisions. Bringas' iron control over household expenditures: "...that sovereign function, which is the most obvious attribute of domestic authority..." ("...aquella soberana función, que es el atributo más claro de la autoridad doméstica...") [p. 166], is reinforced by a daily routine of relentless investigation into his wife's managerial practices.

In order to maintain his position of absolute authority during his illness, Bringas converts his customary scoldings into a public chastisment of his wife's shortcomings:

> ...he would order her to come before him, and once there, with the gestures if not the piercing gaze of the implacable judge, he would make ostentatious and public show (Torres or some other friend was usually present) of the extent of his domestic sovereignty.
>
> (...mandábala venir a su presencia, y allí, con ademanes, ya que no con miradas de juez inexorable, hacía pública ostentación (solía estar presente Torres o algún otro amigo) de su soberanía doméstica.) [p. 187]

By punishing his wife in front of their friends, Bringas draws his own map of private and public domains. Rosalía's humiliating chastisement negates for her the existence of the home as a private refuge from the oppressive vigilance of public opinion. The right to privacy, then, is not only a question of class and the economic power necessary to gain access to privately controlled physical space; it is also a question of male-female relationships of power and dependency within the institution of the bourgeois family – in

---

[11] E. J. Hobsbawm, *The Age of Capital* (New York: Mentor, 1979), pp. 261-62.

the words of Virginia Woolf, the woman's need for "a room of one's own" within patriarchal nineteenth-century society.

Like the criminal who flees the authority of the police, Rosalía contrives to live a clandestine life, evading her husband's importunate surveillance. But unlike the recourses of the public criminal, there is no where to hide within the physical and social confines of matrimony. The only sure evasive tactic is systematic hypocrisy:

> ...the faithful wife would remain at his side, playing her role with the skill acquired during so many years of hypocrisy. But she longed desperately for something else for herself besides mere existence and good health; she wanted a taste, even if it were only a little one, of something she had never had; freedom, and to leave behind, if only symbolically, the narrow constraints of that shameful penury.
>
> (...la esposa fiel seguiría a su lado, haciendo su papel con aquella destreza que le habían dado tantos años de hipocresía. Pero para sí anhelaba ardientemente algo más que vida y salud; deseaba un poco, un poquito siquiera de lo que nunca había tenido, libertad, y salir, aunque sólo fuera por modo figurado, de aquella estrechez vergonzante.) [p. 180]

Since Galdós is careful to provide us with an abundance of monetary facts, we are able to evaluate fairly precisely the family's economic limitations by measuring Bringas' salary against a variety of socio-economic yardsticks. In *Tormento*, we learn that Bringas earns 20,000 *reales* [p. 89], more than three times the 6,000 earned by the nightwatchman and streetcleaners [p. 198], but less than half the 50,000 *reales* enjoyed by the prosperous Manuel Pez [p. 155]. Even more revealing are the figures found in the column of expenditures. Rosalía's friend Milagros, the Marquesa de Tellerías, owes 10,000 *reales* for an intimate supper party, 2,000 to her dressmaker for one gown, not including the fabric, and 1,500 for its trim [p. 158].[12]

---

[12] R. Carr, citing the novelist Valera, states that the decade preceding the Revolution of 1868 witnessed the importation of French luxury items and the imposition of a "cosmopolitan," i.e. French style of fashion among the Spanish aristocracy and the haute bourgeoisie. According to Carr, the middle class was comprised of families with a maximum income of 5,000 to 8,000 *reales* in the year 1857. M. Tuñón de Lara places the salary range for middle-class teachers and employees of commercial establishments at from 7,000 to 10,000 *reales* in the year

It is within this explicit social context that Rosalía, accompanied by the Marquesa, falls from grace in the shop of Sobrino Hermanos and purchases (on credit) a Parisian cape of velvet and corduroy worth 1,700 *reales* or close to 8 & 1/2 % of the family's yearly cash income. This incident occurs early in the novel (Chapter X), and Galdós' masterful description of the act of purchase illuminates many of the emotional elements inherent in the relationship of the consumer with any expensive commodity.

First of all, the purchase of the cape had been preceded by a habit of economy sustained under duress and experienced as constant and painful deprivation. This feeling of deprivation had been heightened by the custom of shopping with an apparently wealthy friend whose authoritative manner with the shop attendants awes the timid Rosalía much in the same way that Manuel Pez's voice and attire seduce her with their insinuation of power. She can demonstrate her equal social status with the Marquesa by imitating her friend. She wants, just once, to sign her name with a flourish to an enormous bill, to say, "I think I'll take it," to say, *"yes."* The intensity of her desire to possess the fabulous cape transforms her into a state of exquisite physical sensibility:

> Rosalía began to feel a coldness in her chest, a burning at her temples, and the nerve ends in her shoulders were prickling so with the imagined sensation of the cape's weight and touch that she felt as if she were wearing it.
>
> (Rosalía hubo de sentir frío en el pecho, ardor en las sienes, y en sus hombros los nervios le sugirieron tan al vivo la sensación del contacto y peso de la manteleta, que creyó llevarla puesta.) [p. 143]

The first shy kiss of two impassioned lovers could not be more erotic.

The narrator explains Rosalía's passion for clothes in accordance with the folklore of the period, that most women are born with an instinct for adornment that necessitates some form of social repression, since women are not capable themselves of controlling their

---

1857, and he specifies that neither day wages nor salaries varied greatly during the following dacade, in spite of an abrupt and substantial rise in basic food prices. See *La España del siglo XIX* (Paris: Librería Española, 1971), pp. 152, 183.

instincts.[13] One taste of the forbidden fruit and they say goodbye to all decorum [p. 141]. But Rosalía's feelings toward her finery: "those bits and pieces of her heart" ("aquellos pedazos de su corazón") [p. 161], are much more complex. Her wardrobe receives the care and enthusiasm she cannot feel for her husband who has given her four children without ever inspiring in her sexual desire.

> That milksop had made her the mother of four children, one of whom had died in infancy. She loved them dearly, and thanks to that, the lively appreciation which she had come to feel for the milksop continued to grow... She wished him long life and health...
>
> (Aquel muñeco hízola madre de cuatro hijos, uno de los cuales había muerto en la lactancia. Ella los quería entrañablemente, y gracias a esto, iba creciendo el vivo aprecio que el muñeco había llegado a inspirarle... Deseaba que el tal viviese y tuviera salud...) [p. 180]

In effect, this is a description of what was considered the optimal emotional bond between a married couple of the period, tied together by economic necessity, love for their children and in the absence of sexual desire, at least some form of respect or affection born of habit and shared experience.[14] But Rosalía's dresses are

---

[13] For example: "that feminine passion that causes more destruction in the world than revolutions" ("esta pasión mujeril que hace en el mundo más estragos que las revoluciones") [p. 142]; "...hurrying from shop to shop under the intoxicating influence of the drunkeness produced by new clothes" ("...corriendo de tienda en tienda, bajo la acción intoxicante de una embriaguez de trapos") [p. 146]; "...her passion for luxury had led her, unconsciously, to a hazardous terrain" ("...su pasión de lujo la había llevado, insensiblemente, a un terreno erizado de peligros") [p. 151]; "Unable to resist the temptation... letting herself be carried along by her burning need" ("Sin poder resistir la tentación... dejándose llevar de su apasionado afán") [p. 168].

[14] The asexuality of the *ángel del hogar* is consistently emphasized in the many magazine articles that pontificate on the virtue of female self-denial. The formula is womanly tenderness devoid of sexual passion. For one example see Antonio Rodó y Casanova, no title, año XXVII, núm. 8 (26 febrero 1877) *El Correo de la Moda:* "Woman, born and educated for the home, and man's inseparable companion, should not aspire to engage in ruinous competition, nor to vague ideals as senseless as they are unachievable in this life... if her submission as a wife is great, later, as a mother, it is all-encompassing..." ("La mujer, nacida y criada para el hogar, e inseparable compañera del hombre, no debe aspirar a una competencia funesta, ni a vagas idealidades tan faltas de sentido como irrealizables en la vida... si su sumisión es grande como esposa, es más tarde inmensa como madre...") The author goes on to enumerate the many satisfactions to be derived from the wife's

even more than a substitution for sexual fulfillment. Her finery is also a visible manifestation of a new precarious and secret autonomy.

Until the moment when Rosalía gains access to the family treasure, her plan of emancipation from her husband's tutelage is limited to vague feelings of dissatisfaction accompanied by even stronger ones of guilt as a result of her growing intimacy with Pez, even though she has kept their friendship within the limits of decorum. The circumstances which permit Rosalía to penetrate into the mysteries of the strongbox are important to our understanding of the novel as a whole, because they constitute a confutation of the naturalistic reading that interprets Rosalía history as a tale of inexorable moral degeneration.[15] Unlike Emma Bovary, or Rosamond Vincy in *Middlemarch*, who are capable of destroying their husbands with a terrifying cynicism, Rosalía Bringas oscillates between a desire to satisfy her own ambitions and the guilty realization that her husband has provided for her and her children to the best of his ability [p. 183]. When Bringas suffers a relapse, Rosalía feels pity and concern. This reversal of fortune acts to bring out the best in her character and she dedicates herself night and day to her husband's comfort. It is this demonstration of tenderness which inspires Bringas to turn over to her the key to the money box.

Galdós has built up a great deal of suspense, and the reader is not defrauded. We find that Bringas has scraped together over the years more than 20,000 *reales*, the equivalent of one year's salary. Rosalía can now consider how she might effectively exert some semblance of control over the family's destiny. Although she still feels the effect of long years of submission, her husband's unaccustomed praise and her own belief that she could manage more productively the family property combine to rationalize the loan of 5,000 *reales*, exactly one quarter of the treasure, to her friend, the Marquesa.

At this point, Galdós moves definitively away from what might have been a Zolaesque treatment of women's fascination for luxury

---

submission to her husband and children's needs, among them "that virtuous love which warms but does not burn, which does not flare up but which never dies..." ("el mismo amor honrado que calienta pero no abrasa, que no deslumbra, pero que jamás se apaga...").

[15] For a comprehensive discussion of the nineteenth-century medical concept of physical and moral degeneration see George F. Drinka, *The Birth of Neurosis: Myth, Malady and the Victorians* (New York: Simon & Schuster, 1984), *passim*.

goods. The image of the consuming woman out of control (like the sexually insatiable woman) is the diabolical other of the *ángel del hogar*. At one extreme we have Zola's *Nana*, at the other, Dickens' *Little Dorrit*. Galdós breaks with the literary stereotype, because Rosalía is capable, like a man, of regaining her lost self-control. Unlike the fatal trajectory of events in *L'Assommoir* or *Nana*, Rosalía's plunge into the world of conspicuous consumption – her purchase of the cape – had *not* been followed by more expensive and numerous purchases. Rather she had attempted, by robbing Peter to pay Paul, to incorporate the purchase of the cape into a fairly realistic assessment of the family's financial situation.

Since Rosalía's obsession with dress is motivated by more than a desire to experience pleasure, it comes as no surprise that she does not plunder the domestic treasury when she does gain control over it. Rosalía is aware that social status is defined by the capacity to conform to a standard of fashionable respectability: "...she considered that her decorum and her contact with important people imposed upon her unavoidable duties." ("...consideraba que su decoro y el contacto con altas personas le imponían deberes ineludibles") [p. 154]. Class status permits access to power, which is, in turn, the prerequisite for entering into the game of power. Her wardrobe has become a kind of capital investment for this woman who longs to play "the woman behind the man," seeing in Manuel Pez a possible Bonaparte to her Josephine [p. 155].

Unlike the purchase of the luxurious Parisian cape, Rosalía's loan to the Marquesa fulfills a different need, although both acts demonstrate her longing to exercise control over her life. But the loan is connected with a desire to earn money, not to spend it, with an ambition of entrepreneurship. She wishes to enter the public sphere through the male entrance that opens into the world of finances, rather than entering through the lady's side door that opens into a sphere restricted to consumption. Prevented, however, by both her sex and her economic circumstances from entering directly into the creation of wealth, Rosalía has developed the characteristics of the ambitious but insecure social climber. What provides the comic element in *La de Bringas* is Galdós' caustic depiction of the Madrid society which Rosalía has set out to conquer.

The privatization of social existence is an important factor in the creation of bourgeois class-consciousness. One of the emblematic forms of this privatization is the social function in the home. Even though the Marquesa may serve only the shank end of the ham, Rosalía is flattered by an invitation to her soirée. But the power to carve out a privatized social space for the elite only begins with the social use of the private home. Of even greater importance to the *arriviste* mentality is the ability to penetrate the sacred space appropriated from the public domain by the economically and socially privileged. The custom of renting a box at the theatre, for example, guarantees permanent access to a public function, but more important, assures a separation between the private box and the public gallery. The enjoyment of the spectacle in the private space is derived from the existence of the people in the gallery. Their location at a distance from the enclosed box testifies to the elite who they are *not*, thus reassuring them of who they are.

Galdós criticizes the pretentiousness of Madrid's precarious middle-class through the voice of Agustín Caballero, who condemns the practice of theatre subscriptions as "immoral, a negation of the home" ("una immoralidad, la negación del hogar") [p. 81]. The Galdosian ideal of domesticity is a standard of comfort that prefers "what is useful to what is decorative" ("lo útil a lo brillante") [p. 75], that is, consumption for personal use rather than the conspicuous consumption of the *nouveau riche* designed to advertise one's economic and social rank. In Madrid, the underdevelopment of the middle and upper class manifests itself in the eating of endless *cocidos* in order to finance the façade of bourgeois respectability. The sacrifice of the children's diet, health and general welfare on the altar of fashion – a constant theme in Galdós' Contemporary Novels – is in turn a reflection of the underdevelopment of the values inherent in the ideology of the child-oriented bourgeois family. The essence of the bourgeois domestic ideal lies in a belief in the social autonomy of the nuclear family unit, structured around the child's physical and moral education.

In *Tormento*, Caballero describes his own picture of family life when he insists to Amparo that: "They would only have a few very close friends, they wouldn't give big dinners, everyone could eat in their own house..." ("Tendrían pocos pero buenos amigos, no darían comilonas, cada cual que comiera en su casa...") [p. 81]. In the Bringas household, the idea of the pleasure to be derived from a quiet evening at home with the family is manifestly absent. Rosalía describes the flat on the Costanilla de los Ángeles as "a parked carriage" ("un coche parado") [p. 19], an apt metaphor that expresses succinctly her social aspirations – to live in the public eye, but effectively protected from the lower classes by her privileged status, symbolized in the private and exclusive space of the upper-class carriage.

Galdós brings into comic relief the inadequacy of Madrid's hybrid elite in a scene towards the end of *Tormento* in which Bringas discovers that the sacred space of the Royal Palace has been violated by sinister forces that have dared to abscond with his brand-new overcoat. "It doesn't seem possible that they would permit that kind of people to attend such majestic ceremonies." ("Parece mentira que cierta clase de gente se meta en esas solemnidades augustas") [p. 118], he complains. The lack of definitive class contours produces instability and uncertainty in the means by which the upper class defines itself through the exclusion of "outsiders," the *pueblo* (the people), the masses, the lower classes.

During the tedious heat of the long Madrid summer, the aristocracy and the haute-bourgeoisie abandon the city, and Rosalía's solitude becomes the prison of isolation as the streets are taken over by the *pueblo:*

> When she saw the inhabitants of the poorer neighborhoods in possession of the sidewalks: the men in shirtsleeves, the women skimpily dressed, the little kids half naked, playing in the gutter streams, she thought she had stumbled into a Moorish town, such being her idea of African cities.
>
> (Cuando veía a los habitantes de los barrios más populares posesionados de las aceras: ellos en mangas de camisa, ellas muy a la ligera, los chiquillos medio desnudos, enredando en el arroyo, creía hallarse en un pueblo de moros, según la idea que tenía de las ciudades africanas.) [p. 199]

The "people," like the "noble worker" or the "noble savage" can only be idealized from the safe distance of a secure status of privilege. The distinction between civilization and barbarism is a class distinction. Rosalía pulls back her skirts in horror, for her sense of class identity has been overwhelmed by the commanding presence of the lower classes. Madrid, without her circle of friends to vindicate her place in society, is Africa. Her determination to maintain her social pretensions increases with her terror of being forced to return to the *ancien régime* of "Bringas' Laws." She decides to act.

But before Rosalía can offer herself to Manuel Pez, she must make the moral adjustment that comes with placing herself on the market.[16] She learns to disregard the social façades of her male acquaintances, and to calculate their worth in the only true measure of value, hard cash [p. 205]. Two additional lessons must be learned in order to prepare herself for her new career. She must give up the romantic ideal of the male protector in order to avoid the emotional involvement that might lead to her own exploitation. Pez himself teaches her this lesson: "Men! She had had the illusion that at least some of them knew how to act like gentlemen... It was humiliating enough to sell oneself; but to give oneself away for nothing!..." ("¡Qué hombres! Ella había tenido la ilusión de figurarse a algunos con proporciones caballerescas... Ignominia grande era venderse; pero ¡darse de balde!...") [p. 211]. And we can assume from the concluding hints of the narrator that Rosalía has learned another necessary lesson. Indeed, she probably remembered her husband's advice: never deal in credit.

The Revolution of 1868

La de Bringas ends with the confrontation scene between Rosalía Bringas and Refugio, and a final chapter in which the narrator reappears and from his vantage point within the newly-established government of the September Revolution, sums up for the reader the history of the Bringas family. Galdós' assessment of the Revolution of 1868 is inserted into his analysis of the relation between individual existence and the collective experience and the narration of each; or in other words, the relation between private historiography (the genres of autobiography or memoirs) and public historiography (History or official biographies).

Galdós reinforces the basic structure of the memoir in *La de Bringas* by fleshing out the narrator's personal biography. Although he is never identified by name, he is a man of property, Pez's confidante and an intimate friend of Máximo Manso (author of his

---

[16] Rosalía's experience with Pez will force her to readjust a highly inflated assessment of the market value of her sexual favors: "aren't I giving him a treasure for a mere pittance..." ("no le doy un tesoro por una miseria...") [p. 210], an assessment derived from the erroneous premise that she is living in an economy of scarcity.

own autobiography). Thus, the narrator-witness is firmly established as the source – although necessarily limited to the narrator's personal perspective – of a history that is oral rather than written, and personal or private rather than public and official. Even though it is a private history based on the science of *chismografía* (gossip-mongering), it is a history documented by facts: it is not fiction. Galdós employs the framework of the memoir to create the atmosphere of verisimilitude required by the realist genre. He goes to a fair amount of trouble to establish the narrator as a fictional character who is a credible although cynical witness of the novel's events, so it comes as a shock to find that the narrator bids the reader farewell by signing his name with the linguistic signature of our romantic (and very unreliable) scribe, Don José Ido del Sagrario: "Frankly, naturally, I was very sorry to see them leave." ("Francamente, naturalmente, los vi salir con pena.")[17]

The sudden introduction of Ido's voice must cause the reader a momentary sense of confusion, since its presence seems both arbitrary and contradictory. We have no reason not to assume one single and continuous narrative perspective, nor is there the slightest possibility that the narrator – intimate friend of the powerful Manuel Pez – could also be the debt-ridden and harried author, José Ido. At the same time, it is even more doubtful that Galdós would

---

[17] Galdós makes sure that the reader is aware of Ido's linguistic idiosyncracy by having Refugio say in *Tormento:* "frankly, naturally, as Ido would say" ("francamente, naturalmente, como dice Ido") [p. 39]. Michael Nimetz comments on the reappearance of Ido's voice in his book *Humor in Galdós* (New Haven: Yale University Press, 1968), p. 94. He states that our knowledge of Ido precludes the assumption that he is, or has been, the narrator. This is true; however, we cannot therefore conclude, as so many critics tend to do when faced with an apparently inexplicable element in Galdós' narrative structure, that his insertion of Ido's voice is equivalent to an authorial mistake or lapse. Nimetz' statement that "except for a few seemingly insignificant 'yo's,' (I's) *La de Bringas* reads like a third-person narrative" also ignores the fleshing-out of the narrator-agent (to use Nimetz' own apt phrase). It is of structural importance that the narrator is Pez's intimate friend, for he demonstrates his own fish-like characteristics by emerging from the revolutionary stream as a replacement for none other than Bringas himself. His job is "to administer everything that had belonged to the Crown" ("administrar todo lo que había pertenecido a la Corona") [p. 222]. In effect, he has replaced Bringas in his position as "head deputy of the Treasury Department" ("oficial primero del Patrimonio") [p. 135]. It would seem that he had also replaced Bringas in the domestic sphere, at least on a temporary and *ad hoc* basis. "She wanted to give me proof once more of her calamitous friendship, but I hastened to put an end to the affair..." ("Quiso repetir las pruebas de su ruinosa amistad, mas yo me apresuré a ponerles punto...") [p. 223].

use Don José's linguistic tic unwittingly. Retracing the final chapter, we find this illuminating comment: "The new sketches of this lady [Rosalía] have not yet appeared in our inkwell." ("Las nuevas trazas de esta señora no están aún en nuestro tintero") [p. 223]. Galdós also pays tribute to Ido's function as a literary alter-ego when he discusses the genesis of *Fortunata y Jacinta* in his own *Memorias:*

> At the end of the summer, I returned to Madrid and I had barely arrived home when I received a pleasant visit from my friend, that distinguished gentleman, Don José Ido del Sagrario, who told me the news about Juanito Santa Cruz and his wife Jacinta...
>
> (Expirando el verano, volví a Madrid y apenas llegué a mi casa cuando recibí la grata visita de mi amigo el insigne varón don José Ido del Sagrario, el cual me dió la noticia de Juanito Santa Cruz y su esposa Jacinta...) [18]

José Ido's reappearance, or rather, the fusion of the two narrative voices into one, is both a statement about the creative process and an oblique comment on the "Glorious Revolution." José Ido represents the romantic element in Galdós psychology that cannot be easily integrated into a unified and coherent interpretation of contemporary nineteenth-century Spain. In order to more efficiently analyze this romantic tendency within himself, Galdós exteriorizes and objectifies it, and José Ido – self-confessed romantic – is born. Ido's novels are the apex of a degenerate romanticism: passion cheapened into sentimentalism, idealism brought down to the level of Sunday School preaching. Ido interprets reality through the prism of a moralizing optimism and the result is simply bad literature.

Thus, the intrusion of José Ido's linguistic signature into the text becomes a final exclamation point attached to Galdós' statement about the inadequacy of the Glorious Revolution. Realism as a literary convention may be art imitating life, but life also "imitates" art, the same bad art that helps to shape the values and consciousnesses of the people who produce it, and who must now live with the consequences of their poverty of spirit and narrowness of vision. The insertion of Ido's voice also serves to remind the reader that any narrative: oral or written, private or public, *chismografía* or historiography, will always be mediated by the inevitably subjective

---

[18] Quoted in Montesinos, *Galdós*, II, p. 201.

viewpoint of the author's consciousness. With the creation of José Ido, Galdós has built into the structure of the realist novel the demythification of realism's ideal, that is, the author's posture of objectivity.

And so, when history is transmitted through the mentality of a Manuel Pez, it becomes "a never-ending stream of personal anecdotes" ("un sinfín de anécdotas personales") [p. 164]. If the writing of history, historiography, is the public record of that part of the collective experience that transcends the passage of time, the essence of the anecdote is precisely the opposite. The anecdote is defined by its temporal and spacial uniqueness, its lack of integration into a larger pattern of social forces. Spanish history cannot be written until Spain is capable of producing an historian able to perceive and interpret events in relation to the socio-economic forces that shape the collective destiny. Until that moment, the collective experience will be written as personal anecdote, interpreted and transmitted by the biased and opportunistic Peces and distorted by the false optimism of the Idos.

Rosalía Bringas has gained some insight into the relation between personal idealism and the reality of her specific economic circumstances. "Necessity, she said to herself, is what molds character" ("La necesidad – se dijo – es la que hace los caracteres") [p. 204]. But she wears her middle-class mentality like blinders and is incapable of recognizing or sympathizing with these same sentiments if they originate from a different class perspective: "Make sure I have food and clothing, and you won't have any complaints about me," ("Asegúrame la comida, la ropa, y nada tendrás que decir de mí,") [p. 45], exclaims Refugio. "Have you eaten your fill, are you well dressed? Fine then, now you've got time for morality." ("¿Estás bien comida, bien vestida? Pues ahora... venga moralidad") [p. 205], Rosalía thinks bitterly as she contemplates selling her much-prized virtue.

The characterization of Refugio in the confrontation scene with Rosalía Bringas causes us to regret that we have not been permitted to know her better. Refugio will reappear in *Fortunata y Jacinta*, but she will be sadly reduced from the fiery young woman who responds to Rosalía's arrogance with an unbreakable pride and a penetrating intelligence that will not be blinded by the other woman's self-satisfied posturing. Refugio knows what she is and how society perceives her, and she also knows that her place in society is a result of the actions of others who presume to be morally better than she. Therein lies her strength and the moral outrage that sustains her:

> First-class whores (is what I'd like to tell them), I don't pull the wool over anybody's eyes; I live by my work. But you women deceive half the planet, and you're trying to cut your silk dresses out of the poor people's bread.
>
> (Grandísimas... (les digo para mí), yo no engaño a nadie; yo vivo de mi trabajo. Pero vosotras engañáis a medio mundo y queréis hacer vestidos de seda con el pan del pobre.) [p. 215]

It is not only Refugio's eloquence that persuades. The reader knows – having journeyed to the end of this history – that an endless line of unpaid seamstresses, shopkeepers, and servants such as Amparo and Refugio, support and maintain the *appearance* of wealth that constitutes bourgeois respectability and forms the class barrier separating Refugio and Rosalía Bringas.

Not until this scene are we permitted to see the coming revolution from a different class perspective, and to know what the revolution may have signified to certain sectors of society living outside the protective custody of the Queen. Hope is mixed with a desire for revenge. Refugio exclaims: "...we'll get even with her now... there'll be freedom, liberties" ("...ya le ajustarán las cuentas... habrá libertad, libertades") [p. 216]. But the door that has opened so briefly to reveal deep resentment against the Spanish monarchy slams quickly shut. Refugio will take personal revenge when she uses the powerful weapon of gossip to inform Rosalía that the Marquesa has laughed at her behind her back, and called her *cursi* (vulgar or pretentious): a bitter wound and effective revenge, but one that lacks historical transcendence. The revolt of an individual does not constitute change.

The revolutionaries themselves are seen only from the eyes of the palace denizens. They are not the embodiment of evil, the dreaded horde of *sans-culottes*, the atheistic communistic masonic horned-devils that populated the nightmares of the traditionalists. But neither are they the Byronic heroes that inhabit the landscapes of Delacroix. They are merely "unfortunate people... the salt of the earth" ("unos pobrecillos... unos angelotes") [p. 211].

If History is the record of those moments which transcend the anecdotal because they change or influence the course of events, in the nineteenth century the historiographical subject also tends to take on an aura of transcendence. But even though the narrator is writing his history sixteen years after the Glorious Revolution, the narrative perspective remains frozen in the quotidian, in the immediacy of the present moment. The Revolution of 1868 is reduced to one more anecdote – another story in the abundant supply of gossip that circulates from café to salon, from parliament to bedroom. History does not exist in Spain; there is only *chismografía*. Without the means to create a new future, Spain is condemned to the prison of a never-ending present. The revolutionaries, seen in the light of Madrid's morning sunshine, are neither avenging angels nor redeemers. They are only "one of us," *buena gente*, mediocre. At best they are – like José Ido – that romantic element in all of us that must be shunted aside when daily life is taken in hand.

The concluding chapter constitutes a bitter indictment of the ineptitude of the revolutionary struggle in Spain. The Septembrists are incapable of managing the practical aspects of the revolution and must rely on political opportunists like Pez and his cohorts to guide them through the bureaucratic maze. They will soon be submerged into the bureaucratic machinery that becomes a kind of *deus ex machina*, chewing up well-intentioned but ingenuous revolutionaries and spewing out functionaries with "fish faces" ("caras pisciformes") [p. 222].

Rosalía overthrows her own private tyrant. But her arrogance and her identification with the power of the throne insulate her from any sympathy for the revolutionary project, even though her personal experience of poverty and patriarchal repression has its roots in Spain's political and economic bankruptcy. The revolutionaries' attempt to collectively restructure the state is seen as "social disorder" by Rosalía. Her reaction to Refugio's audacity typifies the reactionary's solution of the iron fist to the problem of rebellion and revolution:

> For that kind of boldfacedness... that shameless disrespect with which you talk about ladies whose shoes you aren't fit to tie, they should tear out that viper's tongue of yours and then whip you the full length of the public streets, naked from your waist up, like that, and that, and that...

> (Por ese descaro... por ese cinismo con que tú hablas de señoras cuyo zapato no mereces descalzar, se te debía arrancar esa lengua de víbora y luego azotarte públicamente por las calles, desnuda de medio cuerpo arriba, así, así así...) [p. 215]

But Rosalía does possess one characteristic which defines both her own future and that of the revolution. Her sense of opportunity reflects the political opportunism of those "fish" who will ultimately come to control the revolutionary process. The revolution fails in part because of its leaders, who are not the "people" (noble or otherwise) but political hacks forced to rely on an entrenched power interested only in lining its pockets. The collective effort of the revolution will disintegrate into the satisfaction of individual ambition. Rosalía will sell her virtue to build her personal future and the future of the revolution will be sold out.

A private solution to a collective problem can never transcend the level of anecdote. At the end, when Galdós directs the reader to consider, not the future of the revolution, but the future of Rosalía Bringas, he is placing the revolution on the same level of historical significance as that of the personal biography of the Bringas family. Sixteen years may pass, but historical time stands still. The revolution is nothing more than an anecdote told to enliven the evening visit at Doña Cándida's, an anecdote to be told and then forgotten; for ultimately nothing has happened and nothing will change.

CHAPTER SEVEN

LO PROHIBIDO: THE LITERARY CREATION OF AN ANGEL

Lo prohibido is Galdós' third novel since *La familia de León Roch* (1878) to be set in the Restoration. The Centeno-Bringas trilogy turns back to the years preceding the Revolution of 1868, and only *La desheredada* is set in the turbulent period of the first Republic, years during which Spain experiences tremendous upheavals in every facet of national life: suffrage, changes in censorship, the University crisis and the events that lead to the founding of the Institución Libre de Enseñanza (The Free Institute of Teaching) in 1876, and also changes in Spain's anachronistic protective tariffs as well as an influx of British and French capital that will help produce the economic expansion of the late '70s and the '80s.[1]

It is evident in the opening pages of *Lo prohibido* that Galdós has reevaluated the years from the Revolution of 1868 to the Restoration in 1875 as a historic period that leaves few if any traces on Spanish society, an idea which he insists upon at the beginning of *Tormento* when the narrator says: "in that kind of society [the Isabeline], or in this one [the Restoration in 1884], since the change in sixteen years hasn't been very great..." ("en una Sociedad como aquélla, o como ésta, pues la variación en diez y seis años no ha sido muy grande...") [p. 20]. But in spite of the fact that any change has been relatively inconsequential, the failure of the Revolution of 1868 is not equivalent to the absence of revolution. Although the liberal legislation of the First Republic is abolished by the architects

---

[1] See Carr, pp. 374-411.

of the Restoration, the Restoration government is not a return to the pre-revolutionary period, but rather a liberal-conservative reaction and solution to the political instability of the revolutionary years. The intransigence of the neo-Catholics and the extreme homage paid to social conventions likewise stems in part from the reaction to the temporary victory of the revolutionary forces. The historian, Raymond Carr, maintains that the fear of falling again into political chaos resulted in a general feeling that the political institutions of the constitutional monarchy were sacrosanct.[2]

Galdós links *La de Bringas* with *Lo prohibido* temporally through the biography of the narrator-protagonist José María Bueno de Guzmán, who left Madrid in 1868 during González Bravo's caretaker government immediately preceding the September Revolution. Guzmán is a personification of the lack of will or moral anemia that defines the so-called syndrome of *mal de siècle*, the moral-medical trope that came into vogue to explain the inability of the new European bourgeois order to control the social upheavals taking place throughout the nineteenth century. This metaphor of collective moral degeneration will be played off throughout the novel against an image of social progress: the love, marriage and domestic life of Camila and Constantino, who represent a constructive solution to Guzmán's destructive inertia.

Prior to *Lo prohibido*, Galdós' treatment of sexuality in *La familia de León Roch* is overtly negative. Sexual love is seductive, antirational and even dangerous for León Roch, and is compared disfavorably with a love defined primarily as compatability of character. But the definitive barrier between the protagonist and domestic happiness is the absence in Spain of civil divorce, together with the general refusal of a Catholic society to even contemplate the possibility of the dissolution of marriage. In *Lo prohibido*, Galdós emphasizes the mutual sexual attraction between Camila and Constantino; however, of equal importance is the fact that both young people are unencumbered by previous attachments, and thus are legally free to marry.

The nineteenth-century novel generally condemned adulterous affairs, even though the heroine might be portrayed sympathetically, as in the case of Tolstoy's Ana Karenina. Adulterous love was either sordid, *Madame Bovary*, for example, or tragic, but in any event, in

---

[2] Carr, p. 336.

the nineteenth-century world it was always more interesting than passion domesticated by marriage. In *Lo prohibido*, the love between Camila and Constantino is an oasis of virtue and respectability in a barren landscape of ego-driven desire and purchased sexual favors rationalized as love. But unlike the tedious (although also very comic) love affairs of Guzmán with his attractive cousins, the socially legitimate love affair between Camila and Constantino turns out to be the more psychologically interesting one.

Friedrich Engels' statement that "...the Catholic Church doubtless abolished divorce only because it was convinced that for adultery, as for death there is no cure whatsoever..."[3] certainly does not speak to all the nuances of the political struggle in Spain between the progressive secularists and the ultramontanes, but it does express succinctly the problem that Galdós attempts to analyze in *Lo prohibido:* the repercussions upon family life of the failure of the First Republic and the absence of a definitive separation between Church and State that would have left a space for civil divorce.

The battle between an intolerant Catholic absolutism and the proponents of ideological pluralism is revolved by "this provisional pact in which we live in order to keep on living" ("este pacto provisional en que vivimos para poder vivir") [p. 250], that is, a rigid adherence to the appearance of virtue (decorum), and a tacit tolerance of what Catholic orthodoxy names as vice. Because divorce cannot be legitimized, adultery is institutionalized. José F. Montesinos maintains that:

> That society's refusal to accept divorce was both a stimulus and a pretext and caused everyone to feel they were heros of classical tragedy, caught between passion and duty.
>
> (La negativa de aquella sociedad a aceptar el divorcio era a un tiempo estímulo y excusa y hacía que todos se sintieran héroes de drama antiguo, entre la pasión y el deber.)[4]

This is probably an exaggeration of the real-life situation in which, for the majority, fear of exposure, frustrated sexual desire, and enforced submission to a loveless marriage would necessarily create

---

[3] Friedrich Engels, *The Origin of the Family, Private Property and the State* (New York: Pathfinder Press, 1973), p. 73.

[4] See Benito Pérez Galdós, *Lo prohibido*, ed., intro. and notes of José F. Montesinos (Madrid: Castalia, 1971), p. 31.

a sordid atmosphere far removed from the transcendent passions of Calderonian drama. Nevertheless, Montesinos emphasizes an important point: the absence of divorce perpetuated the traditional Catholic dichotomy between marriage-duty and the forbidden fruit of sexual passion wrapped up in the obligatory tinsel of romantic love.

One of the most important elements in the ideological construction of the cult of domesticity was the belief that the bourgeois family,[5] unlike the institution of the state, was a "natural" permanent and ahistorical institution, outside of and unrelated to the public sphere where progress, change and the making of history took place. As Richard Sennet points out, the division between public and private spheres was reflected in a popular mentality that relegated "nature" to the private sphere and culture or civilization to the public:

> The more this opposition of nature and culture through the contrast of private and public became tangible, the more the family was viewed as a natural phenomenon. The family was "a seat of nature" rather than an institution like a street or a theater.[6]

This popular concept of the family as a "natural" entity beyond the purview of man-made laws and therefore not subject to transformation, is a myth that is vigorously debuked in *La de Bringas*. Galdós' description of the symbiotic relation between the Bringas' private family life and the social relationships that control the public world of state bureaucracy sets the stage for *Lo prohibido*, in which the novelist widens his lens to observe the world of the Stock Exchange, the drawing rooms of Madrid's *nouveaux riches*, and, from a distance, Parliament and the dilettante philanthropy of the upper class.

---

[5] For an excellent monograph on the ideology of the family and its different repercussions on the working class and bourgeois family, see Jacques Donzelot, *The Policing of Families* (New York: Pantheon Books, 1979).

[6] Richard Sennet, *The Fall of Public Man: On the Social Psychology of Capitalism* (New York: Vintage Books), p. 90.

The Question of Objectivity in Naturalism's 'Scientific Novel'

Galdós applies the full weight of naturalist techniques in this study of the institution of the family. The tenets of French naturalism as exemplified by Emile Zola combined the idea of inherited biological and moral characteristics with a belief in the destructive effect of an unhealthy social environment upon a human organism already debilitated by various inherited pathologies. In Zola's novels, social environment functions as a permanent condition of homeostasis; the concept of environment generally speaks to the way in which the different social classes organize the activities of eating, playing, sexual intercourse and other forms of social interaction. The laundry in *L'Assommoir* or the theatre in *Nana*, for example, are seen as part of a socializing network, rather than a sector of the capitalist economy containing any antagonism between capital and labor.[7] There is, in Zola's novels, no dialectical relationship between the individual and society, since the environment effects the individual, producing both organic and moral disease — tuberculosis and syphilis are placed in the same category as avarice and sloth — but the individual is not able to work any effect upon the social organism. The determinism of Zola's naturalism consists of this: the individual cannot transcend either his inherited pathology or the degenerative effects upon him of a "naturally" pernicious environment.[8]

Galdós refuses to share Zola's dogmatic social Darwinism. M. Gordon, in her article on naturalism in *La desheredada* emphasizes the presence of moral choice.[9] The possibility of free will, of

---

[7] For an excellent comparison of the different techniques of realism of Balzac and Zola, see G. Lukacs, "Narrate or Describe," in Writer and Critic (New York: Grosset and Dunlop, 1971), pp. 110-48.

[8] Zola explains the scientific role of the "experimental novel" in his essay of the same title: "We have experimental physics; we will have experimental physiology; and even further on we will have the experimental novel. [...] since learned men like Claude Bernard have recently shown us that a given set of laws govern the human body, we can announce without fear of being mistaken, the moment in which the laws of thought and of the emotions will be formulated. The same determinism should govern the pathways of the earth and the human brain." (my translation), Emile Zola, "La novela experimental" [1880], in the anthology *El naturalismo*, ed., intro. and notes of Laureano Bonet (Barcelona: Nexos, 1989), p. 42.

[9] M. Gordon, "The Medical Background to Galdós' *La desheredada*," Anales Galdosianos, 7 (1972), p. 75.

personal autonomy, of the existence of the individual as subject, rather than mere object acted upon by social forces, is the key factor that defines Galdós' naturalism. To the extent that he does employ naturalistic techniques, he does so in the service of his own personal reading of reality, rather than imposing them mechanistically upon a reified fictional material.

The structure of *Lo prohibido* represents at least an attempt to imitate that of a controlled scientific experiment. The control factors are environment and heredity, although Galdós places much more emphasis on the determining element of environment, to the point where the concept of inherited moral characteristics becomes, as Arthur Terry has pointed out, mere window dressing or folklore employed by the protagonist as a rationalization for his behavior.[10] J. Casalduero has sketched out the scheme of Galdós' experiment;[11] however, his formula of ABC (the three sisters) who interact in the *same* environment and are then confronted by the same entity N (Guzmán), assumes that the environment is an undifferentiated element – Madrid in 1880 – and that the economic status or class background of the sisters' spouses is irrelevant. Casalduero's reading disregards the role played by the husbands, yet the women define themselves in relation to their husband's economic and social status, and make choices and develop expectations according to the differences in their environment *after* marriage. The three sisters, then, represent three distinct social classes: the aristocracy (economically precarious), the bourgeoisie (economically ascendent) and the petty bourgeoisie (economically dependent). In these very distinct social environments, the three sisters are then put to the same test when they are confronted by their wealthy and seductive cousin. Will the sisters control their destinies? Or will they be controlled – by their passions, by the social mores and values of their specific class, or perhaps by the family's inherited neurotic tendencies?

The character who acts out the role of observer-protagonist is José María Bueno de Guzmán. His autobiography provides the reader with a scientific notebook which affords us the evidence upon which we will draw our own conclusions. It is obvious that the narrator's scientific probity is essential if we are to reach a correct evaluation of the facts. But of even greater importance than

---

[10] Arthur Terry, "*Lo prohibido*: Unreliable Narrator and Untruthful Narrative," in *Galdós Studies*, ed. J. Varey (London, 1970), p. 64.

[11] Casalduero, p. 78.

truthfulness is the scientist's talent for observation. Even if he reports rigorously all that he observes, he cannot know the truth if he is incapable of seeing certain colors or textures, contrasts or dimensions. Inevitably, the quest for scientific truth must confront the fallibility of the scientist. Therein lies the problem.

Any analogy between scientist-laboratory and novelist-narrative that might exist on the ideal plane of scientific-aesthetic theory disintegrates at the moment in which the narrative process is begun. Unlike the scientist, who may choose to stand back and observe the development of his experiment once it has been set in place, the novelist must continue to intervene if he wishes to know the results of his "experiment." The extent to which the narrator of these memoirs is an unreliable witness has been discussed at length by both Terry and K. Engler.[12] Both critics define unreliability as the gap between Guzmán's social and moral values and those of Galdós. This definition presupposes the existence within the novel of a coherent system of values that is identifiably Galdós', thus permitting the reader to use this system as a measure of truth against which the narrator's values can be judged. In addition, a definition of reliability that is based on the relationship of the narrator to the author also assumes that the reader should identify the narrator Guzmán with the author Galdós and therefore accept his interpretation of reality as privileged because it is literally the authorized one.

We do not find in *Lo prohibido* the kind of omniscient narrator whose opinions have often been interpreted by Galdós critics as those of Galdós himself. Nevertheless, the absence of the traditional third-person omniscient narrator does not permit us to conclude that Guzmán, from his privileged position as witness and narrator, has been selected by Galdós to act as his spokesman. In the absence of any designated representative of Galdós, the author's ideas, values and most importantly, his ambivalence, will necessarily be refracted into a multitude of perspectives, fragments of which are embodied in all of the characters. Guzmán's reliability as a witness, then, needs to be discussed both in terms of his relationship to the other characters in the novel, and to the reader.

Realism in fiction depends upon the ability of the author to structure his narrative in such a way that a contract between reader

---

[12] See Terry, p. 66, and K. Engler, *The Structure of Realism: The Novelas Contemporáneas of Benito Pérez Galdós* (Chapel Hill, 1977), pp. 139-41, 164-68.

and author is established in which the reader, to use Coleridge's phrase, can "willingly suspend disbelief" in the fictional illusion and accept it as reality. This contract must, by definition, exclude the presence of the real world outside the literary text, necessarily implying the exclusion of the "real" author. The problem of the prologue is defined by the necessary placement of a boundary between the literary text and "reality." The problematic status of the reader's relationship with the narrator is brought into relief by Engler's conclusion that "José María and the reader together discover the truth, and the conflict between the *narrador-personaje* [character] and the *narrador-testigo* [witness] is resolved."[13] The fact that we may or may not agree with this statement forces us to take into account the subjectivity of the reader as an additional perspective. For if we disagree with Engler's conclusion, it is clear that we are not the same "reader" referred to by Engler, that no ideal or privileged reader exists and therefore no ideal or definitive interpretation of the narrative text is possible.

At the end of the novel, Galdós once again interjects the presence of his faithful scribe, José Ido del Sagrario, cutting short any cathartic process the reader might be experiencing as a result of an identification with Guzmán's sufferings. We are forced out of the fictional illusion and back into the world we share with Galdós. As M. Nimetz points out, "As soon as Ido del Sagrario's shadow is evoked by the narrator, Galdós and his readers become accomplices."[14] The introduction of Ido effectively casts doubt on the reliability of the narrator by casting doubt on the identity of the memoirist. But since José Ido is identified in our minds with Galdós, we also begin to question the sincerity of Galdós, author. In other words, the possibility of an ironic reading is placed before us. For example, does the moralistic ending with its rewards and punishments – Camila's twins, Guzmán's disfigurement and death – fit logically within the overall structure of events? Or is the ending rather a case of being told "the moral of the story," a prescription for what the world would be if morality triumphed? Geraldine Scanlon notes the presence of José Ido and gives the following interpretation:

---

[13] Engler, 167.
[14] M. Nimetz, *Humor in Galdós* (New Haven: Yale University Press, 1968), p. 83.

If the exaggerated emphasis on José María's animal condition suggests a parody of Naturalism, his excessively exemplary punishment and gratuitous moralizing suggest a burlesque of the pseudo-Romantic popular novel, in which vice was always punished and virtue rewarded.[15]

The collaboration of the melodramatic Ido with the inhibited and conventional Guzmán, who has ostentatiously maintained throughout a posture of objectivity, calls into question the validity of the entire text, and consequently the realist aesthetic which posits the possibility and the necessity of a mimetic relationship between narrative and an objectifiable reality. In effect, Galdós' decision to give José Ido final control over Guzmán's memoirs defines the idea of author metaphorically as only one more character whose power to translate reality into its fictional representation is no more omniscient or transcendent than that of any other character in the novel.

Guzmán's frequent insistence that he is telling the truth unvarnished by imagination is a defensive statement that causes us to examine his words more closely. But even if we choose to conclude that Guzmán is sincere, we can never be sure that his manuscript has not been tampered with by José Ido or the publisher to whom he sells the memoirs in order to make them more marketable. Guzmán's limited control as author over what he writes therefore mirrors Galdós' relationship to his novels and to the publishing world. On the one hand, imagination and idealism (represented by José Ido) will interfere with even the most scientific mentality. And on the other hand, once the author has handed his manuscript over to the publishers, he relinquishes control; he ceases to exist as author.

Galdós not only negates the realist premise of authorial detachment by the interjection of José Ido, he asserts the author's presence by removing the curtain of fiction and coming on stage to take a well-deserved bow. Fictional reality is authored by human consciousness which is, by definition, subjective, personal, limited, biased. Therefore, according to realism's same mimetic principle, the characters cannot possess an unrealistic omniscience; they cannot know more than their creator. The problem of reality's defini-

---

[15] Scanlon, "Heroism in an Unheroic Society: Galdós' *Lo prohibido*", *The Modern Language Review*, 79, 4 (October 1984), pp. 831-845.

tion must thus be posed within an epistemological framework, rather than an aesthetic one. However, Galdós' stance of pluralistic relativism does not prevent him from attempting to define reality within the limits circumscribed by individual consciousness. *Lo prohibido* is ultimately an examination of those limits that individual subjectivity imposes upon the mental and emotional capacity to encompass the reality that extends beyond one's own thoughts, feelings, and physical sensations; the limited capacity to transcend the prison of individual isolation, to break through the ego's encirclement.

If we analyze Guzmán's reliability as a narrator in terms of his relationship with the reader rather than with Galdós, our opinion of his sincerity depends in part on Guzmán's successful manipulation of rhetoric in the service of the appearance of truth. Guzmán uses a frequent strategy of accumulating details in support of his statements. In Chapter II, he introduces himself with an exact accounting of his wealth, to "clarify the absurd fairy-tales about my capital that have been passing for gospel truth" ("desmentir las absurdas consejas que corrían como dogma evangélico acerca de mi capital") [p. 237]. This statement establishes a paradigmatic relationship between narrator, reader and the other characters which privileges the narrator. We are being asked to accept the principle that only Guzmán knows and can tell us the truth concerning his personal history, and that other witnesses are less reliable because they do not have access to his knowledge.

One of Guzmán's characteristics that does reinforce his credibility is his willingness to admit his personal lack of omniscience. His inability to decipher the laws that govern human relationships is repeatedly made manifest. He cries to himself at Carrillo's deathbed: "For the rest of my life, ah! I will have in front of me, like a pensive sphinx, Carrillo's image, without discovering the answer to its riddle." ("Toda mi vida, ¡ah! estará delante de mí, como pensativa esfinge, la imagen de Carrillo, sin que me sea dado descifrarla") [p. 313]. His lust for his cousin Eloísa cools and their affair becomes a prison from which he longs to escape. But he had loved her. Or was it love? "Why did I admire her so much then, and later on I no longer did?" ("¿Por qué la admiré tanto en otro tiempo y después no?") [p. 324]. Has he changed, or has she?

Guzmán's inability to decipher the mysteries of human behavior is linked to his self-righteous belief in the unique truth of his own point of view. Or perhaps it would be more exact to say that his inability to recognize another's desire, the existence of any subjective perspective not his own, makes him incapable of understanding his cousins' motives and behavior. This disjunction between a series of conflicting subjective realities creates the tension that propels the novel forward until the climactic scene between Camila and Guzmán in which Camila forces her importunate suitor to accept *her* reality as the definitive one by pounding it into his head with her husband's boot.

What this very brutal and hilarious scene demonstrates clearly is the degree to which the reader may be privy to knowledge that for some unexplicable reason is inaccessible to the narrator. Guzmán's imagination is limited or bound by two beliefs: the first is that any woman can be seduced; and the second, that any woman has her price – two beliefs which operate essentially as one for this wealthy man who is accustomed to buying what he wants. Why should Camila be different from any other woman, if no woman has ever refused him or his money? Guzmán cannot sustain his desire for an *ángel del hogar* because he believes that all women are in reality a potential or real "fallen angel."

In the second half of the novel, structured around Guzmán's nefarious pursuit of his virtuous cousin, Camila, the disparity between Guzmán's lack of understanding of the people around him, and the reader's possibility of seeing beyond Guzmán's limited perspective becomes even more evident. If the reader believes in Camila's virtue, the novel's tension does not arise from the question, when will she fall? but rather, when and how will this decrepit Don Juan realize that his Dulcinea is made of flesh and blood, that she possess a will of her own and is determined to exercise it in her own interests? Because Galdós follows a basically conventional formula and makes use of familiar literary types – the evil Don Juan, the young innocent lovers, Virtue struggling with Vice – it is to be expected that Virtue will triumph and Guzmán will be forced to learn his lesson. During Guzmán's education, the reader must collaborate with the text, imaging answers of his or her own to the questions which mystify Guzmán: why does Carrillo love him? why has he ceased to love Eloísa? and above all, why does Camila love Constantino instead of her cousin, why is she impervious to the temptation of his wealth and person?

The narrator paints a self-portrait of emotional and moral bankruptcy with a skill which ultimately depends on his ability to be as frank with the reader as he is hypocritical with his family and friends. Guzmán's saving characteristic – for his egoism is singularly unappealing – is his apparent willingness to reveal to the reader the hubristic need to manipulate and control which he hides from his family. This apparent honesty with the reader is another form of seduction, and the more terrible the crime, the more interesting (and seductive) his secret. When Guzmán confesses to us the satisfaction he feels in tormenting Eloísa's blind admirer, Manolo Trujillo, we cannot approve, we cannot love him, but he is very credible: "I took pleasure in destroying his illusion by painting him a detailed picture of how disfigured she was... this cruelty came from somewhere deep inside me, and I experienced a strange and vengeful pleasure" ("Me complací en destruir su ilusión pintándole lo desfigurada que estaba... me salía esta crueldad muy de dentro, y sentía un goce extraño y vengativo...") [p. 384].

Although Guzmán portrays his faults to us with convincing consistency, nevertheless he is not a profoundly interesting psychological study. He himself recognizes that his egocentricity defines his character: "I was an egoist, while Carrillo had the mania of *otherism*..." ("Yo era un egoísta, mientras Carrillo tenía la manía del *otroísmo*...") [p. 274]. Guzmán's total self-absorption is both tedious and repelling. The puzzle for the reader, then, is to understand Guzmán's obvious capacity to generate sympathy, interest and love in his friends and family. What is this *"ángel"* [seductiveness, irresistibility] that he possesses? Do they love him for his money or for himself? In order to attempt to answer these questions, and in the absence of the narrator's ability to read the people that surround him, we must take his text and read it from the perspective of the other characters.

Eloísa: The Attraction of the Fallen Angel

In Spanish literature, the Don Juan myth has always functioned as a vehicle for moral censure of libertinage, even while the different versions glorify Don Juan's sexual prowess and irresistibility. Guzmán's donjuanism is a blend of anti-social attitudes – a general disparagement of the society in which he moves and a misogynistic fear of marriage – that combine with an attitude of approving obsequience to social conventions. His donjuanism is, perhaps, the clearest manifestation of his innate conventionality. Vicente Llorens points out in *El romanticismo español* that much of the appeal of the Don Juan myth for the Spanish middle class "whose repressed and sordid erotic life oscilated between a marriage of convenience and the escape of prostitution" ("cuya reprimida y sórdida vida erótica oscilaba entre el matrimonio de conveniencia y la escapada a la prostitución")[16] is the element of fantasy. Galdós, on the other hand, has created in Guzmán a Don Juan whose amorous adventures are bereft of any mythic dimension. The only certain aphrodisiac in the stale ambience of the Restoration is money, and most women are, in the words of Guzmán's colleague, Gonzalo Torres, "no better than they should be" ("unas... tales") [p. 357].

Guzmán presents the three sisters to the reader without idealizing them, in fact, insisting upon the nervous tics and idiosyncrasies that are part of the family heritage of depressive and hysterical symptoms. The physical beauty of the two eldest sisters is reduced to the generic type found in fashion magazines: the prescriptive and necessarily imitable beauty found in the pastel-colored sketches of the latest fashion model: María Juana is "as beautiful as a statue" ("una belleza estatuaria") [p. 232]. Eloísa is "as beautiful as her older sister, but much prettier" ("tan guapa como su hermana mayor... pero mucho más linda") [p. 234]. The differences in their personalities are also reduced to a cliché: María Juana is criticized for her pretentiousness and arrogance – she reads French and Italian novels, and, in translation, Herbert Spencer [p. 360]. It is implied that she is a blue-stocking, a *marisabidilla*. Eloísa, on the contrary, is gentle, sweet-tempered, domestic. Eloísa is an angel.

The youngest sister Camila, however, is described in terms as vivid and specific as they are derogatory. Camila is the polar opposite of the pale anemic Kitty, the dead English woman who was Guzmán's betrothed, and is now his model of femeninity: Kitty was "...lovely, modest, pale, with a subdued voice and unclouded eyes that revealed candour and refinement." ("...graciosa, modesta, descolorida, de voz tenue y ojos claros que revelaban ingenuidad y delicadeza...") [p. 256]. Camila de Miquis is "brown-skinned, extremely slender, vigorous and as healthy as a country girl" ("morena, esbeltísima, vigorosa, saludable como una aldeana") [p. 235].

---

[16] Vicente Llorens, *El romanticismo español* (Madrid: Castalia, 1979), pp. 447-48.

Guzmán explains to himself his attraction for Eloísa by the idea that she is the spiritual reincarnation of the perfect Kitty: "I had started to believe that Kitty's soul had come to inhabit Eloísa's body and appeared at the window of her eyes to look out at me" ("Yo había dado en creer que el alma de Kitty se había colado en el cuerpo de Eloísa y se asomaba a los ojos de ésta para mirarme") [p. 256]. While Kitty was still alive, Guzmán satisfied his sexual desire with the prostitutes of London's *demi-monde*. But instead of fantasizing that his cousin Eloísa is an exotic lady of the night, he transforms her into a nurturing *ángel del hogar* who possesses not only the dead Kitty's virtue, but also the comfort charm and order of an equally absent and idealized family life. He falls in love with his cousin in her role as bedside nurse: not champagne and candlelight, but the cozy sound of a teaspoon clinking against a china cup, the comforting voice and soothing hand of the helpmeet, the wife, or best of all, the mother. The apple that tempts him is not his cousin's voluptuous flesh, but her "domestic wisdom" ("saber doméstico"): she is "the soul of the home, the authority, the executive power..." ("el alma de la casa, la autoridad, el poder ejecutivo...") [p. 248]. There is no doubt that Guzmán has fallen in love, not with the Angel, but with the space which she creates and inhabits, with the Home.

His affair with Eloísa establishes a model of behavior which Guzmán will continue to follow in his pursuit of María Juana and Camila. The battle to gain possession of the delectable Eloísa – "when I saw that delicious piece of fruit, someone else had it in his hand and had taken a bite out of it" ("cuando vi aquella fruta sabrosa, otra la tenía en la mano y le había hincado el diente")[17] [p. 234] – is not waged directly with Eloísa, who offers no resistance, but with the rightful owner of the tempting morsel, her husband. His competitive relationship with the husband is the mirror that defines him, not the reflection of his love in the eyes of Eloísa. His sexual longings turn him in upon himself in a frenzy of doubt concerning his masculinity:

---

[17] Caballero's reaction when he realizes that he would not be the first one to "open" Amparo, makes clear Galdós' use of the image of the apple to signify the female sexual organs: "I thought the apple I had picked was ripe. When I opened it, I saw it was rotten." ("La manzana que cogí parecióme buena. Ábrese y la veo dañada") [p. 119].

> From the moment that invisible tooth began to chew up my insides, the main object of my meditations was the following: Was Carrillo a better man than I? Was I a better man than he?
>
> (Desde que el diente aquel invisible empezó a roerme las entrañas, el objeto principal de mis cavilaciones era el siguiente: ¿Valía Carrillo más que yo? ¿Valía yo más que él?) [p. 254]

He must establish his masculine status publicly; male status belongs necessarily to the public sphere. Once the conquest is complete, the proud Lothario confides in a friend who obligingly spreads the news. The public recognition of his triumph transforms his relationship with Eloísa as well as his fantasies, since he must now give up his dream of living "a normal, legal and religious life" ("una vida regular, legal y religiosa") [p. 255]. Eloísa's role as his mistress precludes her from being an *ángel del hogar*, and with Guzmán's money and expensive presents he transforms her literally into a scarlet woman. She appears at one of her infamous soirées dressed from head to toe in screaming red velvet [p. 277]. However, she now belongs not only to him but also to the public; his fame as a Don Juan is precariously linked to her notoriety as "the avenging angel" ("el ángel del asesinato") [p. 277].

But little by little, the fantasy of the forbidden fruit of the novel's title is replaced by a parody of married life, supported by his family ties and the tacit approval of his friends. From the beginning, Guzmán had confessed to his readers his pragmatic opinion of marriage and family life, one that is completely divorced from his recurrent odysseys into the exciting but controllable world of the imagination. His relationship with Eloísa fulfills his formula for enjoying the intimacy of domesticity without the responsibility of permanent emotional or financial commitment. With Eloísa, he is able to live on the threshold of family life: "near enough to keep warm, but far enough away to keep from suffocating" ("bastante cerca para matar el frío, bastante lejos para que no me sofocara") [p. 240]. In spite of his complaints about Eloísa's profligate Thursdays-at-home, he always attends, for they provide a splendid showcase for his new possession. They also satisfy his need for another kind of commodity, that is, a prefabricated social environment in which he will not be required to take any active part except to exercise his dancing-school manners and to pay the bill.

Carrillo's death forces Guzmán to abandon his game of playing house and to confront his moral obligation to marry Eloísa. He reacts with panic, with the typical symptoms of claustrophobia, or rather, *casa*phobia, he wants neither the Angel nor her House:

> The idea of living in that house and being in charge of it caused me to feel the same anguished terror that I had experienced in other attacks when I felt I was being run over by a train.
>
> (La idea de ser habitante de tal casa y de mandar en ella me producía el mismo terror angustioso que en otros ataques la idea de sentir un tren viniendo sobre mí.) [p. 314]

His ears begin to ring. Employing the feminine defense of manipulation rather than confrontation, the defense of the timid and powerless, he falls ill.

Guzmán's disillusionment brings into evidence the different components – physical, psychological and social – that constituted his love for Eloísa. Sexual desire and the social acclaim afforded him by his male counterparts had enhanced the emotional titillation derived from acting out the narcissistic fantasy of the Wertherian lover.[18] Not surprisingly, imagination's fragile aphrodisiac disappears first: "Pepe's [Carrillo's] death turned out to be like one of those scene-changes in the theatre that destroys all the illusion and undermines the scene's magic." ("la muerte de Pepe había sido como uno de esos giros del Teatro que destruyen todo encanto y trastornan la magia de la escena") [p. 315]. With the illusion of a forbidden love destroyed by the removal of the barrier, Guzmán comes face to face with his real misogynistic fear of Eloísa: "the kind of fear that dangerous animals inspire" ("un miedo como el que inspiran los animales dañinos") [p. 315], a fear caused by his knowledge that he is unable to control her, to control her sexuality, and with that awareness, the fear that she will sell her sexual services to others as she has to him. The measure of masculinity in the conventional role of domestic patriarch is the husband's capacity to police

---

[18] The reference to Goethe's *Sorrows of Werther*, "...I was ready for anything, even to become romantic and *Wertherian*" ("...Estaba dispuesto a todo, hasta volverme romántico y *wertheriano*") [p. 266], becomes even more explicit when Guzmán tells us: "I thought what one was supposed to think in these cases, that is, that she and I were made for each other, that we were designated for each other from birth, to be two inseparable pieces of one unique instrument..." ("Yo pensaba lo que es de cajón en tales casos, es decir, que ella y yo éramos el uno para el otro; que habíamos nacido para unirse, para ser dos piezas inseparables de un solo instrumento...") [p. 254].

his wife: Eloísa exclaims, "You are afraid of tying the Sacred Knot,... you don't trust me, you don't think you can control me." ("El *santo yugo* te da miedo,... Dudas de mí, dudas de poderme sujetar") [p. 323]. And he agrees.

Unlike the complexity and uncertainty of *human* relationships, the commodified relationship between the Fallen Angel and her customer is, for Guzmán, a less threatening one because it is controlled by the clarity of the laws of the market. The medium of exchange between the consumer and the commodity is money which acts as both a distancing agent and a protective barrier between the buyer of sexual services and the reified human commodity. As long as the consumer pays his bill, he has no moral or emotional obligation to the commodity he purchases.

Guzmán's refusal to marry Eloísa leaves him no alternative but that of redefining his relationship with her according to the standards of conventional morality that are his guidelines for interpreting reality. If he will not marry Eloísa, it is because she is a whore, or at least, a potential one:

> With the bad habits that you have acquired, how can you inspire any confidence? Because if I don't approve of selling a husband's honor for the love of another man, how much worse to sell it for a set of diamonds!... and that's where you're headed,...
>
> (Con los resabios que has adquirido, ¿qué confianza puedes inspirar? Porque si no me parece bien vender el honor de un marido por el amor de otro hombre, ¡cuánto peor es venderlo por un aderezo de brillantes!... Y a eso vas tú,...) [p. 326]

Redefining Eloísa as an *ángel caído* [fallen angel] rather than an *ángel del hogar* enables Guzmán to end the relationship by buying her off, but he also is forced to redefine himself. For if Eloísa is a whore, what is he? A very poor version, indeed, of the legendary Don Juan.

Guzmán's refusal to marry Eloísa is just one incident in the life of a man who has not only avoided the bond of matrimony up to this point, but who is very determined to continue doing so. His fear of women, of the patriarch's traditional responsibility for female sexuality motivates all his amorous relationships and explains his identification with the role of lover rather than that of husband. For the two roles define each other in their mutual exclusivity: a man is either the Don Juan, the *burlador* [the joker] or the cuckhold, the *burlado* [the fool]. Guzmán tells himself: "...it was very possible that my appetites and my vanity could induce me to conquer that which is prohibited, but to be myself the prohibition,... never!" ("...bien podían mis apetitos y mi vanidad inducirme a conquistar lo prohibido; pero ser yo la prohibición,... ¡jamás!") [p. 317]. The reduction of women's humanity to two conventional roles, that of the virtuous woman or the whore, finds its counterpart in the reduction of men to the social stereotypes of husband or libertine.

The need to absolve himself of moral responsibility for the outcome of their love affair brings Guzmán face to face with his own inability to act according to the moral standard by which he judges women. He accepts the reality of a dual standard without any emotional turmoil: "But we men are like that... women must be heroines for us, while we do whatever we feel like" ("Pero los hombres somos así... las mujeres han de ser heroínas para nosotros, mientras nosotros hacemos lo que nos da la gana") [p. 327]. However, by taking refuge in the status quo of a double moral standard, one that separates the world of women from the world of men, but also separates feminine moral superiority or heroism from the mediocre morality of the ordinary male, Guzmán must accept the fact that he is not the hero of his fantasies. The hero is capable of "moral acts of tremendous power and effectiveness" ("actos morales de grandísimo poder y eficacia") [p. 328]. Guzmán admits to himself, "I am passive" ("yo soy pasivo"). He is always able to escape: "life's waves do not crash down upon me" ("las olas de la vida no se estrellan en mí") [p. 328]. He prefers the solitude of his bachelorhood which he protects by systematically raising the protective shield of his wealth, using it to control and limit all human relationships both sexual and emotional.

Although the treatment of marriage and adultery from the bachelor's perspective is certainly not unique in the nineteenth-century novel, Galdós departs from the standard explanations for adultery that tended to place the onus of guilt on women. Pope Pius IX's papal encyclical entitled "Concerning Women and Luxury" ("Sobre el lujo de las mujeres") is a typical expression of the popular consensus:

> It is luxury that tends to divorce husband and wife, and with even more frecuency impedes the celebration of matrimony, because there are few men who will agree to take on such an enormous expense.

(Él [el lujo] es el que suele divorciar los esposos, y con más frecuencia impedir la celebración de los matrimonios, porque hay pocos hombres que consientan cargar con gastos tan enormes.)[19]

Galdós' portrait of Eloísa builds on his study of women and conspicuous consumption in *La de Bringas*. Eloísa is depicted as an ambitious woman for whom luxury becomes a substitute for active participation in the productive sphere. She tells Guzmán: "I feel within me sudden attacks of financial genius. I feel I could be a Pereira, a Salamanca if they would let me." ("Yo siento en mí arrebatos de genio financiero. Me parece que sería un Pereira, un Salamanca si me dejaran") [p. 300]. Galdós' attitude towards the world of banking, finance and speculation is ambivalent.[20] Still, he is critical of the kind of shady deals that enrich the private speculator by robbing the state, a specialty of the Marqués de Fúcar and his cronies. Guzmán's comment, that Eloísa possesses "an unhealthy enthusiasm for things that are contrary to women's spiritual nature" ("insano entusiasmo para cosas contrarias a la condición espiritual de la mujer") [p. 300], could be interpreted as a criticism shared by Galdós, except that the authority of Guzmán's right to moralize – for example, his criticism of Camila – is undercut by his participation in many of the very things he chooses to condemn.

Galdós also explains Eloísa's compulsive buying in terms of the relationship between wealth and respectability. In *Tormento*, Caballero's wealth permits him to flout the social code and to live publicly with Amparo, although not in Spain: nor does his sense of propriety allow him to marry her. Eloísa realizes that only the appearance of wealth will prevent social ostracism after her lover has ceased to protect her. She tells Guzmán: "Do you take away my luxury? Then give me your name." ("¿Me quitas el lujo? Pues dame el nombre") [p. 325]. If she maintains an upper-class standard of living, she will still be visited by the more tolerant segments of

---

[19] Breve de Su Santidad Pío IX a María de Gentelles, "Sobre el lujo de las mujeres," *La Familia* (30 octubre 1875), p. 171.

[20] It is difficult to pinpoint Galdós' distinction between the "good" and the "bad" capitalist. Eloísa's plan to foment a civil war in order to profit from contracts for supplies, is certainly meant to be a critique of the capitalist's cynical opportunism. Nevertheless, Caballero, Galdós' "good" capitalist, made his fortune precisely in that way, selling goods on the Mexico-United States border during the Mexican-American War of 1848.

society, although it is clear by the end of the novel that she has gradually transformed her home into a bordello for the rich.

Donjuanism and the Prison of Romantic Rhetoric

Guzmán's refusal to marry Eloísa is only partially explained by his fear that her spendthrift habits would ruin him. This rationalization is also a pretext to justify the fact that he has simply lost interest in her. Galdós uses Guzmán's love affair with Eloísa as a means of analyzing the mystery of ephemeral sexual desire, and the obsessive behavior of the Don Juan; that is, his psychological need to renew sexual desire through the compulsive conquest of new and different female bodies. For the Don Juan, there is no other stimulus to love. Not until we have observed Guzmán in a variety of social situations are we able to deduce the extent to which he has repressed his emotions and to observe his inability to feel emotional commitment. Guzmán's psychological self-portrait is more empirical than it is analytical, but clearly, his lack of emotional maturity is linked to the repressive effects of a social education that emphasizes conformity to the appearance of propriety rather than sincerity.

Guzmán's rejection of Eloísa as a wife is, however, also a rejection of the uncontrolled and for him, frighteningly excessive level of luxury consumption. To fill the gap left by the absence of any family life, he turns to the respectable bourgeois household of his cousin María Juana and her husband, Medina, a broker in the stock market. He discovers, to his surprise, that he feels very much at ease: "I liked their house because in it one breathed a business atmosphere to which I had become very attracted." ("Érame grata aquella casa porque en ella respiraba una atmósfera de negocios a que yo había cobrado bastante afición") [p. 362]. He exchanges Eloísa's gluttonous orgy of consumption, for the productive bustle of the Stock Exchange transferred to the privacy and solid comfort of Medina's dining room. Guzmán tells the reader: "His home was our own Stock Exchange." ("La casa era nuestro Bolsín") [p. 362].

For the first time since his arrival in Madrid, Guzmán's daily existence is defined by his social integration into activities that might be classified as work. The excitement of making money awakens him from his habitual lethargy. The deals he makes privately with Arnáiz, Trujillo and Barragán over Medina's brandy and cigars are consumated in the public Stock Exchange: "the center of commercial palpitations, the enormous sympathetic nerve that reflected the excitement of the entire Madrid financial community." ("el centro de las palpitaciones comerciales, el gran *simpático* que reflejaba la excitación de todo Madrid financiero") [p. 375]. Guzmán's parasitical need for constant artificial stimulation to alleviate his unhealthy state of *taedium vitae* is satisfied with the aphrodisiac of money, with the voyeuristic[21] penetration into the financial secrets of friends and acquaintances:

> ...nowhere else could you find a more complete knowledge of the pecuniary secrets of the people who pass themselves off as rich in Madrid [...] that palpitating truth, all numbers, all alive...
>
> (...en ninguna parte se tenía un conocimiento más completo de las intimidades pecuniarias de toda la gente que se pasa por rica en Madrid [...] aquella verdad palpitante, toda números, toda vida...) [p. 363]

But in spite of the satisfaction that Guzmán derives from knowing that his bank account and his sexual life are once more under control, his incorporation into the financial community is relatively passionless. He plays at playing the market, making cautious wagers that reap moderate winnings. He explains his fear of risk as the virtue of prudence and a dislike of associating with the ill-mannered *parvenus* who make the Exchange their home. But it is not possible to accuse Medina of vulgarity, in spite of his nickname *"el ordinario."* Medina is certainly as well-mannered as he, infinitely more moral – in the conventional meaning of the word – and also more prosperous. Guzmán's fear of losing prevents him from competing openly with Medina on the Stock Exchange, much as his fear of losing control over a wife prevents him from marrying. When Medina beats him in the stock market, he harbors his rancour within him and says "thank you" with a smile when his host proffers him second-rate cigars.

This inability to express feelings of resentment sows the seeds of his desire for revenge. Guzmán sets out to seduce Medina's wife this time without any illusion. María Juana will be another number

---

[21] For an interesting discussion of Guzmán (and Galdós) as voyeur, see Lois Baer Barr, "Voyeurism in *Lo Prohibido", Kentucky Romance Quarterly,* 31 (1984), pp. 169-75.

in the column of his conquests placed in the account book that measures the extent of his masculinity. He will control the terms of the seduction:

> ...that she would come to me, begging me to make the move; I would only have to stretch out my hand,... forget about everything else, that man so upright and sanctimonious would pay me all at once for every vulgar offense.

> (...que ella venía hacía mí, solicitándome para que la jugase; yo no tenía más que alargar la mano,... nada, nada, que aquel hombre íntegro y juicioso me pagaría juntas todas sus groserías.) [p. 372]

Carrillo was morally superior. Constantino is stronger, and Medina makes more money. But they, not he, will wear the cuckhold's horns.

Guzmán has become an expert at separating the satisfaction of his sexual needs from the world of romantic fantasy, now constructed around his adoration of the youngest sister, Camila. After Eloísa takes the Marqués de Fúcar as a lover and the danger of matrimony is definitively removed, he resumes the affair; but now Camila, not Kitty, provides the psychological stimulus that Eloísa's body satisfies:

> Camila never left my mind for even a minute, and the closer I was to Eloísa, the more I was aware of her presence, or if you want, at the moment of greatest proximity. The idea that they were sisters excited me, penetrating my imagination to the point where they became in my mind one and the same person.

> (Camila no se me apartaba del magín ni un solo rato, y tanto más presente la tenía cuanto más cerca de Eloísa estaba, o, si se quiere, en el mayor grado de proximidad posible. La idea de que eran hermanas me cosquilleaba la mente, violentando la fantasía para que llegase a la figuración de que eran una misma persona.) [p. 355]

As Guzmán explains to the reader, it is his own fantasy – with its incestuous overtones – that makes love to him, breaking in and taking control of an otherwise passive imagination. His need to fantasize that Eloísa is someone else – Kitty, Camila – forms part of a pattern in which fantasy is consistently substituted for material reality. For Guzmán, the act of love is an act of self-gratification, of mental masturbation, in which the object of sexual desire is not another human being but the projection of his own narcissism.

María Juana's seduction underlines the extent to which Guzmán is emotionally constricted by the need to measure his social stature with other men through the conquest of women. For not only does she not attract him sexually or emotionally, he actively dislikes her:

> ...it was as if I were wrapping up in straw my true feelings for her, in order to send them off by rapid post. I was packer of the contempt she inspired in me.
>
> (...me parecía que estaba volviendo en paja la verdad de mis sentimientos con respecto a ella, para remitirlos en gran velocidad. Yo era el embalador del desprecio que me inspiraba.) [p. 374]

The story of his love affair with María Juana marks a turning point in Guzmán's moral degeneration. He has become capable of initiating a sexual relationship motivated only by a desire for revenge and without the framework of any fantasy. But the respectable Mrs. Medina does need to justify her actions by imagining that she is an involuntary prisoner of her love. She becomes a feminine Don Juan who uses her cousin's weapon, romantic rhetoric, in order to make her conquest. The reader is allowed to see the illusion of romantic love from the inside out. We see inside the magician's hat, we look up his sleeve. And what we find is the silken skein of words: "phrases invented on the spot, artificial confections of words, something like the castles made of caramel and almond paste that they give you on your birthday" ("invenciones del momento, palabras confitadas y artificiosas, semejantes a esos castillos de caramelo y guirlache que se regalan el día del santo") [p. 388]. The disjunction between Guzmán's verbal love-making and his real emotions towards Eloísa, María Juana, Victoria, and also Camila, compels the reader to question the validity of Guzmán's insistence that if he is false with his friends, he is sincere with his readers. For his sincerity is no longer a question of intent, but of the capacity to *be* sincere; that is, the capacity for self-knowledge.

Guzmán's seductive power is dependent on his capacity to dissemble, and to evade emotional confrontations that might provoke rejection. Although he relies on money when necessary, his seductions are primarily verbal, the dialogue of the Don Juan who lives his own *mise en scène*. He tell us that he speaks to María Juana in "...elaborate sentences just like hers that I prepared beforehand..." ("frases rebuscadas como las suyas que de antemano preparaba...") [p. 397]. And remembering his affair with Eloísa, he is struck by its irreality:

> If we had been characters in a play, instead of living human beings, they would have dismissed us as false, without taking into account the complexity of the human character.
>
> (Si hubiéramos sido personajes de teatro, en vez de ser personas vivas, se nos habría tachado de falsos, sin tener en cuenta la complejidad de los caracteres humanos.) [p. 324]

And yet this complex personality behaves as if he were confined within the very limited role of male vamp, perhaps a charming Don Juan when he was young, but now condemned to play out the comic role of *viejo verde* [dirty old man] assigned to the aging character actor.

The ironic posture of the Don Juan that is Guzmán's refuge not only from marriage but from any emotional confrontation is not without its own hidden dangers. The seduction of the pompous Mrs. Medina provides the reader with a hilarious comic interlude that relieves the tedium of Guzmán's self-centered histrionics. Guzmán finds out that he has met his match, as María Juana puts into practice her literary education. She is Madame Warrens, saving the young Rousseau from the coils of evil prostitutes. And Guzmán is forced not only to make love to her but to listen to her and to respond as she makes verbal love to him:

> I was in no condition to make any sense out of philanthropic love and twisted psychologizing that not even God himself could understand! And what else could I get but a headache from the whole thing about loving me in order to save me, and sacrificing the lesser honor to the greater.
>
> (¡Buena tenía yo la cabeza para sacar virutas de amor filantrópico y de psicologías enrevesadas que ni el Verbo las entendía! Ni qué otra cosa sino mareos podía producirme aquella de amarme por salvarme, y el sacrificio del honor pequeño al honor grande.) [p. 397]

Don Juan has been beaten at his own game.

Guzmán is aware that the basis of his most intimate relationships is a tissue of lies, because his expertise as a Don Juan requires an awareness of his methods of conquest – in the scene with Victoria, he tells us: "I repeated to her the same rubbish I always said" ("Repetíle las mismas tonterías de siempre") [p. 366] – but he continues to maintain to himself and to his readers that his love for Camila is different: it is real, not artificial, it is something more than rhetoric. But where does rhetoric stop and feeling begin? His sexual desire for Camila ebbs and flows without any apparent reason. When he sees Camila nursing the sick Eloísa, he assures us that his is a platonic and ideal love. But he can no more convince us than he can convince Camila, because we know that he is only capable of assimilating his emotions through a web of meaningless clichés. By now, even his sacred and private love for Camila is a prisoner of rhetoric. He can do nothing more than repeat to her mechanically the same words spoken to Eloísa, Victoria and María Juana:

> I don't remember if I also trotted out *'my precious little mink'* which is obligatory, but you can be sure I didn't forget to use *'the altar of my heart'* and other suitable metaphors.
>
> (No recuerdo si saqué a relucir también lo del *armiño*, que es de reglamento pero de fijo no se me quedó por decir lo del *altar de mi corazón* y otras imágenes muy al caso.) [p. 384]

His identification with the stereotype of the romantic lover has reduced him to a straw man. And we know that Camila has been correct to answer: "nonsense, nonsense" ("papas, papas").

SILENCE: THE LANGUAGE OF HYSTERIA

The Bueno de Guzmán family provides a clinical model of what the narrator describes as "a family diathesis" ("una diátesis familiar"), that is, a congenital susceptibility or liability to certain diseases. [22] Galdós seems to pick off diseases from J. J. Moreau de Tours' "Tree of Nervosity," the title of the graph that appears in the medical treatise, *La psychologie morbide* [1859] [23] in order to replant them onto

---

[22] L. Braier, *Diccionario Enciclopédico de Medicina* (Barcelona: Editorial JIMS, 1982).

the genealogical tree of the Guzmán family. Uncle Rafael suffers from *astasia-abasia* (tottering and swooning) – the agoraphobic's fear of falling into the infinite space of the public square. Cousin Raimundo has all the characteristics of the *idiot-savant*, and the narrator himself suffers from "mild attacks of hypochondria" ("achaquillos de hipocondría") and periodically, "a state of tremendous panic" ("un acceso de miedo inmenso") [p. 229]. Galdós reserves for the women the prototypical hysterical symptom of the *globus hystericus*, Eloísa chokes on an imaginary feather caught in her throat, and María Juana is condemned to chew on a piece of cloth, "until she has undone the weave and can swallow the wool" ("hasta deshacer el tejido y tragarse la lana") [p. 231].[24]

In *Lo prohibido*, the forbidden fruit of illicit sex is consumed in gluttonous proportions by the female as well as the male protagonists. Unlike the eminent Spanish hygienist, Dr. Pedro Felipe Monlau, who recommended against marriage for women suffering from hysteria for fear that they might contaminate their future daughters,[25] Galdós does associate the symptoms of hysteria with unsatisfied sexual desire. María Juana's attacks of the *globus hystericus* subside after her marriage [p. 232]. And Guzmán tells us that on one occasion, after their affair is well-established, she becomes symptomatic when, in an obvious state of sexual arousal – "my cousin's lips were dry, her eyes were beginning to close" ("mi prima tenía los labios secos, la vista un poco adormecida") [p. 412] – he sends her home without making love to her.[26] But on the other hand, the two characters who are the least self-controlled sexually, either by necessity or desire, Eloísa and the narrator himself, are also the most afflicted with nervous symptoms.

---

[23] See George F. Drinka, M.D., *The Birth of Neurosis: Myth, Malady and the Victorians* (New York: Simon & Schuster, 1984), p. 55. See also José Luis Peset and Rafael Huertas García-Alejo, "Del 'ángel caído' al enfermo mental: Sobre el concepto de degeneración en las obras de Morel y de Magnan," *Asclepio*, vol. 38, 1986, pp. 215-40.

[24] See Bridget A. Aldaraca, "The Medical Construction of the Feminine Subject in Nineteenth-Century Spain," in the anthology *Cultural and Historical Grounding for Hispanic and Luso-Brazilian Feminist Literary Criticism*, ed. H. Vidal (Minneapolis: Ideologies and Literature, 1989), pp. 395-413.

[25] P. F. Monlau, *Higiene del matrimonio, o el libro de los casados*, séptima edición considerablemente aumentada (Paris, 1892), pp. 30-31, 500-503.

[26] See Bridget A. Aldaraca, "El caso de Ana O: La histeria y sexualidad en *La Regenta*," *Asclepio* (núm. monográfico: *La sexualidad y sus límites*, vol. 42, July, 1990), pp. 51-61.

The experiments of J.-M Charcot with hypnotism and his hysterical patients in the clinic of the Hospital of the Salpêtrière produced contradictory results in the terrain of public opinion, both scientific and popular, concerning the enigmatic disease of hysteria. On the one hand, the classification of the hysterical symptoms and the identification and description of the famous four stages of the hysterical fit, *la grande hystérie,* raised hysteria to the category of a disease, separating it out from other well-established diseases such as epilepsy or dementia and the kinds of paralysis which had an organic etiology, often associated with the final stages of syphillis.[27] But on the other hand, the proof through the use of hypnotism that hysteria (and the hysteric) had the ability to imitate other diseases: epilepsy, blindness, certain kinds of muscular weaknesses, and even the hysterical symptoms of other patients – in a word, that "the disease of hysteria imitates almost all the illnesses that are the patrimony of our species" ("la afección histérica imita a casi todas las enfermedades que son patrimonio de nuestra especie")[28] – called into question not so much the validity of the disease itself but that of the patients. The idea that hysteria was defined by its capacity to simulate other diseases reinforced the traditional idea that hysteria was a disease of fakery, a fake disease, and that the hysterical woman was therefore an imposter, garnering undeserved sympathy and attention. Certainly the idea that women simulated this emotionally-charged illness fitted well into the misogynistic tradition that women acted out emotions and feelings (love, orgasmic response) that they did not experience, and were therefore untrustworthy.

Galdós would seem to share this lack of confidence in those who suffer from "nerves." For example, Raimundo's compulsive stuttering is quickly cured by an application of *pesetas* from his cousin's wallet. Guzmán makes an accurate diagnosis of his uncle's *astasia-abasia:* "Without knowing why, it ocurred to me that there was something else behind the nervous symptom of his feeling of suspension." ("Sin saber por qué, se me antojó que detrás del síntoma

---

[27] See Drinka, pp. 74-107. See also, Henri F. Ellenberger, *The Discovery of the Unconscious: The History and Evolution of Dynamic Pyschiatry* (New York: Basic Books, 1970), pp. 89-102; Paul Bercherie, *Génesis de los conceptos freudianos* [1983] (Buenos Aires: Editorial Paidós, 1988), pp. 69-97; and Etienne Trillat, *Histoire de L'Hystérie* (Paris: Editions Seghers, 1986), pp. 127-65.

[28] Dr. J. Grasset, *Enfermedades del sistema nervioso,* tomo II (Barcelona, 1880), p. 465.

de la suspensión había otra causa") [p. 339]. Again, a small loan is an effective cure. Camila's tantrums and suicide threats force her family to accede to her marriage:

> ...the child manipulated so artfully the recourse of her nerves, her spoiled demands, and her terrifying unpredictability, that her parents were forced to give in for fear that they might have to call on Dr. Esquerdo. [29]

> (...la niña manejó con tal arte el resorte de sus nervios, mimos, y de sus temibles espontaneidades, que los papás hubieron de ceder por miedo a que llegara el caso de llamar al doctor Esquerdo.) [p. 236]

The key words are: "manipulated so artfully the recourse of her nerves." Camila gets her husband, Raimundo gets his loan, and in every instance, hysterical behavior produces sympathy, special privileges and solicitous concern for the health of the sufferer. Can we conclude, as some contemporary feminist theorists have done, [30] that Galdós views hysteria as a form of rebellion against the domestic restraints which limited the power and social mobility of women, not only in the bourgeois society of Victorian England, but also in the *sui generis* version of that society in Restoration Spain? If we were to base our opinion on the description of hysteria in *Lo prohibido*, it would be difficult to arrive at this conclusion. The three sisters, in spite of manifesting occasionally some of the hysterical symptoms listed in the medical text books of the period, are anything but hysterics, for the disease was, above all, one that incapacitated its victims, either periodically or consistently.

---

[29] Dr. José María Esquerdo was a disciple of the well-known forensic specialist, Dr. Pedro Mata; he was also director of the insane asylum at Carabanchel and editor of the *Revista Clínica de los Hospitales* (1889-91). The first volume includes his article "De la locura histérica," in which he insists that the hysterical woman is better treated in a mental institution rather than at home, because she is morally harmful to her family (p. 276).

[30] See Elaine Showalter, *The Female Malady: Women, Madness and English Culture, 1830-1980* (London: Virago Press, 1985), pp. 147-164. Showalter comments on the interpretation of hysteria as a form of female rebellion against patriarchal restrictions and concludes that: "In its historical contexts in the late nineteenth century, hysteria was at best a private, ineffectual response to the frustrations of women's lives. Its immediate gratifications – the sympathy of the family, the attention of the physician – were slight in relation to its costs in powerlessness and silence" (p. 161).

What makes Galdós' depiction of hysteria in *Lo prohibido* interesting is that the cliché of the manipulating female hysteric is virtually eclipsed by the more subtle psychological study of the narrator, whose memoirs provide the reader with a well-drawn case study of male hysteria, including as a kind of *grand finale,* an hysterical attack which might well have been pulled from Charcot's *Tuesday Lectures.* Galdós contrasts the strong-willed women who push and pull against the circumstances of their lives with Guzmán's *abulia* or loss of willpower. In nineteenth-century medical discourse, will and emotion cohabit in an eternal struggle. If lack of control is linked to mental illness, self-control through will-power is the definition of sanity. In a lecture read in Granada's Royal Academy of Medicine and Surgery and titled "Hysterical Women and Responsibility" ("La responsabilidad en las histéricas") [1893], hysteria is described as the lack of will-power to control one's emotions:

> ...these sick women [are] slaves to what they feel, at the mercy of their irresistible impulses, without energy to fight against them, they are impelled to commit extreme acts or acts condemned by morality [...] they are scatter-brained and obsessive...
>
> (...esas enfermas [son] esclavas de sus sensaciones, a merced de sus irresistibles impulsos, sin energía para oponerse a ellos, son impelidas a la realización de actos extremos o reprobados por la moral [...] carecen de voluntad para fijar las ideas movibles y rechazar las fijas...)[31]

Guzmán laments his lack of will-power: "I am passive, I myself do not control the situations in which events and my own weakness place me, no, I do not. It is they that control me." ("Yo soy pasivo, no domino yo las situaciones en que me ponen los sucesos y mi debilidad, no. Ellos me dominan a mí") [p. 328].

Guzmán's main nervous symptom is *taedium vitae,*[32] or depression. It is characterized by the incapacity to maintain a sustained interest in life, resulting in melancholy, apathy, irritability, lack of affect, and hypochondriacal fears. Depression (feelings of sadness)

---

[31] Dr. Velázquez de Castro, 1893, p. 39.
[32] The term *taedium vitae* is used by Freud in his case history of Frau Elizabeth von R. [1892] and is related to the patient's state of depression and melancholy. See Joseph Breuer and Sigmund Freud, *Studies on Hysteria,* trans. J. Strachey (New York: Basic Books, n.d.), p. 163 n.

was associated both with hysteria and neurastenia or nervous exhaustion.³³ Galdós contrasts the emptiness of Guzmán's emotional and spiritual life with the plenitude of his material existence: his great wealth, social connections, and the physical beauty of the ideal lover. Why, then, is he not happy? A perplexed Guzmán asks himself: "Why wasn't Camila mine? Just tell me, why not?" ("¿Por qué Camila no era mía? Vamos a ver. ¿Por qué?") [p. 347].

But it is more interesting to reverse the man's question and to ask, why does Eloísa love him so much, when he clearly does not love her? And María Juana, does she truly love him? Or is she using him to take, like a man, the sexual satisfaction she may not find within her decorous marriage. Even after the narrator has confessed the weariness bordering on repulsion that he feels toward both women, they continue to pursue him. Is he, then, truly irresistible? We know that he is rich and that he is handsome. But what really entices the women is his indefinable charm, his ability to please. He is a good listener: he listens not only to the women, but also to the men. He gives them advice and little presents of money; he soothes and flatters them. He is gentle kind and loving. He understands them. Indeed, he is truly angelic. His cousin tells him, "Because you are so irresistible..." ("Como tienes ese ángel...") [p. 406]. In a word, José María Bueno de Guzmán is a perfect nineteenth-century woman, exercised in the art of pleasing others.

If female hysteria manifests itself as transgressing the prescribed model for proper feminine comportment – in willfulness and a lack of docility –, male hysteria, according to Charcot, is identified primarily by symptoms of depression and melancholy.³⁴ In the case of

---

³³ The confusion between the symptoms of neurasthenia, hypochondria, hysteria, and depression (melancholy, sadness or *taedium vitae*) is evident in the various medical charts, even after Charcot's nosological work. Thomas D. Savill's chart of medical symptoms lists sadness as a defining symptom of neurasthenia, also present in hypochondria and fleetingly in hysterical patients. Hysteria is distinguished by "deficient will power" and neurasthenia by "mental exhaustion and inability to think or study." See. I. Veith, op. cit., pp. 242-43.

³⁴ J.-M. Charcot, *L'hystérie*, Textes choisis et présentés par E. Trillat (Toulouse: Privat, 1971). "...in the male, in particular, one observes depression and a tendency to melancholy most frequently, in the most pronounced and least questionable cases of hysteria. One does not usually observe with men [...] the caprices, the changes of character and mood that appear more customarily, although not necessarily always, in women's hysteria." ("...chez le male, en particulier, la dépression et la tendance mélancolique s'observent le plus communément dans les cas d'hystérie les plus accusés, les moins contestables. On n'observe pas ordinairement, chez

women, pathological symptoms of mental and physical inervation may easily be interpreted as the self-abnegation which in turn defines the feminine ideal. But the virtue of feminine docility or submissive behavior is, in the male, diagnosed as illness. To cede one's will to another in order to please contradicts the model of patriarchal masculinity.

It is impossible to always please without repressing one's own interest, needs and desires. Guzmán is a timid man who fears rejection because he fears solitude; he must not alienate anyone's affections. Seduction for him is a preventive medicine against solitude's claustrophobia. But in order to be always agreeable, always lovable – that is to say, to seduce everyone – Guzmán must repress his boredom, his impatience, his anger, his disgust: "I was forced to control myself and to feign indifference." ("Tuve que reportarme y disimular") [p. 346]. "There was a secret anger inside me." ("En mi interior había una ira secreta") [p. 315]. "I considered it more correct not to say anything." ("Creí más correcto no decir nada.") [p. 310]. "...I hid my true feelings and managed to portray the indifference or superficial interest which is common among gentlemen" ("...disimulé y supe afectar la indiferencia o el interés superficial que es propio, entre caballeros") [p. 334]. And again and again he silences: his fear of marriage to Eloísa, his disgust and boredom with María Juana, his guilt over Carrillo's death, and above all, his childish jealousy of Camila and Constantino's passionate sexuality and mutual loyalty which is a constant affront to the emotional poverty of his own love affairs.

Repression demands its price and it is the body that pays, not only during the moment of hysterical crisis, but also the daily symptoms of headache, exhaustion, shortness of breath, all the limps and tics and unexplicable heart pains, the *globus hystericus* that strangles and suffocates, the *tos nervosa* that is the hysteric's fretful attempt to rid his throat of this impediment. The hysteric expresses with the body the unutterable. Throughout the novel, Guzmán is tormented by a humming in his ears.[35] Is it the echo of his own false

---

lui [...] ces caprices, ces changements de caractère et d'humeur qui appartiennent plus habituellement, bien que non nécessairement, toutefois, à l'hystérie de la femme."), p. 160.

[35] The sound of humming in the ears was considered a typical symptom of hysteria and, in particular, one that announced the onset of the convulsive attack. See Velázquez de Castro, op. cit., pp. 18-19.

words? "I couldn't have felt less like conversation. But I had no alternative. I talked, I talked about a thousand stupid pointless things." ("Yo que no tenía malditas ganas de plática. Pero no había más remedio. Hablé, hablé de mil cosas tontas y hueras") [p. 392]. Or is it the stifled sound of his own anger, waiting to explode? The French psychiatrist, Lucien Israël, writes in *Hysteria, Sex and the Physician*, in the chapter on male hysteria:

> In the male we find another kind of crisis, fits of rage, [...] fits provoked by "disappointments" *["contretemps"]* or a series of them, [...] It is rather a question of obligations, often unchangeable, imposed by normal life, and which take away from the subject the ability to employ himself freely. To be obliged to take into account everyone else to one's own detriment, produces a growing feeling of malaise which, when it becomes intolerable, and is unable to express itself by other means, explodes in a crisis of rage. Nevertheless, this rage constitutes an authentic demonstration of impotence because it does not represent a real orgasm nor does it bring about any expansion. It is not very far off from appearing to be a "solitary" pleasure. [36]

It needs to be noted that Israël's description of the hysterical male prior to his "fit of rage" conforms precisely to the model of behavior required of the *ángel del hogar:* "to be obliged to take into account everyone else to one's own detriment" and especially, "the obligations, *often unchangeable,* imposed by normal life." The fact that hysteria was considered above all a woman's disease points a finger at the coercive elements of the ideology of domesticity, which emphasized, above all, women's submission to duty. The kind of feminine intuitiveness which always anticipates the other's desire is not a quality that society generally requires of the masculine roles, except that of the Don Juan, who must make himself lovable if he is to be loved: "The hysteric loves and longs to be well-considered." ("El histérico ama y ansia ser estimado"), insists the famous alienist, Dr. José María Esquerdo, in an ambivalent attempt to defend the hysteric's reputation for immorality. [37]

---

[36] Lucien Israël, *L'Hystérique, le Sexe et le Médicin,* Spanish trans. by Aurelio Lopez Zea, *La histeria, el sexo y el médico* (Barcelona: Toray-Masson, 1979), p. 63. I have translated from the Spanish version.

[37] Esquerdo, see op. cit. in note 28, p. 4.

In the scene of Guzmán's final hysterical crisis, Galdós unleashes all the force of his satire, painting a kind of epileptic fit that brings on an incapacitating stroke which ultimately results in the narrator's death. It is important to note that Galdós is much more lenient with Eloísa. When her *globus histericus* is made flesh in the form of a loathsome disfiguring boil on her neck, she cries piteously: "Dear God, I've been bad, but this is too much..." ("Dios mío, yo he sido mala; pero no para tanto...") [p. 381]. Galdós agrees and rescues her so that she may continue to ravish the bodies and pocketbooks of Madrid's decadent aristocracy. But Galdós is not so gentle with his male hysteric, for after all it is the strong sex and not the weaker one who is the true exemplar of bourgeois morality, a morality that is cruel and inexorable. Justice must be done. Galdós takes out his pen and castrates his protagonist.

Guzmán recognizes the justice of his punishment, and he resigns himself to becoming a true angel, with neither the desire nor the capacity for sexual activity. The absence of his virility does not disturb the poor invalid, but he is horrifed at the loss of his true source of power, his voice. He is barely able to speak:

> The truth of the matter was, ladies and gentlemen, what remained of my voice after the terrible crisis was intolerable; a shrill screeching high-pitched voice that made me think of the *castrati*'s soprano.
>
> (La verdad, señores, la voz que me quedó después de la horrible crisis era inaguantable; una voz atiplada, chillona y aguda, que me recordaba la de los cantares de capilla.) [p. 436]

The voice of a castrated man; the voice of a woman: the scolding voice of Shakespeare's nagging harridan, Kate; the whiny invalid voices in the novels of Edith Wharton and Henry James; the impossible-to-silence female soprano that haunted the plays and the imagination of Samuel Beckett; the demanding voice of the hysteric that irritates simply because she speaks and one must listen to her, regardless of the content of her words.

Guzmán tries to regain control over his life in the only way he knows how, by manipulating his illness to attract, by using his symptoms to make himself interesting. He stops talking: "My silence had turned into a form of coquetery for me." ("Mi silencio había venido a ser en mí como una coquetería") [p. 428]. Are we, the readers, finally seduced by his quiet resignation?

To write or to imagine one's own death-bed scene is pleasurable: it is an opportunity to fantasize love, revenge, and the ideal and desired responses of those who have remained resistent to our seductiveness. The fantasy of the death-bed scene is a happy ending to the narrative of our life because we image the perfect ending – perfect because we control it and it is not imposed upon us. Galdós' frantic comic death-bed scene imposed upon the life of his protagonist works as his own form of coquetery. The humor of the scene may distract us from our disapproval of the degenerate Don Juan and safe-guard Galdós from the ultimate rejection – the possibility that we might set aside Guzmán's memoirs without finishing them. For if we cannot love Guzmán, and that is too much to ask, then perhaps he will amuse us and we will read to the end and not abandon him alone on his death-bed. To be seduced is to permit oneself to be manipulated. Each reader will ultimately decide for her/himself how seductive he or she finds Guzmán's story of love and repentance.

CAMILA: GALDÓS' *ANGEL DEL HOGAR*

The theme that plays the counterpoint to Guzmán's monotonous melody of false love, rejection and disillusion is the love story of Camila and Constantino. If Amparo in *Tormento* is Galdós' critique of the romantic feminine ideal, Camila is Galdós' personal model of ideal womanhood. This model conforms in important aspects to the dominant bourgeois ideal of feminine domesticity, but there are significant deviations.

Guzmán is awakened to Camila's virtue upon the death of her first-born child. He had been unable to accept Camila's loyalty to her husband as either meritorious or even credible, but he cannot deny the strength of the mother's character during her child's illness. Until the appearance of Guillermina Pacheco in *Fortunata y Jacinta*, the popular belief that maternity is the essence of womanhood is implicit throughout Galdós' Contemporary Novels.[38] What distin-

---

[38] In *La familia de León Roch*, the Marqués de Fúcar comments that his daughter Pepa has reformed since the birth of her son: "Fortunately, she became a mother, and her regeneration dates from the time of her maternity." ("Felizmente fue madre, y de la maternidad data su regeneración") [p. 864]. The sterility of two such dissimilar women as María Egipcíaca and María Juana can be read as Galdós'

guishes Camila from the nineteenth-century stereotype of the self-abnegating mother is both her physical strength and her indomitable spirit that refuses to recognize an exclusively hierarchical and patriarchal authority.

Although passion had been traditionally associated with sensual pleasure and denigrated as sinful, maternal passion is exonerated in the nineteenth century and defined as the quintessential female characteristic, thus permitting the male to retain hegemony over intelligence, rationality and other cerebral functions. Camila, seen through the eyes of her cousin, José María Bueno de Guzmán, conforms to the contemporary prejudice that men think, and women feel. According to Guzmán, "...only her feelings were deep and long-lasting..." ("...sólo el sentimiento era en ella duradero y profundo...") [p. 318]. Camila becomes Guzmán's mirror-other whose reflection permits him to define himself as essentially intellectual: "...that damnable savage female; happy teasing and always incomprehensible to my intellectual blindness..." ("...aquella maldita hembra salvaje, feliz, burlona y siempre incomprensible para mi ceguera intelectual...") [p. 395]. Guzmán rationalizes Camila's refusal to be seduced as the incapacity of Man, the representation of intellect and civilization, to dominate Nature, a primitive female force. Guzmán's interpretation of Camila as "a wild headstrong little savage who had grown up in society as if to provide us with an example of all the lack of civility that civilization can encompass" ("una fierecilla indócil criada dentro de la sociedad como para ofrecernos una muestra de todo lo incivil que la civilización contiene") [p. 261], and also "authentic Nature" ("la naturaleza auténtica") [p. 319], is not so much a definition of Camila, the woman, as it is a reiteration of Guzmán's prissy white-glove definition of civilization as decorum and emotional restraint.

The key word in Guzmán's depiction of Camila as "natural" rather than "civilized" is "headstrong" [indócil]. When Camila screams at him: "You're out of your mind... shameless thing!... Leave me in peace." ("No estás tú mal... ¡sinvergüenza!... Déjame

---

punishment for the exercise of their sexuality divorced from the sentiment of maternal love. On the other hand, both Isidora in *La desheredada* and Eloísa in *Lo prohibido* reveal an innate femininity by producing children, even though both become prostitutes. Galdós underlines their similarity by having each woman sell herself to the same man, the repulsive Sanchez Botín, and for the same "noble" purpose, to provide economic support for their "true love."

en paz") [p. 384], he is unable to understand why she rebuffs him. Her anger merely acts as a challenge, as a provocation for further pursuit and he thinks: "I'll tame you yet" ("Ya te irás domando") [p. 384]. The concept of "to tame" [domar], to dominate, to control has throughout the novel an overt sexual content, as does the word "passion." María Juana, in her self-appointed role as Guzmán's guardian angel, tells him:

> ...when you gain control of yourself, you will experience the chaste satisfaction of being the master of your own passions and of being in charge of them, like the lion tamer who enters the lions' cage and whips them into shape.
>
> (...cuando te domines, experimentarás la satisfacción purísima de ser dueño de las propias pasiones y mandar en ellas, como ese domador que entra en la jaula de los leones y les sacude.) [p. 388]

But Guzmán has no wish to renounce his sexual life nor his self-image as the perfect lover. He rejects the model of male virtue personified in Carrillo:

> To die without ever having loved or hated anyone! To die without experiencing passion, without having anyone to pardon, anything of which to repent! Dull, monotonous and miserable death!
>
> (¡Morir sin haber querido o sin haber odiado a alguien! ¡Morir sin despedirse de una pasión, sin tener alguien a quien perdonar, algo de que arrepentirse! ¡Sosa, incolora y tristísima muerte!) [p. 311]

He will annihilate, by violating it, a standard of virtue — sexual control — that he cannot maintain and that is a constant reminder of his moral inferiority.

Galdós' explanation for the frequent incidence of adultery among the respectable middle and upper classes goes beyond the causes usually cited of *el lujo* and *la lujuria*. He takes into consideration the sexual relationship between husband and wife, and the importance of the wife's lack of sexual satisfaction within an otherwise happy and respectable marriage. The love between Camila and Constantino begins with the element of sexual attraction, unadorned by any romantic fantasy. Camila explains candidly to her cousin: "If you were to ask me why we got married, I wouldn't know how to answer you. It was something that just came over us..." ("Si me preguntas que por qué nos casamos, no te sabré contestar. Nos entró muy fuerte a los dos...") [p. 348]. What interests Galdós as he constructs the step by step progress of their marriage are the elements that combine to produce "that blind faith which they had in each other..." ("aquella fe ciega que tenían el uno en el otro...") [p. 350]. For it is this trust in each other's love which provides a human social dimension to their sexual passion.

The formula for an enduring marriage becomes *mutual* sexual attraction reinforced by *mutual* respect. Galdós emphasizes that both husband and wife seek and find in the other the approval and admiration that is denied them by their families. When Guzmán declares his love for the first time, Camila surprises him by replying: "I'm glad, I'm glad, so that Constantino will realize the treasure he has at home... because he adores me, even if he thinks neither one of us count for anything" ("Me alegro, me alegro... para que sepa Constantino el tesoro que tiene en casa... él que me adora, creyendo que ni él ni yo valemos un comino") [p. 331]. Their love for each other forms a protective wall against the general disdain in which they are held and it is bolstered by the pride they take in playing the socially respected roles of husband and wife.

Camila is also aware that Constantino's respect for her has great value in a society in which a woman's reputation is as fragile as it is precious. A loyal husband protects her against treacherous Don Juans. When Guzmán asks her why she loves Constantino, she replies: "because he's my husband, because he loves me... and all you're interested in is having a good time with me and turning me into a bad woman" ("que es mi marido, que me quiere... Y tú no vienes más que a divertirte conmigo y a hacer de mí una mujer mala") [p. 337].

Camila's intelligence shows itself as the wisdom of common sense that is acquired from living within certain social boundaries and learning how to find real solutions to real problems. She rejects Guzmán because she is repelled by his affected manners and his reputation as a ladies' man – a possibility that never seems to occur to Guzmán – but also because she is motivated by a sense of honor and a wife's duty to her husband that is firmly entrenched in the Spanish tradition. The trust that defines the young couple's love depends on their acceptance of the social norms of Spanish society.

They are not romantic rebels fleeing from society's repression; on the contrary, they are completely and willingly integrated into it.

Although Guzmán persists in describing the marriage of Constantino and Camila as a kind of romantic paradise, Camila is hard at work adjusting to the difficult demands of housekeeping on a very limited budget. Galdós returns to the theme of social education of the individual in his description of Camila's self-education as she teaches herself to cook, to sew, and even to add and to subtract: "Necessity is the mother of invention" ("La necesidad obliga") [p. 319], she tells her cousin. Her lack of formal training in the career of housewife is given comic relief in Chapter VII, "Dinner at Camila's House" ["La comida en casa de Camila"]. The food is oversalted and undercooked. The hostess receives her guests, first in her dressing gown, and then, in the middle of the day, in a low-cut evening gown. Like the dinner, she is either under or over-dressed. The house is freezing, Constantino has forgotten the wine, and worst of all, the coffee is undrinkable. Three years later, Guzmán visits them and finds:

> The man from the Mancha [Constantino] was making coffee in a Russian coffee urn, and she was sewing on the new Singer's sewing machine which she had purchased with part of the money she had saved for his [Constantino's] horse.
>
> (El manchego estaba haciendo café en la cocinilla rusa, y ella cosiendo en una máquina nueva de Singer, que había adquirido con parte de los ahorros destinados al caballo.) [p. 350]

Coffee brewed properly and served decently in the privacy of one's home rather than in a public café, the fabulous Singer sewing machine, both are symbols of progress, of the modern technology on which the standards of comfort and civilization depend.

But how has this miraculous transformation taken place? For Camila has somehow transformed herself, without any education, into a model housewife, an authentic *ángel del hogar* – industrious, prudent, frugal, and also modest, since an essential element of modesty is knowing one's place in society and not aspiring to imitate the superior classes. Equally important, under Camila's tutelage, Constantino has given up gambling and drinking; he has learned to respect his superiors, to help with the housework, and even to wash his neck and ears.

Galdós' explanation of this miracle breaks with the social determinism of Naturalism. When Camila repays her cousin a loan of 500 pesetas, she tells him how difficult it was to save the money: "But where there's a will, there's a way..." ("Pero todo se aprende con voluntad...") [p. 377]. Constantino informs him that they have given up meat, because it is a luxury they cannot afford, but he insists: "...you can get used to anything" ("...a todo se *jace* uno") [p. 338]. Camila's will power infused into her husband has transformed them into a model couple. But Galdós' analysis does not depend solely on a belief in the moral education acquired through perseverance in the face of adversity. The marriage of the Medinas is also structured upon the bourgeois values of industriousness, thrift and the virtue of living within one's income. Nevertheless, the couple's respectability evidently hides secret dissatisfactions which are sufficiently profound to leave María Juana vulnerable to sexual seduction and willing to risk her status as a virtuous wife. In turn, the source of Camila's moral strength lies both within her and at her side in the much maligned Constantino. She tells her cynical cousin "he loves me terribly, he idolizes me" ("me quiere muchísimo, me idolatra") [p. 330]. When Guzmán laughs at her, she tries to explain her experience of love to a man whose deepest feelings have always been systematically filtered through romantic clichés:

> You're just so *dissipated* you can't understand something like this. No matter how lofty an idea you might have of a man's love for a woman, you have no idea how much Constantino loves me. He would die a hundred deaths for his wife. He never lies to me, and he trusts me so much that if anyone were to tell him I'd been a bad woman, he wouldn't believe it.
>
> (Es que tú eres un *tísico*, y no comprendes esto. Por muy alta idea que tengas del amor de un hombre, no sabes cómo me quiere Constantino. Se dejaría matar cien veces por su mujer. Jamás me dice una mentira, y tiene tal fe en mí, que si le dijeran que yo era mala, no lo creería.) [p. 330]

Guzmán is incapable of understanding this kind of unconditional love, because he assumes, like the philosophers and the Church Fathers, that women are the morally weaker sex. He considers all women capable of "falling" because up to now, no woman has resisted him.

The emphasis that Galdós places on the importance of the husband's fidelity in a marriage is unusual for the nineteenth century. The dyad of mother and child embodied trust, maternal love and loyalty but also deemphasized the importance of the father-husband's emotional bonds within the family unit in spite of his power in the home as principal authority. The salient characteristic of Camila and Constantino's relationship is the absence of a hierarchy of power. Camila says: "I rule him and he governs over me." ("Le domino y me tiene dominada") [p. 348]. The only chink in this armour of mutual trust is the possibility that one or the other might break their contract of absolute fidelity. When Camila is led to believe that Constantino has been unfaithful to her she explodes in a diatribe that leaves no doubt as to the precise limits of her self-abnegation and her dedication to the institution of matrimony:

> I want to be left alone, I'm tired of working so hard. I'm a slave: I sew, I cook the dinner; I do the washing, I do the ironing; I brush his clothes, I clean his boots; I dress him; I wash him; I sweep the house while he sleeps the morning away; I write letters for him to his family; I make the coffee; I fill his cigarette case with cigarettes and count out for him how many he should smoke each day; I teach him a thousand things he doesn't know, even how to walk, and explain to him what he should say when we go calling; I do his thinking for him; I teach him, I take care of him as if he were a child and go without food so he can go to the bullfights... well he can go straight to hell!

> (Quiero estar sola, quiero descansar de tanto trabajo. Soy una esclava: yo coser; yo hacer la comida; yo lavar; yo planchar; yo cepillarle la ropa; y embetunarle las botas; yo vestirlo; yo lavarlo; yo barrer mientras él duerme la mañana; yo escribirle las cartas a su familia; yo hacer café; yo ponerle los cigarrillos en la petaca y contarle los que se ha de fumar cada día; yo enseñarle mil cosas que no sabe, hasta el modo de andar, y darle lección de lo que ha de decir cuando va a una visita; yo pensar por él, educarle, criarle como a un niño y dejar de comer para que él se vaya a los toros... ¡Que se vaya con mil demonios!) [p. 391]

Camila's capacity for self-sacrifice is clearly dependent on her husband's loyalty and love. If she is not a respected and beloved wife, she is nothing more than an unpaid servant. But the value of Camila's services cannot be quantified in terms of money. What defines the essence of the *ángel del hogar* is that she is not for sale. Guzmán is incapable of understanding human relationships outside the purvue of commodity exchange. The story of Camila and Constantino serves to demonstrate a clear moral message: sexual services (like domestic service) can be bought and sold, but love is given freely or not at all.

In *Lo prohibido*, Galdós rewrites the romantic formula of love that is based on narcissistic fantasy and thrives on the absence of the beloved because the lover prefers his own creation to the human imperfections and contradictions of real women. He underlines the healthy self-interest in a love relationship that demands as its right the full and active participation of the beloved. Camila explains matter-of-factly, in words liberated from the weight of romantic rhetoric, the reciprocity that is her experience and definition of love: "Well, I fell in love with him because he fell in love with me, and I love him because he loves me." ("Pues le quise porque me quiso, y le quiero porque me quiere") [p. 236].

THE PARADISE OF DOMESTICITY

Galdós contrasts Guzmán's gradual psychological regression with Constantino and Camila's slow process of emotional and social maturation. In the final scene of Guzmán's expulsion from the "paradise" of the young couple's home, he is reduced to the status of a screaming child caught in the throes of rage and self-pity:

> Love me or I'll kill you – I told her in a fit of epileptic excitement – [...] love me or I'll kill you! He has no right to have it all, give me some, too. Here I am loving you like a child, and you, nothing...
>
> (¡Quiéreme, o te mato – le dije con desazón epiléptica – [...] quiéreme o te mato! Que no todo sea para él, algo para mí. Te estoy queriendo como un niño, y tú nada...) [p. 402]

This scene represents one of the few moments in the novel in which Guzmán expresses spontaneously and openly his true sentiments. Throughout the novel, Guzmán's compulsive mendacity condemns him to a state of emotional isolation. His slow psychological disintegration testifies to the prejudicial effects of the Spanish Restoration's hypocritical moral ambience on men as well as on women. His furious attempt to break into the Miquis home is essentially an attempt to break out of the solitary confinement of his own psyche, the façade of lies behind which he is dying. But ironically, when Guzmán finally tries to break through the barrier of his lies by spewing out the truth of Camila's fidelity, he communicates this truth to the one individual who is as cynical as he, María Juana. And she laughs in his face and calls him a liar; he is now irrevocably alone:

> My true emotions, and the lies which I had employed to give to my false passions the pretense of truth, formed a thick net around me from which I could not escape. I was, as she [María Juana] had said, despicable and monstrous.
>
> (Mis pasiones verdaderas, las mentiras con que cohonestaba las falsas, habíanme formado una espesa red de la cual no podía salir. Era, como ella dijo, despreciable y monstruoso.) [p. 411]

Camila's physical and mental health functions throughout the novel as an ideal standard against which Guzmán's physical and psychological degeneration is measured. The healthiness and virtue of matrimony are placed in contrast to the immorality of bachelorhood, with its barren and diseased promiscuity. In Spain, the Catholic Church's critique of bachelorhood is reinforced by the secular authority of medical and public health institutions as a result of the inability to control veneral disease and its consequent encroachment on the family institution. According to Dr. P. Hauser, whose monograph *Madrid bajo el punto de vista médico-social (Madrid Seen from a Medical-Social Perspective)* appeared at the turn of the century, the growing awareness of the secondary and tertiary stages of syphilis and of the consequences wrought upon the children of syphilitic parents had a profound and definitive effect upon the movement of hygienists and moralists during the last quarter of the nineteenth century:

> The spread of syphilis is seen by all as a social danger, since it is not only a matter of the harm and danger to one's health and other concerns, along with the secondary and tertiary symptoms, but also the unhealthy influence which extends to the descendants, weakening their vital resistance and predisposing them to rickets and tuberculosis. In recent times, numerous statistics

have shown the disasterous effects upon those individuals of nervous temperament, predisposing them to *general paralysis* and *progressive locomotor ataxia*, serious diseases which have become so prevalent in modern times.

(Todos ven en la propagación de la sífilis un peligro social, pues no sólo se trata del daño y perjuicios en su salud y en sus intereses, con los accidentes secundarios y terciarios, sino de la influencia nociva que ejerce en los descendientes, disminuyendo su resistencia vital y predisponiéndolos al raquitismo y a la tuberculosis. En los últimos tiempos, numerosas estadísticas han puesto en evidencia sus efectos desastrosos en los individuos de temperamento nervioso, predisponiéndolos a la *parálisis general* y a la *ataxia locomotriz progresiva*, enfermedades graves que han tomado tanto incremento en los tiempos modernos.)[39]

Although the symptoms of Guzmán's illness are deliberately ambiguous, specific allusions to possible symptoms of venereal disease abound. Camila's rage at her husband's supposed transgression is colored by the fear that he will contaminate her: "...you've brought that nasty smell in with you, that rotten *bouquet*... get out of here, get away from my sight. I don't want to catch that plague from you..." ("...traes pegado el tufo o el *bouquet* podrido... lárgate, quítate de delante de mí. No me pegues esa peste...") [p. 391]. Eloísa, disfigured and reeking, tells her former lover that she feels "As if all my sins were consuming every part of me" ("Como si los propios pecados me estuvieran comiendo por todas partes") [p. 382]. More telling yet is Camila's scorn for Guzmán's physical weakness, for she relates it directly to the libertine habits of the promiscuous *señorito*:

> You're nothing but a milksop; you have no blood in your veins; your vices have worn you out, you're no good to a real woman, all you're good for is visiting those women that are just as decrepit and consumptive as you are... you miserable man.
>
> (Si eres un muñeco; si no tienes sangre en las venas; si los vicios te tienen desainado, no sirves para una mujer de verdad, sino para esas tías tan tísicas, tan fulastres como tú... perdido.) [p. 403]

---

[39] Philip Hauser, *Madrid bajo el punto de vista médico-social*, first published in 1902, ed. Carmen del Moral (Madrid: Editora Nacional, 1979), p. 131.

The idea of moral regeneration through marriage evidently has, in the nineteenth century, a clear and specific material dimension. Sexual access to a healthy wife prevented the need to use diseased prostitutes. Guzmán's expulsion from the "healthy" social organism of the Miquis home thus becomes a commentary on his "unhealthy" status as a bachelor, a status considered both amoral and anti-social.

Another important aspect of middle-class family life is the new bourgeois luxury of privacy, the power to recuperate from the public sphere those hours of daily living that are left over from work-time. Galdós emphasizes that the right to privacy in the home is a prerogative that must be exercised. Eloísa and María Juana open their homes to their guests for reason of business and social status. The gatherings in the Miquis' modest living-room take place for their own pleasure. The narrator describes these social events with his customary snobbery:

> Some of their friends were usually there, and they would talk about a thousand silly things, or they would play cards and lotto. I've never seen anything so stupid in my whole life! The life of the party was Camila, the center, heart and soul of everything.
>
> (Solían ir algunos amigos, y charlaban de mil tontadas, o jugaban a la brisca y a la lotería. ¡Cosa más necia no he visto en mi vida! Lo simpático de tal reunión era Camila, alma, centro y núcleo de ella.) [p 329]

The concept of privacy, that is, the right to dispose as one sees fit of at least a portion of one's time and the right to be protected from unwanted interference with one's person or property, does not signify isolation from the public sphere. R. Williams explains the evolution of the term private from a general meaning in the sixteenth century of hidden and secret to its modern use in the nineteenth century as a word which describes the rights of the individual in relation to other individuals and to the state:

> But this general movement in *private* (the association with *privilege*) has to be set alongside an even more important movement, in which 'withdrawal' and 'seclusion' came to be replaced, as senses, by 'independence' and 'intimacy'. It is very difficult to date this. [...] In C17 and especially C18, seclusion in the sense of a quiet life was valued as *privacy*, and this developed beyond the sense of solitude to the senses of decent and dignified

withdrawal and of the *privacy of my family and friends*, and beyond those to the generalized values of *private life*. [...]

Private, that is, in its positive senses, is a record of the legitimization of a bourgeois view of life: the ultimate generalized privilege, however abstract in practice, of seclusion and protection from others (the public); of lack of accountability to 'them'; and of related gains in closeness and comfort of these general kinds. [40]

The tranquility of the Miquis' private life is not only dependent on their ability to exclude from their home the public world of capitalist competition (the Medina's world) and of sordid sexual scandal (Eloísa's world); it is equally dependent on the couple's public integration into society. Paradoxically, they are able to create a private life because they have nothing to hide; they live in intimate *privacy*, not in fearful *secrecy*. When the scandal of Camila's supposed adulterous affair with Guzmán breaks over their heads, the fearful ogre of 'what people will say' shatters their privacy and threatens their marriage. Galdós' depiction of their tense unhappiness is subtle and sympathetic. The malicious gossip and the snubs of her friends make Camila cry and her husband is powerless to defend her. They were able to close their door against Guzmán, the agent of their misery; can they also close out the powerful specter of public opinion?

Galdós writes the habitual open-ending. Even though the prince and the princess live happily-ever-after only in fairy-tales, Camila's words encourage us to hope for the best:

> Aren't we at peace with our own consciences? Don't you and I both know, like day is day and night is night, that he never took advantage of me and that there never was any affair nor anything of the sort...? Well if there's some fool around who thinks differently, that's up to him; he can go ahead and think what he wants.
>
> (¿No estamos bien tranquilos en nuestra conciencia? ¿No sabemos tú y yo, como este es día, que ni él pudo conquistarme, ni había tales carneros, ni Cristo que lo fundó...? Pues si hay algún necio que crea otra cosa, déjalo y con su pan se lo coma.) [p. 434]

---

[40] Raymond Williams, *Keywords: A Vocabulary of Culture and Society* (New York: Oxford University Press, 1976), p. 204.

Camila has learned to pardon her transgressor, one more example of maturity. Yes, people will continue to gossip but we are left with the impression that Camila, protected by her husband's love and busy with the care of her children will be too occupied to notice. Unlike the submissive and anemic bourgeois ideal, Galdós has created an *ángel del hogar* who is strong-willed, energetic, and blessed with a mind of her own. She won't allow herself to made into anyone's muse, and she doesn't have time to sit still on anyone's pedestal. "Nonsense, nonsense," she laughs at us, and without bothering to see whether or not we answer, she turns away and goes on about her business.

EPILOGUE

TRISTANA: THE DEATH OF AN IDEAL

> In those days – the last of Queen Victoria – every house had its Angel. And when I came to write, I encountered her with the very first words. The shadow of her wings fell on my page; I heard the rustling of her skirts in the room.... And she made as if to guide my pen.... I turned upon her and caught her by the throat. I did my best to kill her.... She died hard. Her ficticious nature was of great assistance to her. It is far harder to kill a phantom than a reality.
>
> Virginia Woolf, *Professions for Women* (1931)

In 1892, in the midst of preparing the production of his play, *Realidad,* Galdós pens a curious novel about a young woman who thinks that she might be, in the future, an artist or perhaps an actress. She learns to play the organ brilliantly, as if endowed with a natural talent or genius. She is also fascinated with words, words as play and the power to create new imaginary worlds; words above all to communicate, to express an artistic self which is stillborn upon the pages of this all-too-brief novel. However, *Tristana* frustrates the reader, not because of its brevity, but because it is absolutely and irrevocably finished. When the final page is read, we cannot avoid recognizing that there is no recourse to its ending. Unlike the relatively open endings of *Tormento, La de Bringas,* and *Lo prohibido,* the ending of *Tristana* records a final judgement laid down by the laws of nature, of man-made patriarchal society, and finally, of the Spanish tradition: *"La mujer honrada, pierna quebrada y en casa"* [The decent woman, at home with a broken leg], a phrase that combines the authority of the bourgeois expression "A Woman's Place is in the Home" – restrained, correct but dictatorial – with the threatening rednecked male chauvinism of "keep 'em barefoot and pregnant."

Since the feminist movement of the 1970s, *Tristana* has inspired a substantial list of diverse, thoughtful and contradictory readings. While these articles treat different aspects of the novel, one question seems to be inevitable, and almost every critic would seem compelled to answer it to her/his own satisfaction: why does Tristana fail to realize any of her dreams?[1] Asking this question implies that Tristana's marriage to Don Lope represents a failure in her life,

---

[1] The key question of why Tristana fails to achieve her goals has been posed from the very beginning within the context of Tristana's possible responsibility (or guilt) for this failure. Leopoldo Alas, in his brief review of the novel, agreed with the narrator's opinion that Tristana's own weakness of character prevented her from attaining her goals. Leopoldo Alas, *Galdós (Obras Completas,* vol. I) (Madrid: Renacimiento, 1912), pp. 251-52. Doña Emilia Pardo Bazán insists that Galdós insufficiently develops the theme of: "...the awakening of the understanding, the consciousness, of a woman in rebellion against a society which condemns her to endless infamy, and provides no honorable means through which she might earn her own livelihood, extricate herself from the power of her decrepit lover and not see her concubinage as her only protection, her only support." ("...el despertar del entendimiento, la conciencia de una mujer sublevada contra una sociedad que la condena a perpetua infamia y no le abre ningún camino honroso para ganarse la vida, salir del poder del decrépito galán, y no ver en el concubinato su única protección, su apoyo único.") "Tristana," *Nuevo Teatro Crítico,* II, núm. 17 (mayo 1892), p. 81.

I believe that the narrator's habit of both criticizing and defending Don Lope (and also Tristana) sets a polemical framework which is partially responsible for provoking a judgmental tendency on the part of the critics, directed principally towards Tristana. For example, Roberto Sánchez judges the heroine: "With her egocentric obsession, Tristana is equally guilty." "Galdós' *Tristana,* Anatomy of a Disappointment," *Anales Galdosianos,* XII (1977), p. 123. (I am not certain if Sánchez means that Tristana is guilty of *being* egocentric, or of actions that result from her egocentricity.) Noel Valis states: "The truth is, Tristana simply doesn't have the staying power to become a great artist." See her "Art, Memory, and the Human in Galdós' *Tristana,*" *Kentucky Romance Quarterly* 31 (1984), p. 212. Leon Livingstone comes out against what he sees as Tristana's exaggerated and "unnatural" feminism: "Tristana condemns herself in this respect [...] in her statements about being [...] more like a man than a woman." "The Law of Nature and Women's Liberation in *Tristana,*" *Anales Galdosianos,* VII (1972), p. 97.

In support of Tristana, Ruth A. Schmidt maintains that: "The forms of repression and conformity are too formidable to be deflected by the spirit of an idealistic woman..." in "Tristana and the Importance of Opportunity," *Anales Galdosianos,* IX (1974), p. 143. John H. Sinnegan agrees with this position: "...the role society plays in repressing women is clear in the lack of alternatives available for a woman to gain economic independence and in Horacio's unwillingness to grant Tristana anything more than a supporting role." "Resistance and Rebellion in *Tristana,*" *Modern Language Notes,* 91 (1976), p. 287. Emilio Miró interprets the novel as a struggle between the stronger and more experienced male to dominate the unexperienced younger woman: "Una mujer indefensa ante un mundo hostil es Tristana." "Tristana o la imposibilidad de ser," *Cuadernos Hispanoamericanos,* 250-52 (1970-71), p. 521.

although the marriage of a penniless orphan who cannot be considered by community standards to be a decent and therefore marriageable woman, to a respectable gentleman who is economically well off, would be a textbook "happy ending" for the nineteenth-century novel, and indeed, is the ending Galdós attaches to *Tormento*.

Another question also puzzles the critics: if Tristana's subjugation by Don Lope is implicated in her lack of self-realization, as it certainly is in the restrictions and humiliation of her daily existence, why does she not leave him? Tristana's desire for something more than the prescribed domestic role, as well as her refusal to marry her young lover Horacio, has provided a pretext to consider the novel's possible feminist message, as well as Galdós' position on feminism.[2] Other critics have identified the principal theme as Tristana's lack of self-realization,[3] and her failure to gain independence in a society which was hostile to women's efforts to enter into the professions or to move out of the socially approved domestic role of *ángel del hogar*.[4] Linking the theme of self-realization to narrative structure, Farris Anderson maintains that Tristana's lack of a stable personality creates a missing core or center which in turn informs the novel's organization.[5]

The idea of reading *Tristana* as a novel structured around an absence rather than a presence is very suggestive. Certainly, the narrative is framed by the young girl's lack of personality at the beginning and, at the end, an even more definitive annihilation of her presence. However, if we focus only on Tristana, either as presence or absence, we are drawn away from the dominating and very present personality of her adoptive father, putative protector and self-righteous seducer, Don Lope Garrido. On the other hand,

---

[2] It is refreshing to read Roberto Sánchez's blunt assertion that "it is idle to speculate whether Galdós was or was not a feminist and at which point he may have become one," Roberto Sánchez, op. cit., n. 1, p. 112. Certainly, Galdós' support or lack of support for feminist goals must be judged by something more than the content of one or even all of his novels.

[3] Kay Engler has written a lengthy and very interesting article on the concept of Tristana's self-realization from a Jungian perspective. See "The Ghostly Lover: The Portrayal of the Animus in *Tristana*," *Anales Galdosianos*, XII (1977), pp. 95-109.

[4] See Carlos Feal Deibe, "Tristana de Galdós: capítulo en la historia de la liberación femenina", *Sin Nombre*, 7, no. 3 (1976), pp. 116-29. See also, Sinnegan and Schmidt, n. 1.

[5] Farris Anderson, "Ellipsis and Space in Tristana," *Anales Galdosianos*, XX (1985), pp. 61-76.

by confronting the incestuous relationship between this father-grandfather surrogate and the naïve orphan girl, it is possible to evaluate Tristana's supposed "failure of will" in terms which encompass not only the social limitations but also the psychological effect upon middle-class women whose lives were bound by the beliefs and values of the feminine ideal and the cult of domesticity.

As our previous discussions have shown, nineteenth-century society identified women, valued them, and judged them by their performance as daughters, wives and mothers. Tristana's desire to live her life as a woman who is "free but respectable" (*"libre pero honrada"*) is an expression of her need to disengage her sense of self from her socially mandated place in a male/female dyad. Yet not only does she lack the support of family, education and money to forge an unconventional position of female autonomy, her conventional social identity has already been undermined and perverted by her ambivalent relation to Don Lope. John H. Sinnigan, who emphasizes the social and psychological effects of Don Lope's seduction upon Tristana's psychological development, makes the important point that Tristana's solipsistic reliance upon her own fantasy results in part from her inability to transcend the condition of social isolation resulting from her guardian's seduction:

> Tristana is unable to overcome this initial isolation. Never confronted by any character or group of characters who embody or defend the institutions and values of the status quo, the development of her consciousness is restricted. [...] Thus, although she rebels against the social norm and seeks to achieve a new role [...], that quest ultimately remains abstract because she lacks an adequate vision of the society whose conventions she seeks to overcome.[6]

In *Tristana*, the theme of incest is continually being introduced, only to be displaced, discounted and covered up by the novel's shifting focus on the heroine: Tristana's love affair, her ambition, her illness, and finally, her marriage and psychological death. Not until the novel's end is the horror and perversity of Don Lope's amoral behavior finally given complete expression in the detailed description of a senile old man tied forever by marriage bonds to

---

[6] Sinnegan, op. cit, n. 1, p. 278.

an aging and silent woman who has apparently suffered not only a physical mutilation but also severe psychological trauma.

It is not surprising that the question of incest in *Tristana* has not previously been discussed in the critical bibliography. Of all the so-called women's issues – rape, domestic violence, child abuse, including sexual assault – incest probably provokes the most repulsion and therefore the most denial. If the "natural" is normality, sanity and, in general, social behavior which can be explained logically according to accepted canons of belief, acts of violence such as heterosexual rape or child abuse can still be rationalized; in the first case, as the logical outcome of frustrated male sexual desire or of a woman's provocative behavior; and in the second, as punishment "for the child's own good." But incest, and especially father-daughter incest, is such an all-pervasive and entrenched cultural taboo, that its "unnaturalness" is almost universally assumed. A recognition of the prevalence of incestuous behavior and the harm inflicted upon the victims of incest is one result of the resurgence of feminism since the 1970s. The now extensive bibliography of both clinical studies and personal testimonies has also provided a context within which the theme of incest in literature can be studied.[7]

Dr. Julie Herman, in her study of father-daughter incest, defines incest as "any sexual relationship between a child and an adult in a position of paternal authority. From the psychological point of view, it does not matter if the father and child are blood relatives."[8] According to Dr. Herman, the paradigmatic incestuous family has several essential characteristics: the mother is either powerless or absent, often as a result of illness (frequently mental illness) or death. The fathers are invariably responsible family providers who also feel entitled to be nurtured at home by the wife, and in her absence, by the daughters.[9] The father's feeling of entitlement to his daughters' services dominates and structures the familial relationship. The incestuous father/daughter dyad is also colored by

---

[7] See James B. Twitchell, *Forbidden Partners: The Incest Taboo in Modern Culture* (New York: Columbia University Press, 1987), pp. 281-301 for one of the more complete and up-to-date bibliographies. His list of readings includes personal testimonies, clinical literature and literary and cultural studies.

[8] Judith Lewis Herman with Lisa Hirschman, *Father-Daughter Incest* (Cambridge: Harvard University Press, 1981), p. 70.

[9] Herman, pp. 44-49.

the father's tyrannical jealousy, which is most intense at the moment when the daughter begins to attempt to establish a relationship with any male of her own age. One psychological effect of the father's sexual dominance of his daughter is her tendency to idealize men.[10]

Until the decade of the seventies, the absence of any substantial bibliography on the subject reveals that the existence of incest in advanced Western societies was generally ignored, denied or relegated to the social practices of the "lower classes." More recently, Jeffrey Moussaieff Masson's provocative and, at times, very questionable book, *The Assault on Truth: Freud's Suppression of the Seduction Theory* [1984],[11] became a kind of litmus test for the capacity of historians, psychoanalysts and interested laypeople to engage the subject of the father's seduction of his children, both in Freud's *fin de siècle* Vienna, and now. But in spite of a general tendency to deny the fact of incest, its possibility was (and is) continually and systematically reinforced through the patriarchal values which we have discussed under the rubric of the ideology of domesticity: that women exist to please men and that men are entitled to receive the services of the women whom they protect from male predators outside their family nucleus. Dr. Herman affirms that:

> It is this attitude of entitlement – to love, to service and to sex – that finally characterizes the incestuous father and his apologists. In a patriarchal society, the concept of the father's right to use female members of his family – especially his daughters – as he sees fit is implicit even in the structure of the incest taboo.[12]

In *Tristana*, Don Lope's need to possess and to control Tristana absolutely and permanently represents the paradigmatic incestuous romance. Tristana is more than his "final trophy," and their relationship is more than the Don Juan's typical conquest. Don Lope recognizes this difference, and he begs Tristana: "...let me do with you what I have never done with any other woman, look upon you as a loved one [...] as if you were someone of my own blood..."

---

[10] Herman, p. 103.

[11] The 1985 Penguin edition includes a new preface in which Masson engages his critics and also a short but interesting bibliography of adult writings by incest victims. See *The Assault on Truth: Freud's Suppression of the Seduction Theory* (New York: Penguin Books, 1985).

[12] Herman, p. 49.

("...déjame hacer contigo lo que no he hecho con mujer alguna, mirarte como un ser querido, [...] como un ser de mi propia sangre...") [p. 374]. In a word, the most important thing is the family. And in order to become a *"padre de familia"* ["the head of a family"] this depraved old man will create, like Frankenstein's monster, a daughter.[13] Having made Tristana his mistress, he will seduce her once more into playing the role of daughter to his role of self-sacrificing good father. Finally, when their relationship has been purified of sexuality, when they are truly father and daughter, he will take her as a wife. The respectable bourgeois family, patched together at the end of the novel, is engendered out of the act of incest, the purest act of patriarchal violence.

To solve or at least trace the novel's conundrum of causality, both the reasons for the sudden surge of Tristana's artistic ambitions as well their abrupt decline, three factors must be weighed: first of all, Tristana's lack of social support; second, her illness and the brutal amputation of her leg; and finally, the narrator's viewpoint, frequently shared by the critics, that Tristana fails to realize her goals because of "a lack of willpower (or self-confidence)" ("una falta de fe") [p. 414].

Tristana is nineteen when her father dies, and twenty-one when she loses her mother. During the two years prior to her mother's death, the young girl must exercise the role of protector or parent to her mother, whose obsessive fear of germs causes her to suffer a kind of exaggerated Freudian "housewife's psychosis."[14] Upon her

---

[13] Galdós plays with the idea that Tristana is a kind of daughter-monster of the old man's creation: "...Don Lope,... had made her his disciple, and some of the ideas which flourished so tenaciously in the young girl's mind had as their source seeds of ideas planted there by he who was both her lover and unfortunately, her teacher." ("...don Lope,... habíala hecho su discípula, y algunas ideas de las que con toda su lozanía florecieron en la mente de la joven procedían del semillero de su amante y por fatalidad maestro") [357]. Twitchell, op. cit. n. 7, comments on the Frankenstein myth as a gothic form with the sub-text of "sexual confusion (after all, how can just one person create life?)," and also the abandonment of the monster by its creator, or "love deprivation." (pp. 164-65) Galdós does not really develop this theme of Frankenstein and his monster, probably because the idea of Don Lope as Tristana's progenitor or creator would have refocussed the question of responsibility for Tristana back on her "protector."

[14] Freud uses the term to refer to the behavior of Dora's mother in *Dora: An Analysis of a Case of Hysteria* [1905] (New York: Macmillan, 1963), p. 34. Freud also emphasizes how this syndrome represents the mother's emotional abandonment of the children. On the other hand, Dora's father suffered from syphillis, a fact which certainly could explain both his wife's disgust for sex and her obsession with purifying rituals.

mother's death, Don Lope, a family friend or titular uncle, who has known Tristana since she was a baby, takes the young girl under his protection. After two months residence in his house, he takes her into his bed, employing her both as mistress and as servant. She passes the day cleaning the house in the company of her only female companion, the cook Saturna. Eight months later, having reached her twenty-second birthday, Tristana begins to feel a strong repulsion for the person of Don Lope, now almost 60 years old, and for the sexual obligations which he imposes upon her: "...the methodical continuance of her dishonor..." ("...la continuidad metódica de su deshonra...") [p. 356].

The question of the age difference between Tristana and Don Lope, the difference between innocence and experience, is important in establishing the father/daughter dyad. Tristana is old enough when the seduction takes place that the incestuous nature of their sexual affair can be camouflaged behind the more ideologically acceptable comic literary stereotypes of the maiden and the old man or the romantic narrative, Don Juan's seduction of the virgin. Nevertheless, Tristana's childlike innocence is not so much chronological as a lack of social/psychological development. She has lived completely isolated from society, first by her mother's insanity, then by her ignominious status as Don Lope's paramour. Still, it is Tristana's gradual awareness of their physical age difference, Don Lope is almost 40 years older than she, which finally provokes feelings of repulsion towards his sexual advances.

At this point, the father/daughter relationship is highlighted through Don Lope's possessive jealousy and his refusal to cede control over her. He threatens Tristana: "I will look upon you as my wife and as my daughter, whichever suits me best." ("Te miro como esposa y como hija, según me convenga") [p. 374]. His rights as a father are expressed as the right to exercise total psychological and physical control: "So now I have decided to be her father, and to keep her just for myself, for myself alone, [...] let nobody touch her, by God! let nobody even look at her." ("Ahora me da la gana de ser su padre, y de guardarla para mí solo, para mí solo, [...] que nadie la toque, ¡vive Dios!, nadie la mire siquiera") [p. 396].

Don Lope argues to himself that he has earned the favors of the young woman by paying her father's debts and the expenses of her mother's illness [p. 355]. He is entitled to possess her, it does not matter whether she be his wife or his daughter. The right to control her, including the right to use her sexually is rationalized as a father's obligation to protect her from other men:

> I don't care what anybody says – he would mumble to himself, remembering the sacrifices he had made to support the mother and to rescue the father from dishonor – I earned her the hard way. Didn't Josefina [Tristana's mother] ask me to protect her? Well, she can't be more protected than she is now. She's safe from any danger; now nobody will dare to touch a hair of her head.
>
> (Dígase lo que se quiera – argüía para su capote, recordando sus sacrificios por sostener a la madre y salvar de la deshonra al papá – bien me la he ganado. ¿No me pidió Josefina que la amparase? Pues más amparo no cabe. Bien defendida la tengo de todo peligro; que ahora nadie se atreverá a tocarle el pelo de la ropa.) [p. 355]

The narrator makes an almost *pro forma* recognition of the indefensibility of the seduction: "it is necessary to say it, however harsh and shameful it might be" ("hay que decirlo, por duro y lastimoso que sea") [p. 354]. But at the same time, the narrator criticizes Tristana's rejection of the old man: "Don Lope wasn't as old as Tristana thought, nor was he so worn out as to be put upon the shelf like a useless piece of crockery" ("Y no era don Lope aún tan viejo como Tristana lo sentía, ni había desmerecido hasta el punto de que se le mandara recoger como un trasto inútil") [p. 356]. The ambivalence of Tristana's relation to Don Lope is commented upon by the neighbors, and also recognized by Tristana herself who tells her lover Horacio: "I'm not married to my husband...; I mean, to my father...; I mean, to that man..." ("No estoy casada con mi marido...; digo, con mi papá...; digo, con ese hombre...") [p. 371].

Tristana's attempt at self-definition by rebelling against her father/husband never transcends the confusion of her psychological and affective ties with Don Lope as he shifts from good-bad father to jealous husband to tyrannical father/husband and back to good father. Even after falling in love with Horacio and although she dreams of being "free but respectable," she can only imagine changing her role from wife/mistress to daughter. Her sense of obligation to the man who has paid her family's bills, reinforced continually by Don Lope himself, prevents her from imagining a total rebellion.

At the beginning of her love affair with Horacio, she feigns headaches to escape from the sexual duties required of her by her guardian. In her prayers, she bargains with God for release from Don Lope's sexual demands:

> ...if it were only possible to erase the word love from our relations, and to establish between the two of us another kind of relationship, I would love him, [...] I would even forgive him the evil he has done to me, my dishonor, I would forgive him for it from the bottom of my heart, yes, yes I would, if he would only leave me alone, dear God, make him leave me alone, and I will forgive him, and I will even feel affection for him, and will be like one of those terribly humble daughters who is mistaken for a servant, or the loyal servant who sees a father in the master who gives her food.

> (...si borrase la palabra amor de nuestras relaciones, y estableciera entre los dos... otro parentesco, yo le querría, [...] Hasta le perdonaría yo el mal que me ha hecho, mi deshonra, se lo perdonaría de todo corazón, sí, sí, con tal que me dejase en paz... Dios mío, inspírale que me deje en paz, y yo le perdonaré, y hasta le tendré cariño, y seré como las hijas demasiado humildes que parecen criadas, o como las sirvientas leales, que ven un padre en el amo que les da de comer.) [p. 369]

Tristana's need for a sense of autonomy finally finds expression in her decision to go to bed with Horacio. Her love gives her the courage to rebel against Don Lope's authority. She tells Horacio, "Since I fell in love with you, [...] I'm not afraid of anything, neither bulls nor thieves. I feel brave to the point of heroism." ("Desde que te quiero [...] no tengo miedo a nada, ni a los toros ni a los ladrones. Me siento valiente hasta el heroísmo...") [p. 368]. (Implicit in this defiant statement is Tristana's awareness of her prior incapacitating fear of Don Lope.) The young woman exercises control over her sexuality by sleeping with the man that she loves and at the same time defying the man that she does not. Before she can redefine herself socially, she must know with certainty to whom her body belongs, to herself or to Don Lope. But the male/female dyad is impossible to escape. A woman's identity derives from her relation to a man, not to a profession; and Tristana's "profession" exists only in her imagination. Once Tristana sleeps with the handsome painter, her independence will then become inextricably entwined with her new self-definition as Horacio's beloved. And although she goes from one artistic pursuit to another, each change also represents her choice of emotional dependence on either Horacio or Don Lope.

Tristana first dedicates her interest to painting, reinforcing her decision to establish a bond with Horacio rather than with her guardian. Her dependency on Horacio's love and attention is very explicit; she tells him in her letters: "...I'll keep you with me, I'll tie you up, because my craziness needs your love to make it become reason." ("...te retengo, te amarro, pues mis locuras necesitan de tu amor para convertirse en razón") [p. 398]. To counteract Horacio's influence, Don Lope attempts to seduce her once again, to tie her to him, this time under the guise of the good father. Tristana writes Horacio that Don Lope is sorry for his neglect, his parental "abandonment" and that he has bought her new books. She is certain that he would sell his shirt to provide her with a profession. Don Lope's conversion to the role of good father lessens the onus of his previous abuse and Tristana begins to trust him and to believe that the losses she has suffered in time and intellectual training because of Don Lope's lack of interest in her welfare, can be recuperated. "He curses his neglect of me... But there's still time; we can still make up for the lost ground." ("Maldice su abandono... Pero aún es tiempo; aún podremos ganar el terreno perdido") [p. 391].

Don Lope has taught Tristana that marriage will stifle her talents, but this lesson has also been reinforced by her new lover. Horacio admires Tristana's interest in art (he is after all an artist), but he also expresses a firm belief that a woman finds self-realization in the role of the *ángel del hogar:*

> Give yourself to me without reserve. To be my life's companion; to help me and support me with your love!... Do you think there is any better profession, or any more beautiful kind of art? To make happy the man who will make you happy, what else is there?
>
> (Entrégate a mí sin reserva. ¡Ser mi compañera de toda la vida; ayudarme y sostenerme con tu cariño!... ¿Te parece que hay un oficio mejor ni arte más hermoso? Hacer feliz a un hombre que te hará feliz, ¿qué más?) [pp. 384-85]

Tristana responds by choosing the role of daughter to Don Lope over that of Horacio's wife, hoping that in this role she will be able to pursue her intellectual goals. And the role of daughter is one which should lead, in the normal course of maturation, to the status of adult woman. With Horacio away in the country, she begins to learn English, to read Shakespeare, to ask herself "To be or not to be" and to dream of a career on the stage, a profession in Spain which was certainly a viable one for talented women. As her interest in her studies intensifies, Horacio becomes more and more idealized; that is, more distant from her. Nevertheless, she still cannot trust Don Lope completely; she needs her lover to keep open the door into a world of independence. She writes to him: "Because in spite of all my *bluestockingness* (I want you to keep a list of all the words I invent), I will kill myself if you leave me." ("Porque con todo mi *marisabidillismo* (ve apuntando las palabras que invento), yo me mato si tú me abandonas") [p. 390].

At this point, approximately two-thirds into the novel, Tristana's leg is amputated, apparently as a result of bone cancer. The scene of the actual amputation operates symbolically as a rape scene and is internalized by the victim as such. Tristana is surrounded by three men, Don Lope, Dr. Miquis and his assistant, who propose, first of all, to deceive her in their violent intentions and who then anaesthetize her so that they may perform their will upon her body. She fights the anaesthesia, the drug producing a confused dream sequence in which she is assaulted by indecent men who come and pinch her legs while her hands are occupied in playing the piano. The violation of her body causes her to feel shame and she hopes that Horacio will not arrive to see what is being done to her: "He'll think something immoral is going on." ("Se figurará cualquier cosa mala") [p. 404]. She cries out to a woman, Saturna, for protection, but Saturna is powerless to help her. Finally, she is completely immobilized and unconscious, only capable of whimpering her pain and distress. Throughout the operation, Don Lope sits in a corner and watches.

The amputation of Tristana's leg is generally seen as an arbitrary plot intervention and therefore a weak element in the construction of the novel; certainly Tristana's illness strikes without reason or warning and the reader, like the protagonist, is simply forced to assimilate it. Tristana does seem to associate, at least subconsciously, the perverse sexual control Don Lope had exercised over her with her sudden illness. She writes to Horacio that Don Lope has given her his rheumatism. She then hastens to reassure him that the old man cannot "give" her anything, because they are no longer sleeping together. She also interprets her illness as Don Lope's punishment, through supernatural means (a hex or *mal de ojo*), for her refusal to grant him sexual favors [p. 392].

Ultimately, Tristana's mutilation only makes sense in the context of the dénouement, since her lack of mobility can be read as the cause of her conversion to domesticity. The image of Tristana's reduced and painful mobility also lends itself to a symbolic interpretation. She becomes less and less of an individual with a specific history, possessing her own needs and desires. Her personal history is subsumed into her symbolic function as generic woman, the mutilated male, always inferior, always dependent. At the end of the novel she will disappear entirely into a cliché, the obedient and submissive *ángel del hogar*, dividing her time between the Church and her kitchen.[15]

Nevertheless, during the operation, Tristana does not fear for the legs that enable her to leave Don Lope and run up the stairs to Horacio's studio, there to pass idyllic afternoons of lovemaking; rather she fears for the hands that represent her artistic potential, her newly envisioned, independent self:

> Don't let them take my hands too, because then... No, I won't let them take this hand; I'll hold it tight with the other one so they can't take it away from me, and my other one, I'll grab on to with this one, and that way they can't take either one away from me.
>
> (Que no me quiten también las manos, porque entonces... Nada, que no me dejo quitar esta mano; la agarro con la otra para que no me la lleven..., y la otra la agarro con ésta, y así no me llevan ninguna.) [p. 404]

And they do not take her hands away from her. Why then does she stop painting, and play her organ only in Church? The hands that might have been used to write, to create music or art, make only delicious pastries and nothing more. What has she lost, beyond her

---

[15] This point has been made by several critics. See Edward H. Friedman, "'Folly and a Woman': Galdós' Rhetoric of Irony in *Tristana*" in *Theory and Practice of Feminist Literary Criticism*, eds. G. Mora and K. S. Van Hooft (Ypsilanti, Michigan: Bilingual Press, 1982), p. 222. See also, Sinnegan, op. cit., n. 11, p. 287 and Miró, op. cit., n. 1, pp. 520-21.

physical mobility, that she loses faith in herself and interest in her artistic potential?

After the amputation, Don Lope thinks triumphantly: "Tied down forever! No more getting away from me now!" ("¡Sujeta para siempre! ¡Ya no más desviaciones de mí!") [p. 404]. Don Lope then tells Horacio: "From now on, she's useless as a woman." ("Es ya mujer inútil para siempre") [p. 410]. Since Tristana does go on to fulfill the conventional role of a pious pastry-making wife, "useless as a woman" is obviously referring specifically and only to a woman's role as object of male sexual desire. (She does still retain the capacity to bear children.) Tristana also agrees with this assessment of her mutilation; that henceforth no man will desire her sexually, regardless of whatever sexual desire or physical possibility of experiencing sexual satisfaction she may herself still retain. When Horacio attempts to compliment her on her wit *and* her beautiful bustline, she tells him to be quiet: "I am a seated beauty, seated forever now, a woman with half a body, a bust, nothing more." ("Soy una belleza sentada..., ya para siempre sentada, una mujer de medio cuerpo, un busto y nada más") [p. 412]. We are reminded of the luminous white marble busts that line the corredors of museums: cold, motionless, monumental, dead; existing to be seen, to give satisfaction to others with their beauty, and needing neither voice nor eyes nor extremities to fulfill their aesthetic function.

Tristana's amputation, then, effectively signifies her death as a sexual being and the result is a kind of psychological castration,[16] a destruction or fragmentation of the will, as well as a complete rejection of the new asexual self. The narrator comments: "She didn't seem like the same person and refused to acknowledge her very being." ("No parecía la misma, y denegaba su propio ser...") [p. 405]. Throughout the novel, Galdós links sexuality to creativity but

---

[16] The operation scene has been strangely ignored in the critical bibliography, yet it may be considered both the turning point of the novel and its most dramatic scene. Galdós inserts the castration motif rather crudely with his explicit description of the leg's removal from the operating room: "An hour and a quarter after the patient had been chloroformed, Saturnina left the room hurriedly with a long narrow object wrapped up in a sheet." ("A la hora y cuarto de haber empezado a cloroformizar a la paciente, Saturnina salía presurosa de la habitación con un objeto largo y estrecho envuelto en una sábana") [p. 405]. Tristana's precipitous and rapid aging also reinforces the idea of castration, since a real female castration, or ovariotomy, could have produced similar physical results. Carlos Feal Deibe also interprets the operation as a symbolic castration of women's aspirations by a masculine society. See op. cit, n. 4, p. 126.

there is an inverse relation between them according to gender. In the woman's case, Tristana's love for Horacio awakens her from a lethargic submission to her domineering guardian, and this sexual awakening inspires her to creative outbursts. She tells Horacio: "since I fell in love with you, it's as if my intelligence had awakened, and I find myself surprised by sudden bursts of inspiration" ("desde que te quiero, como se me ha despertado la inteligencia y me veo sorprendida por rachas de saber...") [p. 378]. Horacio, on the other hand, begins to feel that their love affair is costing him time. He experiences "The worker's remorse..." ("Los remordimientos del trabajador...") [p. 379], and when he is in the country, without the distraction of his beloved, he begins to paint again. According to the narrator, "He was overcome by a feverish desire to work" ("Entróle la fiebre del trabajo") [p. 388].

After the operation, Tristana's emotional dependence on Horacio as a mentor is re-established. The loss of her leg means that the public world must come to her. Don Lope, because he has placed himself in the role of father, cannot represent the world beyond the family. Instead of returning to her study of Shakespeare (the theatre can no longer serve as an opening into the public world) Tristana begins to paint again. But what she does esssentially is to shift her place in the male/female dyad from Don Lope's daughter to Horacio's pupil, preferring to practice by copying his paintings rather than attempting any original work. Horacio attempts to reinforce this new de-sexualized relationship of male mentor and female disciple. And the narrator insists that Horacio is not lacking as a teacher:

> The patience and care which Horacio exercised in his role as teacher were beyond words. But something very strange happened; not only did the young lady show little inclination for painting, but also her talent, so clearly displayed several months before, had become dull and lifeless, *no doubt for lack of self-confidence.* (my underlining)
>
> (La paciencia y la solicitud con que Horacio hacía de maestro no son para dichas. Mas sucedió una cosa muy rara, y fué que no sólo mostraba la señorita poca afición al arte de Apeles, sino que sus aptitudes, claramente manifestadas meses antes, se obscurecían y eclipsaban, *sin duda por falta de fe*). [p. 414] (subrayado mío)

In spite of Horacio's patience, the possibility of transforming their love affair into an asexual teacher/pupil relation is poisoned by the history of sexual dominance which defined Tristana and Don Lope's perverse bond of father/daughter, mentor/disciple. In addition, the social conventions ruled by the ideology of domesticity leave no room for any asexual male/female relation outside the family; or rather, the angel's purity exists only within the home. In the public world, the male/female pair is defined by its sexual component since there is no other reason for such a pairing to exist. Tristana, having experienced only a sexualized father/daughter relationship, needs Horacio's love for her as a sexual being. If he desires her sexually, she exists as a woman who is *not* Don Lope's possession. Given the impossibility of leaving Don Lope's home, Horacio's sexual love, and not his interest in her as an art student, is her only remaining defense against her guardian's renewed attempts at psychological seduction, this time in the supposedly innocuous role of benevolent father.

Tristana's affair with Horacio had liberated her from her seducer by creating the illusion of a space in the public world where she could live protected from the contaminated environment of the home, from both Don Lope's threats but more importantly, from the renewal of his seductive behavior. Don Lope, now stabilized in the role of Tristana's father, can only represent the claustrophobic world of the family, and therefore her participation, whether unwilling or not, in the socially abhorrent crime of incest. The vulnerability of the affective ties between Tristana and Horacio, who is now her only link to the public world, is depicted in the scenes of his final visits. Without the motive of sexual gratification, his love for her has weakened. The privacy of their world together, a privacy which is essential to Tristana's sense of an autonomous self, can now be breached by the incestuous father, who interjects himself between them:

> The painter behaved in a very friendly manner, but without saying a word about love. When they least expected it, Don Lope came into the room, and began to take part in their conversation, which was concerned exclusively with art.
>
> (El pintor se mostró muy amable; pero sin decir una palabra de amor. Introdújose don Lope en la habitación cuando menos se pensaba, metiendo su cucharada en el coloquio, que versó exclusivamente sobre cosas de arte.) [414]

Don Lope's entrance onto the scene is a repetition of his successful violation of Tristana's privacy at the moment when she had been weakened by the pain of her illness and could no longer defend the contents of her secret correspondence with Horacio [p. 403]. The old man's obsessive need to know everything about Tristana's affair with Horacio constitutes the psychological equivalent of his sexual aggression, and his invasion of her fantasy world parallels Tristana's prior incapacity to establish limits to the use of her body. In addition, the reader possesses knowledge which has been concealed from Tristana: the two men have discussed the disposal of her affairs, how, when and under what conditions Horacio will visit her, who will pay for the expenses of her illness, how her future is to be constructed, and the fact that Horacio will not be required to marry her [p. 413].[17] Without her knowledge, she has been transformed once more into *"una petaca"* [literally, a trunk or valise] to be placed here or there at the convenience of the gentlemen. And she responds by becoming again the passive victim introduced to us by the narrator with these hopeless words: "She seemed so resigned to being a piece of furniture and nothing more than a piece of furniture!" ("...parecía tan resignada a ser petaca, y siempre petaca!") [p. 350].

The public world, represented by Horacio, vanishes with him, and all that remains is the daughter's deadend within the prison walls of the family. Tristana begins a strategic retreat into herself, first through her music, then through her prayers, and finally, into the mindless role of the domestic. Her internal, spiritual death is not even apparent, because her façade is that of the perfect nineteenth-century *ángel del hogar:* obedient, submissive and sexually pure. And even the problem of children is resolved, for Don Lope has entered his second childhood, and she has, to all effects, become his angel-mother.

In James B. Twitchell's fascinating book on the incest taboo in modern culture, he differentiates between the Don Juan romance and the gothic:

> In the gothic, young women live in constant risk of defilement not by a breathless Don Juan, as in the romance tradition, but

---

[17] Noel Valis comments insightfully on the atmosphere of paternal complicity between the narrator and Don Lope, which is paralleled at the novel's end by a similar complicity between Don Lope and Horacio. See op. cit. note 1, p. 217.

by a father or uncle.[18] [...] the gothic deals with sin, guilt, and immediate retribution. The most particular sin is family sex, the most guilt-producing arrangement is of the father-daughter variety, and the retribution is unambiguous and almost without exception.[19]

Galdós creates gothic overtones in a variety of ways. The decay of Don Lope's fortune and especially, the depiction of his dark and gloomy, barely furnished house is a typical gothic motif. According to Twitchell, this image is a representation of the results of the "family romance run amok" which have wrecked havoc upon the family, and have brought about its downfall.[20] Striking the gothic chord, the narrator also insists on the mysterious power which Don Lope exercises over Tristana, and to a lesser degree, over the young man Horacio as well. He speaks of Don Lope's "mysterious despotism" ("el misterioso despotismo") [p. 396], and describes how "Don Lope imposed his will upon her so absolutely and fascinated her with such mysterious authority..." ("Don Lope se le imponía de tal modo, y la fascinaba con tan misteriosa autoridad...") [p. 373]. Don Lope's power is also linked to "...an almost miraculous youthfulness" ("...una conservación casi milagrosa") [p. 356]. In a similar manner, Tristana's childlike innocence is depicted as an uncanny ability to remain personally clean in spite of all the filth with which she comes in contact in her daily household tasks [p. 350] (and by association, her ability to remain unbesmirched by the sexual tasks she is also obliged to perform).

Since Tristana is twenty-two years old when the novel begins, an interpretation of her obedience to Don Lope's authority and her acquiescence to his sexual demands as "mysterious" behavior, assumes that she is an adult woman in control of herself, her life and her future and that she chooses, inexplicably or "mysteriously," to act against her own interests. This idea, that Tristana has somehow

---

[18] The designation of "uncle" to disguise the biological father and to protect him with what Freud calls "a veil of discretion" is a device used by Freud himself in the case history of hysteria, "Case 4: Katharina —." Freud adds a note to this study in 1924, in which he criticizes himself for this lapse of sincerity and insists upon the importance of the closer biological tie in the trauma to the daughter. See J. Breuer and S. Freud, *Studies on Hysteria* (New York: Basic Books, n.d.), pp. 125-34, and n. 2, p. 134.

[19] Twitchell, p. 155.
[20] Twitchell, p. 176.

chosen her own fate is also implicit in the narrator's explanation of Tristana's artistic failures as a "lack of self-confidence" or *"falta de fe,"* following the amputation of her leg. Galdós uses a gothic lexicon of mystery and the supernatural to cover up the truth of Don Lope and Tristana's perverse "family romance." On the other hand, Galdós has written a psychological portrait which conforms accurately to recent studies done of incest victims.[21] We note at the beginning of the novel Tristana's infantilization, her extreme passivity and indecisiveness. Later, her relation with Horacio is colored by her notable lack of any reliable, interiorized sense of self-esteem, a lack which she demonstrates by her constant anxious need for reassurance from her lover, as well as her inability to trust Horacio's love. Finally, at the end of the novel, she reverts to her previous passive state with her apparent submission to the fate of remaining her "father's" daughter. But in spite of the verisimilitude of Tristana's psychological reaction to Don Lope's aggression, the real evil of her guardian's uncontrolled and unmediated exercise of patriarchal power remains safely disguised as gothic horror.

If we continue to read *Tristana* as a gothic narrative, we must confront the question of the necessary retribution demanded by the crime of incest. At this point, our reading of *Tristana* as primarily gothic breaks down. Only if their marriage is considered a punishment, can the ending be interpreted as a gothic ending. Yet this interpretation, at least in the case of Tristana, is not untenable. The marriage of the crippled woman and the old man is depicted as a vegetative life filled with a child's or an old man's instinctual and innocent satisfactions – food, bodily warmth, the sunny patio filled with poultry and flowers. It is a pre- or post-sexual world, devoid of passion, bereft of any bothersome creative urges.

But in order to attain this state of connubial bliss, the incestuous couple must be castrated.[22] Don Lope's castration is a natural one, the inevitable results of senescence. Tristana's castration, however, is accomplished by joining her forever to an impotent and by now

---

[21] See Herman, Ch. 6, "The Daughter's Inheritance," pp. 96-108, for a more detailed discussion of the psychological effects of father-daughter incest.

[22] Twitchell insists on the importance of retribution in the gothic form of the incest narrative: "Do 'it' just once, the gothic seems to say in its own particular vernacular, and you will do nothing else, ever again." op. cit., p. 155. This gothic castration motif ties in with Don Lope's insistence that he and Tristana no longer have sexual relations (p. 418), as well as Tristana's frequent statements to Horacio that she is no longer sleeping with her guardian.

virtually senile "father." Her marriage institutionalizes her asexuality, both physically and psychologically. The words of the narrator recreate the ambience of victimization experienced by Tristana in the amputation scene. He says of her marriage: "She didn't feel the act. She accepted it as something imposed upon her by the outside world, like the census, or taxes, or police laws." ("No sentía el acto, lo aceptaba como un hecho impuesto por el mundo exterior, como el empadronamiento, como la contribución, como las reglas de policía") [p. 418].

Tristana's purifying absence of sexual and artistic desire becomes the background which illuminates the virtue of her decrepit but now exemplar husband/father. Her pyschological death provides the framework for Don Lope's moral salvation. The old man's obsessive need to dominate Tristana can now be justified as the reason for his "moral regeneration" for he has conformed to the patriarchal (feudal) contract of protection in exchange for service. Don Lope has fulfilled his prophetic and threatening promise made to Tristana at the beginning of the novel: "...you aren't a victim; I cannot abandon you, I will never abandon you," ("...tú no eres víctima; yo no puedo abandonarte, no te abandonaré nunca,") [p. 374]. The couple's marriage can also be interpreted as Galdós' attempt to rehabilitate his aging Don Juan in the eyes of the reader, because in marrying Tristana, Don Lope has performed an act of "self-abnegation," sacrificing his supposed radical opposition to marriage in order to provide for his ward financially after his death.

Inside the house, Tristana has been shut away forever from any male-gendered intellectual and artistic creativity, and also from female-gendered sexuality grounded in the female body. Unlike Ibsen's Nora, the door of matrimony closes in on Tristana, entombing her forever inside the suffocating respectability of bourgeois marriage. Her dream of personal autonomy cannot transcend her economic limitations, but she has also been doomed by her attempt to imagine a "new woman" in a state of social isolation.[23] Deprived of psychological and material support necessary to combat the influence of the traditional definition of femininity, she remains

---

[23] For an interesting discussion on the theme of the "new woman" see Mary Ellen Bieder, "Capitulation: Marriage, Not Freedom: A Study of Emilia Pardo Bazán's *Memorias de un solterón* and Galdós' *Tristana,"* *Symposium*, 30 (1976), pp. 93-109.

dependent throughout the novel on a male mirror to achieve a sense of self.

Tristana's final solipsistic retreat into her solitary ruminations parallels the retreat of many nineteenth-century women into the many forms of invalidism: hysteria, hypochondria, neurasthenia, and the paralyzing effects of depression. Hysterical women, however, commanded great attention: they were often vocal (employing screams and cries, if not language) and given to bizarre behavior that provoked a visceral reaction in the medical establishment and in their husbands and male guardians. Tristana's silence and passivity, symptoms more related to melancholy or depression than to female hysteria, effectively give control of the narrative back to the narrator. From his safe vantage point outside the domestic realm, the narrator uses this power to connect himself to the reader in the public world and to appropriate for himself the text's final act of speech. Just as Don Lope and Horacio manipulated Tristana, the narrator attempts to manipulate the reader's emotional reaction to the marriage by asking her/him to view the marriage from a distance which serves to prevent an empathic participation in Tristana's fate or her possible pain. We are enjoined to respond to the narrator's mild curiosity concerning the couple's future happiness. However, rather than being asked our opinion, we are asked to accept the narrator's own answer of "tal vez" (perhaps) and to retreat with him from the moral issues raised during the course of the novel: Tristana's needs, struggles and painful losses, Don Lope's amoral cruelty.

The final epigraph by Virginia Woolf is encouraging to read because we know that Woolf did succeed in killing her own personal phantom, her resident Angel. Testimony to this happy event is the long list of novels, essays, letters and memoirs left to us by the author. But as she tells us, the Angel in the House is a phantom that "dies hard" in both the individual and the collective mentality. We can never know what price Woolf paid for the artistic aggressivity which made her a great writer. She has also left us the testimony of her suicide. In 1929, Woolf published *A Room of One's Own*, a study of the economic dependency of middle-class women which permitted the ideology of domesticity to flourish. Woolf's own financial independence, her social class, and a supportive husband enabled her to struggle with the Angel in the House, and ultimately, to write her famous essay. Woolf also enjoyed the friendship and professional support of strong-minded women who discussed feminism and women's rights openly and in an atmosphere of solidarity in opposition to patriarchal power.

Galdós wrote *Tristana* a mere 37 years prior to the appearance of *A Room of One's Own* and yet, it would seem, at a cultural distance of centuries. One additional effect of the novel's gothic overtones is a kind of displacement of the events into an ahistorical time and space, at least up to the moment of Tristana's marriage. Yet during the nineteenth century, as recent scholarship has documented in detail,[24] there existed in Spain many women writers who, like Galdós, wrote novels, poetry and plays, contributed regularly to the popular press, and also edited their own magazines. It can be argued that the intellectual and professional future of middle-class women, in the urban capital of Madrid, in the year 1892, was not as entirely hopeless as this novel portrays it.

Tristana has been criticized as a faulty novel and also defended as a successful one; there is no need to ennumerate once again the various opinions of the readers. However, one thing can be said with certainty: Galdós wrote the only novel that he, as author, was capable of imagining. At the end of this narrative, Tristana still remains an elusive character. And perhaps, "tal vez", her retreat into silence needs to be read as a final, desperate and, yes, successful escape from the intrusive voice of the narrator who has stood in judgment upon her and condemned her for her "lack of self-confidence."

---

[24] See introduction, n. 2.

SELECTED BIBLIOGRAPHY

"Advertencia al público." *La Mujer,* 1, 1 (8 junio 1871), pp. 1-3.
Alfredo. "El lujo", *La familia,* II, 22 (agosto 1876), pp. 253-54.
Alas, Leopoldo. *Galdós (Obras Completas,* vol. 1). Madrid: Renacimiento, 1912.
Aldaraca, Bridget A. "El caso de Ána O: La histeria y sexualidad en *La Regenta.*" *Asclepio* (julio 1990), núm. monográfico: *La sexualidad y sus límites. Asclepio:* vol. 42, 1990, pp. 51-61.
―――. "The Medical Construction of the Feminine Subject in Nineteenth-Century Spain." In *Cultural and Historical Grounding for Hispanic and Luso-Brazilian Feminist Literary Criticism,* ed. H. Vidal. Minneapolis: Ideologies and Literature, 1989, pp. 395-413.
"Algo para las mujeres." *El Correo de la Moda* (2 julio 1881), pp. 195-98.
Álvarez, Cirilo. "Del divorcio." *La Defensa de la Sociedad,* 9 (1 enero 1876), pp. 389-412.
Amar y Borbón, Josefa. *Discurso sobre la educación física y moral de las mugeres.* Madrid, 1790.
Anderson, Farris. "Ellipsis and Space in *Tristana.*" *Anales Galdosianos,* XX (1985), pp. 61-76.
Andreu, Alicia. *Galdós y la literatura popular.* Madrid: Sociedad General Española de Librería, 1982.
―――. "El Folletín como intertexto en *Tormento.*" *Anales Galdosianos* XVII (1982), pp. 55-61.
A. P. "Influencia de la mujer en la sociedad." *El Museo de las Familias,* 21-22 (1863), pp. 125-28.
A. P. A. "La emancipación de la mujer." *El Correo de la Moda* (2 noviembre 1875), p. 231.
Aranguren, José Luis L. *Moral y sociedad: introducción a la moral social española del siglo* XIX. Madrid: Editorial Cuadernos para el Diálogo, 1967.
Arbiol, Antonio. *Estragos de la lujuria, y sus remedios, conforme a las Divinas Escrituras, y Santos Padres de la Iglesia.* Zaragoza, 1786. Written in 1725 and published posthumously.
―――. *La familia regulada con doctrina de la Sagrada Escritura y Santos Padres de la Iglesia Católica.* First published in 1715. Madrid, 1783.
Arenal, Concepción. *La mujer de su casa.* First published in 1881. In *La emancipación de la mujer en España.* M. Armiño, ed. Madrid: Ediciones Júcar, 1974.
Ariès, Philippe. *Centuries of Childhood: A Social History of Family Life.* New York: Alfred A. Knopf, 1962.
Armiño de Cuesta, Robustiana. "La mujer emancipada." *La Moda Elegante Ilustrada,* 30, 2 (1871), p. 15.

Auerbach, Nina. *Woman and the Demon: The Life of a Victorian Myth.* Cambridge: Harvard University Press, 1982.
Azcárate, Gumersindo de. *Estudios filosóficos y políticos.* Madrid, 1877.
Baer Barr, Lois. "Voyeurism in *Lo prohibido.*" *Kentucky Romance Quarterly,* 31 (1984), pp. 169-75.
Bataillon, Marcel. *Erasmo y España: Estudios sobre la historia espiritual del siglo XVI.* 2 vol. México: Fondo de Cultura Económica, 1950.
Bercherie, Paul. *Génesis de los conceptos freudianos.* Trans. Jorge Piatigorsky. Buenos Aires: Paidós, 1988.
Bermejo, J. A. "Instrucción y educación." *El Museo de las Familias,* 12 (febrero 1854), pp. 25-28.
Bieder, Maryellen. "Capitulation: Marriage, Not Freedom. A Study of Emilia Pardo Bazán's *Memorias de un solterón* and Galdós' *Tristana.*" *Symposium,* 30 (1976), pp. 93-109.
Blanco, Alda. "Domesticity, Education and the Woman Writer." In *Cultural and Historical Grounding for Hispanic and Luso-Brazilian Feminist Literary Criticism.* ed. H. Vidal. Minneapolis: Institute for the Study of Ideologies and Literature, 1989, pp. 371-94.
———. "Dinero, relaciones sociales y significación en *Lo prohibido.*" *Anales Galdosianos,* XVIII (1983), pp. 61-73.
Bly, Peter A. "The Use of Distance in Galdós' *La de Bringas.*" *Modern Language Review,* 69 (1974), pp. 88-91.
Bossy, John. "The Counter-Reformation and the People of Catholic Europe." *Past and Present,* 47 (May 1970), pp. 51-70.
Braier, L. *Diccionario Enciclopédico de Medicina.* Barcelona: Editorial JIMS, 1982.
Braudel, Fernand. *Capitalism and Material Life 1400-1800.* Trans. Miriam Kochan. New York: Harper and Row, 1974.
Breuer, Josef and Freud, Sigmund. *Studies on Hysteria.* New York: Basic Books, n.d.
Burgos Seguí, Carmen de (Columbine). *El divorcio en España.* Madrid, 1904.
C. "Influencia de la mujer en la vida del hombre." *La Familia* (11 julio 1875), pp. 82-83.
Caballero, Fernán. Letter to Teodoro Guerrero. *El Correo de la Moda* (2 mayo 1877). Published posthumously.
Campomanes, Pedro Rodríguez de. *Discurso sobre la educación popular de los artesanos.* Madrid, 1775.
Canons and Decrees of the Council of Trent. Trans. Rev. J. Waterworth. London, 1848.
Carr, Raymond. *España (1808-1939).* Barcelona: Ariel, 1969.
Casalduero, Joaquín. *Vida y obra de Galdós.* Madrid: Gredos, 1974.
Catalina, Severo. *La mujer, apuntes para un libro,* 2nd. ed. Madrid, 1862.
Charcot, Jean Martin. *L'hystérie.* Textes choisis et présentes par E. Trillat. Toulouse: Privat, 1971.
Charnon-Deutsch, Lou. "*La de Bringas* and the Politics of Domestic Power." *Anales Galdosianos,* XX (1985), pp. 65-74.
Christ, Carol. "Victorian Masculinity and the Angel in the House." In *A Widening Sphere: Changing Roles of Victorian Women.* Martha Vicinus, ed. Bloomington: Indiana University Press, 1977.
Dash, Condesa. "De la castidad conyugal." *La Guirnalda* (20 marzo 1876).
Díaz, Elías. *La filosofía social del krausismo español.* Madrid: Edicusa, 1973.
A Dictionary of Marxist Thought. Eds. Tom Bottomore, Lawrence Harris, V. G. Kiernan, Ralph Miliband. Cambridge: Harvard University Press, 1983.
Doctrina pontificia. Vol. II: *Documentos políticos.* José Luis Gutiérrez García, ed. Intro. Alberto Martín Artajo. Madrid: Biblioteca de Autores Cristianos, 1958.

Donzelot, Jacques. *The Policing of Families*. Trans. Robert Hurley. New York: Pantheon Books, 1979.
Drinka, George F. *The Birth of Neurosis: Myth, Malady and the Victorians*. New York: Simon & Schuster, 1984.
Drumen, Juan. *Tratado elemental de patología médica*. Vol. 2. Madrid, 1850.
Editors. "Sobre el lujo". *La Mujer*, 1, 52 (julio 1852).
Editors. "Sobre el lujo". *La Mujer*, 1, 38 (18 abril 1852).
Ellenberger, Henri F. *The Discovery of the Unconscious: The History and Evolution of Dynamic Psychiatry*. New York: Basic Books, 1970.
Engels, Friedrich. *The Origin of the Family, Private Property and the State*. New York: Pathfinder Press, 1973.
Engler, Kay. *The Structure of Realism: The Novelas Contemporáneas of Benito Pérez Galdós*. Chapel Hill: University of North Carolina, 1977.
―――. "The Ghostly Lover: The Portrayal of the Animus in *Tristana*." *Anales Galdosianos*, XII (1977), pp. 95-109.
Esquerdo, José María. "De la locura histérica." *Revista Clínica de los Hospitales*, tomo I (1889), pp. 1-9; 274-81; 337-40; and tomo II (1890), pp. 1-6.
Fábreques, S. M. "La mujer casada y San Pablo." *La Moda Elegante Ilustrada*, 30, 27 (1871), p. 215.
Fabre y D'Huc. *Tratado elemental de las enfermedades de la mujer y el niño*. Ed. and Trans. Rogelio Casa de Baptista. 3rd. ed. Madrid, 1872.
Feijóo y Montenegro, Benito. "La defensa de las mugeres." In his *Teatro crítico universal*. Vol. 1, Discurso XVI. Madrid, 1765.
"La familia y la moda." *La Guirnalda* (16 octubre 1874), p. 154.
Feal Deibe, Carlos. *"Tristana* de Galdós: Capítulo en la historia de la liberación femenina." *Sin Nombre*, 7, 3 (1976), pp. 116-29.
Fernández García, Antonio. "La mujer." *El Correo de la Moda* (2 octubre 1877).
Foucault, Michel. *The History of Sexuality: Volume I, An Introduction*. Trans. R. Hurley. New York: Pantheon Books, 1978.
Freud, Sigmund. *Dora: An Analysis of a Case of Hysteria*. Intro. Philip Rieff. New York: Macmillan, 1963.
―――. "Case 4: Katharina ―――." in *Studies on Hysteria*. New York: Basic Books, n.d.
Friedman, Edward H. " 'Folly and a Woman': Galdós' Rhetoric of Irony in *Tristana*." In *Theory and Practice of Feminist Literary Criticism*, Eds. G. Mora and K. S. Van Hooft. Ypsilanti, Michigan: Bilingual Press/Editorial Bilingüe, 1982.
Frontaura, Carlo. "Las amas de cría." *El Museo Universal* (1 febrero 1863), p. 39.
García Cañas, Ruperto. "Sobre la influencia de la mujeres en nuestras sociedades modernas." *El Museo de las Familias*, 3 (1845), pp. 72-74.
Gernsheim, Alison. *Fashion and Reality: 1840-1914*. London: Faber and Faber, 1963.
Giedion, Siegried. *Mechanization Takes Command: A Contribution to Anonymous History*. New York: Norton and Company, 1969.
Gimeno Agíus, J. "La moralidad en España." *El Museo Universal*, 10, 31 (1866), p. 358.
Gimeno de Flaquer, Concepción. "La mujer estudiosa." *El Correo de la Moda* (2 diciembre 1882), p. 358.
―――. "La mujer médico." *La Moda Elegante Ilustrada* (22 junio 1884), p. 187.
―――. "No hay sexo débil." *La Moda Elegante Ilustrada* (22 junio 1884), p. 187.
Gómez de Cádiz, Dolores. "Carta a María sobre la emancipación de la mujer." *El Museo Universal*, 6, 24 (15 junio 1862), pp. 187-93.

González Serrano, Urbano. "Una cuestión de la actualidad." *Revista de España*, 31, 29-30, no. 113, 115, 118 (1872-1873), pp. 84-95; 340-52; 191-205.
Gonzalo Morán, Fermín. "La mujer." *El Correo de la Moda* (10 noviembre 1877).
Gordon, Mary. "The Medical Background to Galdós' *La desheredada.*" *Anales Galdosianos*, 7 (1972), pp. 67-77.
Grasset, J. Dr. *Enfermedades del sistema nervioso.* tomo II, Barcelona: 1880.
Guy, Alain. *La Pensée de Fray Luis de León.* Limoges: Imprimerie A. Bontemps, 1946.
Hauser, Philiph. *Madrid bajo el punto de vista médico-social.* Carmen del Moral, ed. 2 vol. Madrid: Editora Nacional, 1979. First published in 1902.
Hemmings, F. W. J., ed. *The Age of Realism.* London: Penguin Books, 1974.
Herman Lewis, Judith. *Father-Daughter Incest.* Cambridge: Harvard University Press, 1981.
Herr, Richard. *The Eighteenth Century Revolution in Spain.* Princeton: Princeton University Press, 1969.
Hill, Christopher. *Society and Puritanism in Pre-Revolutionary England.* London: Secker and Warburg, 1964.
Hobsbawm, E. J. *The Age of Capital.* New York: Mentor Books, 1979.
Israël, Lucien. *La histeria, el sexo y el médico.* Trans. Aurelio López Zea. Barcelona: Toray-Masson, 1979.
Izquierdo Hernández, M. *Historia clínica de la Restauración.* Madrid: Editorial Plus Ultra, 1946.
Jiménez de Pedro, Justo. *Carácter moral de la mujer.* Madrid, 1854.
Kany, Charles E. *Life and Manners in Madrid: 1750-1800.* Berkeley: University of California Press, 1932.
Lasch, Christopher. *Haven in a Heartless World: The Family Besieged.* New York: Basic Books, 1977.
Latorres, R. de. "Estudios filosóficos sobre la mujer." *El Pensil del Bello Sexo* (18 enero 1846).
Keller Fox, Evelyn. *Reflections on Gender and Science.* New Haven: Yale University Press, 1985.
Kirkpatrick, Susan. *Las Románticas: Women Writers and Subjectivity in Spain 1835-1850.* Berkeley: University of California Press, 1989.
Lefebvre, Henri. *Everyday Life in the Modern World.* Trans. S. Rabinavitch. New York: Harper Torchbooks, 1971.
León, Fray Luis de. *La perfecta casada.* First published in 1583. Reimpresión de la tercera edición, con variantes de la primera, y un prólogo. Elizabeth Wallace, ed. Chicago: University of Chicago Press, 1903.
Livingstone, Leon. "The Law of Nature and Women's Liberation in *Tristana.*" *Anales Galdosianos* 7 (1972), pp. 93-100.
Llorens, Vicente. *El romanticismo español.* Madrid: Castalia, 1979.
López-Morillas, Juan. *Hacia el 98: literatura, sociedad, ideología.* Barcelona: Ariel, 1972.
López Piñero, José. "El testimonio de los médicos españoles acerca de su tiempo." In *Medicina y sociedad en la España del siglo XIX.* Madrid: Sociedad de Estudios y Publicaciones, 1964.
Losada, Ramón. "El magisterio de la mujer." *La Defensa de la Sociedad*, 2 (1872), pp. 390-94.
Lukács, Georg. "Narrate or Describe." In *Writer and Critic.* New York: Grosset and Dunlop, 1971.
―――. *Realism in Our Time: Literature and the Class Struggle.* Preface George Steiner. Trans. John and Necke Mander. New York: Harper Torchbooks, 1964.
Luz, Juan de. "Una receta casera." *La Margarita* (30 julio 1871).

Maravall, José Antonio. *Estado moderno y mentalidad social.* 2 vol. Madrid: Revista de Occidente, 1972.
Martín Gaite, Carmen. *Usos amorosos del dieciocho en España.* Madrid: Siglo Veintiuno, 1972.
Martínez Giniesta, M. "La educación de la mujer." *La Familia* (30 mayo 1875), p. 44.
Marx and Engels on Literature and Art. L. Baxandall and S. Morawski, eds. St. Louis: Telos Press, 1973.
Masson Moussaieff, Jeffrey. *The Assault on Truth: Freud's Suppression of the Seduction Theory.* New York: Penguin Books, 1985.
Mata Fontanet, Pedro. *Tratado de medicina y cirugía.* 5th ed. Vol. II. Tetuán de Chamartín, 1874.
Michelet, Jules. *Priests, Women and Families.* Trans. C. Cocks. London, 1845.
Miró, Emilio. "Tristana o la imposibilidad del ser." *Cuadernos Hispanoamericanos.* 250-52 (1970-71), pp. 505-22.
Monlau, Pedro Felipe. *Higiene del matrimonio o el libro de los casados.* 3rd ed. Madrid: 1865. Also, the 7th ed. (considerablemente aumentada). Paris: Garnier Hermanos, 1892.
Montesinos, José F. *Galdós.* 4 vol. Madrid: Castalia, 1969.
———. *Introducción a una historia de la novela en España en el siglo XIX.* Madrid: Castalia, 1955.
Moore, Katherine. *Victorian Wives.* London: Allison and Busby, 1974.
Moratín, L. Fernández de. *La comedia nueva. El sí de las niñas.* Dowling and Andioc, eds. Madrid: Clásicos Castalia, 1968.
Moreno Fuentes, José. "Reparos y obligaciones acerca del destino natural de la mujer." *El Correo de la Moda* (26 septiembre 1885). pp. 285-86.
"La mujer y la política." *La Guirnalda* (20 agosto 1883), pp. 125-26.
Nimetz, Michael. *Humor in Galdós.* New Haven: Yale University Press, 1968.
Olivares, Baronesa de. "La vida en familia." *El Correo de la Moda* (2 diciembre 1884).
Oñate, María del Pilar. *El feminismo en la literatura española.* Madrid: Espasa-Calpe, 1938.
Palacio Atard, Vicente. *Los españoles de la Ilustración.* Madrid: Ediciones Guadarrama, 1964.
Pardo Bazán, Emilia. "Tristana." *Nuevo Teatro Crítico,* II, núm. 17 (mayo, 1892), pp. 77-90.
Peset, José Luis and Huertas García-Alejo, Rafael. "Del 'ángel caído' al enfermo mental: Sobre el concepto de degeneración en las obras de Morel y de Magnan." *Asclepio,* 38 (1986), pp. 215-40.
Peraza de Ayala, Trino. *La psiquiatría española en el siglo XIX.* Madrid: Consejo Superior de Investigaciones Científicas, 1947.
Pérez Galdós, Benito. *Ensayos de crítica literaria.* Selección, intro. y notas de Laureano Bonet. Barcelona: Ediciones Península, 1972.
———. *La familia de León Roch, Tormento, La de Bringas, Lo prohibido, Tristana.* 3 vol. Madrid: Aguilar, 1973.
———. *Lo prohibido.* Edición, intro. y notas de José F. Montesinos. Madrid: Castalia, 1971.
Pío IX, Pope. Breve de su Santidad Pío IX a María de Gentelles. "Sobre el lujo de las mujeres." *La Familia* (30 octubre 1875), p. 171.
Pirala, A. "De la influencia e instrucción de la mujer." *La Moda Elegante Ilustrada* (30 abril 1873), p. 125.
Pulido, Ángel F. Dr. *Bosquejos médicos-sociales para la mujer.* Madrid: 1876.

Pulido Martín, Ángel. *El Dr. Pulido y su época*. Madrid: Imprenta Doménech, 1945.
Putman, Emily J. *The Lady: Studies of Certain Significant Phases of Her History*. New York: G. P. Putman and Sons, 1910.
Quevedo, J. de. "Estudios morales: la moda." *El Museo de las Familias*, 1-2 (1844), pp. 288-91.
———. "La moda en sus relaciones con la política." *El Museo de las Familias*, 3 (1845), pp. 233-35.
Rodó y Casanova, Antonio. n.t. *El Correo de la Moda*, 28, 8 (26 febrero 1877).
Rodríguez, Alfred. "Algunos aspectos de la elaboración literaria de *La familia de León Roch.*" *PMLA*, 82 (1967), pp. 121-27.
Rodríguez-Solís, E. *La mujer defendida por la historia, la ciencia, la moral*. Madrid, 1877.
Round, Nicholas G. "Rosalía Bringas' Children." *Anales Galdosianos*, 7 (1971), pp. 43-50.
Rousseau, Jean Jacques. *Emile or On Education*. Intro. and trans. Allan Bloom. New York: Basic Books, 1979.
Ruiz Salvador, Antonio. "La función del trasfondo histórico en *La desheredada.*" *Anales Galdosianos*, 1 (1966), pp. 53-62.
Sackett, Theodore A. *Pérez Galdós: An Annotated Bibliography*. Albuquerque: The University of New Mexico Press, 1968.
Sáez de Melgar, Faustina. "Deberes de la mujer." *La Mujer*, 16 (agosto 1871), pp. 3-4.
———. "La mujer política." *La Mujer*, 1 (8 junio 1871), pp. 3-4.
Sánchez, Roberto. "Galdós' *Tristana*, Anatomy of a 'Disappointment.'" *Anales Galdosianos*, XII (1977), pp 111-27.
Sánchez de Toca, Joaquín. "El matrimonio." *Revista de España*, 34 (1873), pp. 66-96. Also published in a longer book form as *El Matrimonio: su ley natural, su historia y su importancia social*. Madrid: 1873.
Scanlon, Geraldine M. "*El doctor Centeno*: a Study in Obsolescent Values." *Bulletin of Hispanic Studies*, 55 (1978), pp. 245-53.
———. "Heroism in an Unheroic Society: Galdós's *Lo Prohibido.*" *The Modern Language Review*, 79 (October 1984), pp. 831-45.
———. *La polémica feminista en la España comtemporánea*. Madrid: Siglo XXI de España, 1976. Reedited Madrid: Akal, 1986.
Schmidt, Ruth A. "*Tristana* and the Importance of Opportunity." *Anales Galdosianos*, IV (1974), pp. 135-44.
Segovia, Antonio María. "Del lujo." In *Conferencias dominicales sobre la educación de la mujer*. Discurso IV. Madrid, 1869.
Sempere y Guarinos, Juan. *Historia del luxo y de las leyes suntuarias de España*. 4 vol, Madrid, 1788.
Sennett, Richard. *The Fall of Public Man: On the Social Psychology of Capitalism*. New York: Vintage Books, 1978.
Serrano Sanz, Manuel. *Apuntes para una biblioteca de escritoras españolas*. In Biblioteca de Autores Españoles. Vol. 268. Madrid, 1975.
Showalter, Elaine. *The Female Malady: Women, Madness and English Culture, 1830-1980*. London: Virago Press, 1987.
Simón Palmer, María del Carmen. "Escritoras españolas del siglo XIX o el miedo a la marginación." *Anales de Literatura Española de la Universidad de Alicante*, 2 (1983), pp. 477-90.
Sinnigan, John H. "Resistance and Rebellion in *Tristana.*" *Modern Language Notes*, 91 (1976), pp. 278-89.
Sinués de Marco, María Pilar. "El arte de vestir." *La Guirnalda*, 16, 24 (1882), p. 190.
———. "Contra el lujo." *El Correo de la Moda* (2 septiembre 1883), p. 258.

Sombart, Werner. *Lujo y capitalismo.* Trans. Luis Isabel. Madrid: Alianza Editorial, 1979.
Sontag, Susan. *Illness as Metaphor.* New York: Vintage Books, 1979.
Spell, Jefferson R. *Rousseau in the Spanish World Before 1833: A Study in Franco-Spanish Literary Relations.* New York: Octagon Books, 1969.
Stone, Lawrence. *The Family, Sex and Marriage in England: 1550-1800.* New York Harper and Row, 1977.
Terry, Arthur. "*Lo prohibido:* Unreliable Narrator and Untruthful Narrative." In *Galdós Studies.* J. Varey, ed. London, 1970.
Trillat, Etienne. *Histoire de L'Hystérie.* Paris: Edition Seghers, 1986.
Tubino, F. M. "La mujer y su reforma moral." *La Guirnalda,* 7, 147 (1 febrero 1873), pp. 9-10.
Twitchell, James B. *Forbidden Partners: The Incest Taboo in Modern Culture.* New York: Columbia University Press, 1987.
Ullman Connelly, Joan and Allison, George H. "Galdós as Psychatrist in *Fortunata y Jacinta.*" *Anales Galdosianos,* IX (1974), pp. 7-36.
Valdés, Elisa. "La situación jurídica de la mujer en España." In *La mujer en España.* Barcelona: Ediciones de Cultura Popular, 1968.
Valis, Noel. "Art, Memory, and the Human in Galdós' *Tristana.*" *Kentucky Romance Quarterly,* 31 (1984), pp. 207-20.
Varey, J. E. "Francisco Bringas: nuestro buen Thiers." *Anales Galdosianos,* 1 (1966), pp. 63-69.
Veblen, Thorstein. *The Theory of the Leisure Class.* First published in 1899. New York: Mentor Books, 1953.
Veith, Ilza. *Hysteria: The History of a Disease.* Chicago: University of Chicago Press, 1965.
Velázquez de Castro, A. Dr. *La responsabilidad en las histéricas* (Discurso leído en la Real Academia de Medicina y Cirugía de Granada). Granada, 1893.
Weibel, Kathryn. *Mirror, Mirror: Images of Women Reflected in Popular Culture.* New York: Anchor Books, 1979.
Williams, Raymond. *Keywords: A Vocabulary of Culture and Society.* New York: Oxford University Press, 1977.
Woodridge, Hensley C. *Benito Pérez Galdós: A Selective Annotated Bibliography.* Metuchen, New Jersey: The Scarecrow Press, 1975.
Woolf, Virginia. *Moments of Being.* New York: Harcourt, Brace, Jovanovich, 1978.
———. "Professions for Women." In *Women and Writing.* Michèle Barret, ed. New York: Harcourt, Brace, Jovanovich, 1980.
Wright, Chad C. "Imagery of Light and Darkness in *La de Bringas.*" *Anales Galdosianos,* 13 (1978), pp. 5-12.
Zola, Emile. "La novela experimental." In *El naturalismo.* Ed., intro., and notes of Laureano Bonet. Barcelona: Nexos, 1989.

NORTH CAROLINA STUDIES IN THE ROMANCE LANGUAGES AND LITERATURES

I.S.B.N. Prefix 0-8078-

Recent Titles

RICHARD SANS PEUR, EDITED FROM "LE ROMANT DE RICHART" AND FROM GILLES CORROZET'S "RICHART SANS PAOUR", by Denis Joseph Conlon. 1977. (No. 192). -9192-4.

MARCEL PROUST'S GRASSET PROOFS. *Commentary and Variants,* by Douglas Alden. 1978. (No. 193). -9193-2.

MONTAIGNE AND FEMINISM, by Cecile Insdorf. 1977. (No. 194). -9194-0.

SANTIAGO F. PUGLIA, AN EARLY PHILADELPHIA PROPAGANDIST FOR SPANISH AMERICAN INDEPENDENCE, by Merle S. Simmons. 1977. (No. 195). -9195-9.

BAROQUE FICTION-MAKING. A STUDY OF GOMBERVILLE'S "POLEXANDRE", by Edward Baron Turk. 1978. (No. 196). -9196-7.

THE TRAGIC FALL: DON ÁLVARO DE LUNA AND OTHER FAVORITES IN SPANISH GOLDEN AGE DRAMA, by Raymond R. MacCurdy. 1978. (No. 197). -9197-5.

A BAHIAN HERITAGE. An Ethnolinguistic Study of African Influences on Bahian Portuguese, by William W. Megenney. 1978. (No. 198). -9198-3.

"LA QUERELLE DE LA ROSE": Letters and Documents, by Joseph L. Baird and John R. Kane. 1978. (No. 199). -9199-1.

TWO AGAINST TIME. *A Study of the Very Present Worlds of Paul Claudel and Charles Péguy,* by Joy Nachod Humes. 1978. (No. 200). -9200-9.

TECHNIQUES OF IRONY IN ANATOLE FRANCE. Essay on *Les Sept Femmes de la Barbe-Bleue,* by Diane Wolfe Levy. 1978. (No. 201). -9201-7.

THE PERIPHRASTIC FUTURES FORMED BY THE ROMANCE REFLEXES OF "VADO (AD)" PLUS INFINITIVE, by James Joseph Champion. 1978. (No. 202). -9202-5.

THE EVOLUTION OF THE LATIN /b/-/ṷ/ MERGER: A Quantitative and Comparative Analysis of the *B-V* Alternation in Latin Inscriptions, by Joseph Louis Barbarino. 1978. (No. 203). -9203-3.

METAPHORIC NARRATION: THE STRUCTURE AND FUNCTION OF METAPHORS IN "A LA RECHERCHE DU TEMPS PERDU", by Inge Karalus Crosman. 1978. (No. 204). -9204-1.

LE VAIN SIECLE GUERPIR. A Literary Approach to Sainthood through Old French Hagiography of the Twelfth Century, by Phyllis Johnson and Brigitte Cazelles. 1979. (No. 205). -9205-X.

THE POETRY OF CHANGE: A STUDY OF THE SURREALIST WORKS OF BENJAMIN PÉRET, by Julia Field Costich. 1979. (No. 206). -9206-8.

NARRATIVE PERSPECTIVE IN THE POST-CIVIL WAR NOVELS OF FRANCISCO AYALA "MUERTES DE PERRO" AND "EL FONDO DEL VASO", by Maryellen Bieder. 1979. (No. 207). -9207-6.

RABELAIS: HOMO LOGOS, by Alice Fiola Berry. 1979. (No. 208). -9208-4.

"DUEÑAS" AND "DONCELLAS": A STUDY OF THE "DOÑA RODRÍGUEZ" EPISODE IN "DON QUIJOTE", by Conchita Herdman Marianella. 1979. (No. 209). -9209-2.

PIERRE BOAISTUAU'S "HISTOIRES TRAGIQUES": A STUDY OF NARRATIVE FORM AND TRAGIC VISION, by Richard A. Carr. 1979. (No. 210). -9210-6.

REALITY AND EXPRESSION IN THE POETRY OF CARLOS PELLICER, by George Melnykovich. 1979. (No. 211). -9211-4.

MEDIEVAL MAN, HIS UNDERSTANDING OF HIMSELF, HIS SOCIETY, AND THE WORLD, by Urban T. Holmes, Jr. 1980. (No. 212). -9212-2.

MÉMOIRES SUR LA LIBRAIRIE ET SUR LA LIBERTÉ DE LA PRESSE, introduction and notes by Graham E. Rodmell. 1979. (No. 213). -9213-0.

THE FICTIONS OF THE SELF. THE EARLY WORKS OF MAURICE BARRES, by Gordon Shenton. 1979. (No. 214). -9214-9.

When ordering please cite the *ISBN Prefix* plus the last four digits for each title.

Send orders to: University of North Carolina Press
P.O. Box 2288
CB# 6215
Chapel Hill, NC 27515-2288
U.S.A.

NORTH CAROLINA STUDIES IN THE ROMANCE LANGUAGES AND LITERATURES

I.S.B.N. Prefix 0-8078-

Recent Titles

A CONCORDANCE TO MARIVAUX'S COMEDIES IN PROSE, edited by Donald C. Spinelli. 1979. (No. 218). 4 volumes, -9218-1 (set); -9219-X (v. 1); -9220-3 (v. 2); -9221-1 (v. 3); -9222-X (v. 4).

ABYSMAL GAMES IN THE NOVELS OF SAMUEL BECKETT, by Angela B. Moorjani. 1982. (No. 219). -9223-8.

GERMAIN NOUVEAU DIT HUMILIS: ÉTUDE BIOGRAPHIQUE, par Alexandre L. Amprimoz. 1983. (No. 220). -9224-6.

THE "VIE DE SAINT ALEXIS" IN THE TWELFTH AND THIRTEENTH CENTURIES: AN EDITION AND COMMENTARY, by Alison Goddard Elliot. 1983. (No. 221). -9225-4.

THE BROKEN ANGEL: MYTH AND METHOD IN VALÉRY, by Ursula Franklin. 1984. (No. 222). -9226-2.

READING VOLTAIRE'S "CONTES": A SEMIOTICS OF PHILOSOPHICAL NARRATION, by Carol Sherman. 1985. (No. 223). -9227-0.

THE STATUS OF THE READING SUBJECT IN THE "LIBRO DE BUEN AMOR", by Marina Scordilis Brownlee. 1985. (No. 224). -9228-9.

MARTORELL'S "TIRANT LO BLANCH": A PROGRAM FOR MILITARY AND SOCIAL REFORM IN FIFTEENTH-CENTURY CHRISTENDOM, by Edward T. Aylward. 1985. (No. 225). -9229-7.

NOVEL LIVES: THE FICTIONAL AUTOBIOGRAPHIES OF GUILLERMO CABRERA INFANTE AND MARIO VARGAS LLOSA, by Rosemary Geisdorfer Feal. 1986. (No. 226). -9230-0.

SOCIAL REALISM IN THE ARGENTINE NARRATIVE, by David William Foster. 1986. (No. 227). -9231-9.

HALF-TOLD TALES: DILEMMAS OF MEANING IN THREE FRENCH NOVELS, by Philip Stewart. 1987. (No. 228). -9232-7.

POLITIQUES DE L'ECRITURE BATAILLE/DERRIDA: le sens du sacré dans la pensée française du surréalisme à nos jours, par Jean-Michel Heimonet. 1987. (No. 229). -9233-5.

GOD, THE QUEST, THE HERO: THEMATIC STRUCTURES IN BECKETT'S FICTION, by Laura Barge. 1988. (No. 230). -9235-1.

THE NAME GAME. WRITING/FADING WRITER IN "DE DONDE SON LOS CANTANTES", by Oscar Montero. 1988. (No. 231). -9236-X.

GIL VICENTE AND THE DEVELOPMENT OF THE COMEDIA, by René Pedro Garay. 1988. (No. 232). -9234-3.

HACIA UNA POÉTICA DEL RELATO DIDÁCTICO: OCHO ESTUDIOS SOBRE "EL CONDE LUCANOR", por Aníbal A. Biglieri. 1989. (No. 233). -9237-8.

A POETICS OF ART CRITICISM: THE CASE OF BAUDELAIRE, by Timothy Raser. 1989. (No. 234). -9238-6.

UMA CONCORDÂNCIA DO ROMANCE "GRANDE SERTÃO: VEREDAS" DE JOÃO GUIMARÃES ROSA, by Myriam Ramsey and Paul Dixon. 1989. (No. 235). Microfiche, -9239-4.

CYCLOPEAN SONG: MELANCHOLY AND AESTHETICISM IN GÓNGORA'S "FÁBULA DE POLIFEMO Y GALATEA", by Kathleen Hunt Dolan. 1990. (No. 236). -9240-8.

THE "SYNTHESIS" NOVEL IN LATIN AMERICA. A STUDY ON JOÃO GUIMARÃES ROSA'S "GRANDE SERTÃO: VEREDAS", by Eduardo de Faria Coutinho. 1991. (No. 237). -9241-6.

IMPERMANENT STRUCTURES. SEMIOTIC READINGS OF NELSON RODRIGUES' "VESTIDO DE NOIVA", "ÁLBUM DE FAMÍLIA", AND "ANJO NEGRO", by Fred M. Clark. 1991. (No. 238). -9242-4.

"EL ÁNGEL DEL HOGAR". GALDÓS AND THE IDEOLOGY OF DOMESTICITY IN SPAIN, by Bridget A. Aldaraca. 1991. (No. 239). -9243-2.

When ordering please cite the *ISBN Prefix* plus the last four digits for each title.

Send orders to: University of North Carolina Press
P.O. Box 2288
CB# 6215
Chapel Hill, NC 27515-2288
U.S.A.

The Department of Romance Studies Digital Arts and Collaboration Lab at the University of North Carolina at Chapel Hill is proud to support the digitization of the North Carolina Studies in the Romance Languages and Literatures series.

www.ingramcontent.com/pod-product-compliance
Lightning Source LLC
Chambersburg PA
CBHW030617230426
43661CB00053B/2026